ALCOHOLISM AND THE FAMILY

A Guide to Treatment and Prevention

Gary Lawson, Ph.D.
University of Nebraska
Lincoln, Nebraska

James S. Peterson, Ph.D.
Southern Illinois University
Carbondale, Illinois

Ann Lawson, M.A., M.F.A.
Director
Lincoln and Lancaster County
Child Guidance Center
Children from Alcoholic Families
Program
Lincoln, Nebraska

AN ASPEN PUBLICATION®
Aspen Systems Corporation
Rockville, Maryland
Royal Tunbridge Wells
1983

Library of Congress Cataloging in Publication Data

Lawson, Gary.
Alcoholism and the family.

Includes index.
1. Alcoholics—Family relationships.   2. Alcoholism—
Treatment.   3. Alcoholism—Prevention.   I. Peterson,
James S.   II. Title. [DNLM: 1. Alcoholism—
Prevention and control.   2. Alcoholism—Therapy.
3. Family therapy.   WM 274   L425a]
HV5132.L39   1983   362.8'2   82-24352
ISBN: 0-89443-674-0

Publisher: John Marozsan
Editorial Director: R. Curtis Whitesel
Managing Editor: Margot Raphael
Editorial Services: Jane Coyle
Printing and Manufacturing: Debbie Collins

Library of Congress Catalog Card Number: 82-24352
ISBN: 0-89443-674-0

Printed in the United States of America

3   4   5

To the late Curtis Whitesel

Without his insight and encouragement, this book would not have been written. We are deeply grateful for his faith in us and his support in the writing of this book.

Table of Contents

Preface

Alcoholism currently ranks third, behind cancer and heart disease, as America's leading health problem. It can even be argued that alcoholism is the nation's leading health problem because it is often a direct factor in both cancer and heart conditions.

Alcoholism is a problem of monumental proportions in our culture. Volumes of statistics document the physical, emotional, and cultural effects of alcohol abuse. In terms of suicide, divorce, crime, economic loss, and mental and physical health problems, alcoholism affects our entire society.

Yet, one group probably feels the effects of alcoholism more than any other—the family. The alcoholic family has recently been the subject of much writing and debate. In general, writings about family treatment of alcoholism have underscored the importance of the family as a dynamic system that is the primary source of alcoholism and other related problems. However, mental health practitioners tend to focus rehabilitation efforts on the alcoholic member of the family while simply instructing other family members on how best to work with this person. Generally, the problem drinker goes off for treatment, and the rest of the family is, at best, a secondary consideration. The authors propose a different perspective. Instead of treating just one member, the entire alcoholic family is viewed as the client. Each individual within the family structure should be an integral part of treatment, not just the drinking member. Usually, the development of alcoholism does not happen in a vacuum; it is an outgrowth of an ailing family system. Even if an alcoholic has no current family, it must be remembered that he or she was once a member of a family and is a product of that system. In addition, it may be argued that some families do not cause alcoholism but that alcoholism causes these families' problems. However, this is only an academic point. By the time an alcoholic seeks treatment, the family will most likely be in disarray and in need of treatment.

There are three central reasons for viewing the family system as the client. First, it is less productive, or even harmful, to rehabilitate an alcoholic in isolation and then return him or her to the same destructive family system that created or maintained the problem in the first place. Second, family members may be under as much stress and in as much need of help as the alcoholic. All family members should be encouraged to receive help. Third, only when the family "in toto" participates in the rehabilitation process can family members understand the family dynamics and adopt new behaviors.

The authors' treatment approach attempts to trace alcoholism back to its root origins and describes how the problem is passed from generation to generation. The book describes many ways people perpetuate alcoholism, both consciously and unconsciously, and how it can be identified and treated. Specific procedures are included for prevention and for the diagnosis and treatment of alcoholic families.

This book is primarily designed to aid alcoholism counselors who wish to work with families, as well as family counselors who encounter problems associated with alcohol abuse. Each chapter can be consulted independently for specific information. However, sections were designed to build upon one another so that general background information could be applied to specific methods. The material selected for this book represents a broad spectrum of contemporary thought and intervention approaches, but the intent of the authors was not only to explain this material but demonstrate its application to real life situations.

Part I is a review of alcoholism treatment and etiological theories. It is provided for those readers unfamiliar with these theories. Parts II, III, and IV, covering etiology, treatment and prevention, are based on the family systems model and offer a different and exciting way to view alcoholism and to treat and prevent it. The reader who is knowledgeable in traditional alcoholism treatment may wish to begin with Parts II, III, or IV depending on his or her need.

Although the authors collaborated on each chapter, primary responsibility for various sections was assumed individually. Dr. Gary Lawson was the major contributor in the area of prevention and also made major contributions to the chapters on etiology (Chapters 4, 5, 13, and 14). Ann Lawson was the major contributor in treatment and also made major contributions to the etiology section (Chapters 3, 6, 7, 8, 9, and 10). Dr. James Peterson wrote the introductory chapters and was the primary editor of the book (Chapters 1, 2, 11, and 12).

Part I

Background of the Problem

Chapter 1

Etiological Theories of Alcoholism

The purpose of this chapter is to provide the reader with an overview of existing thought on the etiology of alcoholism. Several major theories of alcoholism will be described and analyzed. The theories to be considered fall into three major categories: (1) physiological theories of alcoholism; (2) psychological theories of alcoholism; and (3) sociological theories of alcoholism. The disease concept of alcoholism will be treated separately.

THE DISEASE CONCEPT OF ALCOHOLISM

When most practitioners in the field are asked to define alcoholism, they often respond categorically that "alcoholism is a disease." And yet, when asked to elaborate many are hard pressed to explain what this phrase really means. This is primarily due to the manner in which this concept has developed and is used. Most advocates of the "disease concept" base their position on various interpretations of the well-known book *The Disease Concept of Alcoholism* by Jellinek (1960).

Jellinek based his concepts on questionnaire studies in 1946 and 1952 along with a synthesis of existing thought on alcoholism (Jellinek, 1946, 1952). His findings can be reduced to two essential concepts: (1) there are several different types (species) of alcoholism; and (2) some types of alcoholics (Delta and Gamma) progress irreversibly through a series of ever worsening stages, unless there is therapeutic intervention. Regarding the first concept, Jellinek used the Greek alphabet for labeling purposes and described five distinct types of alcoholism: Alpha, Beta, Gamma, Delta, and Epsilon.

Alpha alcoholism represents purely psychological dependence on the abusive effects of alcohol. However, the Alpha alcoholic is nonetheless an abusive drinker and is often very resistant to treatment. Since Alpha drinkers are not physically addicted to alcohol, they do not experience withdrawal symptoms if they temporarily stop drinking, nor do they progress through stages.

3

The Beta alcoholic, on the other hand, has physical complications (e.g., gastritis or cirrhosis) related to alcohol consumption. There is no indication of physical or psychological dependence or progression with Beta alcoholics, but heavy drinking often continues in spite of medical complications.

Gamma alcoholism involves physical addiction with withdrawal symptoms (shakes and nausea when drinking is stopped), a definite progression from psychological to physical dependence, and "loss of control," uncontrollable drinking against the alcoholic's own wishes. The Gamma alcoholic experiences a physical craving for alcohol and undergoes marked behavioral and personality changes. The damage to the alcoholic's health and financial and social standing is more prominent than in other types of alcoholism.

Delta alcoholism is similiar to the Gamma variety, but in this case the drinker can control his or her intake in a given situation. However, it is known that Gamma drinkers may abstain ("go on the wagon") from time to time, but Delta alcoholics cannot go a single day without drinking. Delta alcoholism is more prominent in Europe, and Gamma alcoholism is much more common in the United States.

Finally, Epsilon alcoholism refers to the periodic drinker who may drink infrequently but in periodic abusive binges. Although Jellinek only described five different kinds of alcoholism, he felt that many more really exist but have yet to be defined. The key to understanding this aspect of Jellinek's work is that alcoholism is a global concept encompassing many varieties of problem drinking. To simply label someone an alcoholic is to overlook differences that may exist between that person and other drinkers.

Jellinek's second major concept is that many alcoholics go through a series of ever worsening stages or phases. At the first stage, the prealcoholic symptomatic phase, the drinker begins to consume alcohol for relief. As the prealcoholic increases his or her consumption to combat stress, other forms of tension reduction are discarded, and soon alcohol becomes the major response to any stress. Drinking becomes an almost daily habit, and an increase in tolerance is often noted.

The next phase is called prodromal and is characterized by five definite symptoms: (1) blackouts or periods of memory loss while drinking; (2) surreptitious drinking, which involves sneaking drinks; (3) gulping drinks; (4) preoccupation with drinking; and (5) guilt associated with inappropriate behavior while intoxicated. At this phase, a denial or alibi system is formulated.

The next stage, called the crucial phase, involves loss of control and signals physical addiction. Loss of control can be described as a chain reaction—one drink leads to the next. Individuals drink to unconsciousness or until they are forced to quit even though they know the consequences will be negative. This phase may best be understood as the loss phase, loss of job, friends, health, etc.

The final phase is called chronic and is the last phase before death. Alcoholics who progress to the chronic phase have a total obsession with alcohol consumption and have often lost their families, friends, and jobs. In many cases, they have been treated for alcoholism. Major symptoms of the chronic phase are a loss of tolerance for alcohol, morning and day drinking, loss of memory, and ethical or moral deterioration.

It was thought for some time that alcoholics needed to reach the chronic stage ("hit rock bottom") before treatment could be effective because only then would the alcoholic be motivated to quit. Currently most practitioners agree that intervention should take place as soon as possible, at a time when the problem drinker still has the major support systems (job, family, health, friends) intact.

The disease concept of alcoholism has enjoyed wide acceptance by counselors, doctors, and recovering alcoholics, especially those associated with Alcoholics Anonymous. The disease concept is an attractive position for three reasons: (1) it is easy to grasp conceptually; (2) it has, to some extent, removed the negative stigma associated with alcoholism; and (3) it calls for total abstinence from alcohol as the only plausible treatment goal, which is also simple, straightforward, and, therefore, attractive.

The problem with the disease concept, as interpreted from Jellinek's work, is that it has been widely misunderstood and misused. Jellinek himself explained that of all the various types of alcoholism only the Gamma and Delta varieties could be considered diseases. He based this conclusion on the progressive physical and behavioral changes that these alcoholics undergo. However, he felt the other kinds of alcoholism could not really be thought of as diseases.

What does this mean? First of all, not all problem drinkers are alike, and they may require different types of treatment. Based on the goals of the individual client, treatment may range anywhere from training in responsible drinking to complete abstinence. Specific treatment approaches will be addressed in detail in the following chapter.

PHYSIOLOGICAL THEORIES OF ALCOHOLISM

Most research in this area correlates drinking behavior with abnormal biological factors. Many of these studies, however, are flawed with the problem of cause and effect; observed differences in body functioning between alcoholics and nonalcoholics could be the result of years of heavy drinking and not the cause of alcoholism in the first place. Despite this limitation, several areas of biophysiological research relating to alcoholism merit consideration.

Is Alcoholism Inherited?

The theory that alcoholism is genetic has generated a great deal of discussion and research but has not provided a definitive answer to the nature of alcoholism.

Indeed, research on genetics and alcoholism has actually raised more questions than it has answered. For example, it is known that, despite the country of origin, alcoholism consistently runs in families. Without known exception, every family study of alcoholism has shown much higher rates of alcoholism among the relatives of alcoholics than in the general population (Goodwin, 1971). Indeed, a study by Winokur and Clayton (1968) showed a very high prevalence of alcoholism among the full siblings of alcoholics. A full 46% of the brothers and 5% of the sisters of the male alcoholics sampled were also alcoholics. Siblings of female alcoholics had even higher rates of alcoholism; 50% of the male siblings and 8% of the female siblings were alcoholics. However, this research doesn't answer the question. Are these factors due to inheritance of a propensity toward alcoholism or can they be explained through learned attitudes and behaviors that are passed from adults to their offspring?

A second area of genetic inquiry involves comparing the alcohol consumption of identical (monozygotic) and fraternal (dizygotic) twins. Researchers assume that since both identical and fraternal twins are typically raised in the same family environment (same parents, home, etc.) they will differ mostly in regard to genetic makeup. Parenthetically, identical twins share 100% of their genes, but fraternal twins only share 50% and are no more genetically similar than any other brother or sister combination. Therefore, it is theorized that genetic disorders will more often be concordant among identical twins than fraternal twins. Two large-scale studies relating to this subject are cited that represent typical findings in the research literature. The first (Kaij, 1960) was conducted in Sweden and compared 174 male twin pairs in which one member was registered as an alcoholic. In short, Kaij found that the concordance (agreement) rate was higher in monozygotic twins than dizygotic twins. Monozygotic twins showed a rate of 54%, but dizygotic twins had a rate of only 28%. The implication is that heredity accounts for the difference in alcoholism rates. On the other hand, a similar study conducted in Finland by Partanen, Bruun, and Markhanen (1966) compared 902 male twins but found no difference in alcoholism rates between monozygotic and dizygotic twins. Unfortunately, such contradictory research does little to clarify the question of inheritance as a factor in alcoholism.

Research in genetics and alcohol use is also being conducted with laboratory animals. In a study by Rogers and McClearn (1962), strains of mice were identified that seem to voluntarily consume alcohol at varying rates (i.e., high vs. low volumes). A combination of these strains produced offspring that consumed "moderate" amounts, suggesting a genetic predisposition for alcohol preference in these animals.

In another area of genetic research, genetic marker studies have explored associations between inherited characteristics (colorblindness, blood type, etc.) and alcoholism. In general, this research tends to be contradictory. For example, Cruz-Coke and Varela (1966) found that colorblindness, cirrhosis, and alcoholism were associated, and they proposed that alcoholism was transmitted by a sex-linked recessive gene. However, similar research was conducted by Fialkow, Thuline, and Fenster (1966) who concluded that colorblindness was more likely due to the toxic and/or nutritional effects of heavy drinking than to a sex-linked gene.

Although this review of genetic research represents only a tiny sample of the many studies that have been conducted, the unsolved problems are representative. First, as mentioned earlier, the cause and effect relationship is difficult to establish. Second, the age-old "nature versus nurture" controversy is still largely unanswered. Do families inherit alcoholism or learn it? Third, findings with laboratory animals cannot always be generalized to human beings. Finally, conclusions can be hard to draw from the contradictory research studies in this area. Even though genetic research has contributed valuable information, it still has not led to an understanding of the causes of alcoholism.

Is Alcoholism Caused by Abnormal Biophysiological Conditions?

Some researchers have postulated that alcoholism may be due to biophysiological causes. Some of the major biophysiological conditions that have been investigated include: (1) the production of morphine-like substances in the brain (tetrahydropapaveroline); (2) abnormalities in sugar metabolism; (3) food allergies; and (4) endocrine abnormalities. These will be reviewed briefly.

According to the first hypothesis, acetylaldehyde (the first major breakdown product of alcohol) combines under certain unknown conditions with other body chemicals to form a morphine-like addictive substance. This theory could explain the addictive effect alcohol has on some individuals but not others. However, there currently is not enough evidence to prove this reaction actually happens (Editorial, 1972).

The second theory, abnormalities in sugar metabolism, has also become in vogue of late (Lundquist, 1971). It has been noted that many alcoholics suffer from hypoglycemia and other abnormalities related to sugar or carbohydrate metabolism. But nowhere is the cause and effect quandry more evident. Since these problems are discovered in alcoholics with long drinking histories, it seems just as likely that sugar metabolism problems could be the result of abusive drinking and not the cause.

Another hypothesis, alcoholism as a food allergy or craving, has been forwarded by Williams (1981) and others. This theory holds that some people crave or have an appetite for alcohol (it is also felt that this appetite may be inherited). Several alcoholism treatment programs feature specialized diets that include high protein food as well as vitamins and minerals to offset this craving. Again, cause and effect are difficult to determine. Does an appetite for alcohol cause heavy drinking or result from it, as in addiction?

Finally, the concept of an endocrine dysfunction, researched by Senior (1967) and elsewhere, has emerged as a possible contributing factor to alcoholism. In this framework, some individuals lack the enzyme (NAD) that aids in the metabolism of alcohol. When alcohol is insufficiently broken down, an abundance of acetylaldehyde remains in the system and creates symptoms akin to alcohol withdrawal (nausea, shakes, etc.). Therefore the person repeats his or her drinking to alleviate these symptoms, and a vicious cycle is created. In evaluating this theory, two problems arise. First, the cause and effect relationship is unclear; second, this process does not seem to occur in a large percentage of heavy drinkers.

As was the case with genetic research and alcoholism, studies of biophysical abnormalities have contributed to the knowledge base without explaining the *nature* of alcoholism. To resolve the cause and effect problem, research must be conducted with people *before* they become problem drinkers. In this way, those who exhibit biophysical abnormalities, along with a suitable control group, could be followed throughout their lives, and rates of alcoholism could be compared.

PSYCHOLOGICAL THEORIES OF ALCOHOLISM

Psychological theories of alcoholism involve the association of psychological factors and individuals' drinking behaviors. Once again, however, this research area is plagued with the same methodological problem of cause and effect. In this case, it is difficult to determine if psychological factors are the cause of alcoholism or are the result of years of heavy drinking. Another problem inherent in these studies is the imprecise nature of psychological measurement. In order to be concise, only a review of three frequently cited theories will be presented: (1) personality theory; (2) transactional theory; and (3) psychodynamic theory.

Personality and Alcohol Use

The term "addictive personality" or "alcoholic personality" is often used in the field of alcoholism rehabilitation and is meant to describe an individual who is impulsive, aggressive, overly emotional, agitated, and easily frustrated. There is, in fact, some evidence to support these data. Studies seem to show the Sixteen Personality Factor Questionnaire (16PF) and the Minnesota Multiphasic Personality Inventory (MMPI) (Kammeier, Hoffmann, & Loper, 1973) can be used to discriminate personality differences between alcoholics and nonalcoholics. With the MMPI, alcoholics tended to have consistently more depressive profiles, and on the 16PF they score higher aggressiveness and impulsiveness than nonalcoholics (Walton, 1968). And yet, given the limitations of these studies, as cited earlier, it is really not possible to define an alcoholic personality per se. Furthermore, other research has indicated that there is no definite alcoholic personality and that the range of personality types of alcoholics is not different from that found in the general population (Gorad, McCourt, & Cobb, 1971).

Transactional Theory

Steiner's Transactional Analysis (TA) approach (1979) should interest people working with alcoholic families. Steiner maintains that alcoholism is not a disease at all but a series of distorted communications within families that he labels "games." Theoretically, Steiner believes that if an alcoholic was stranded alone on an island, he or she would stop drinking voluntarily even if plenty of alcohol was available because the "alcoholic game" could not be played. This stands in contradiction to the disease concept that maintains that addiction leads to alcoholic behavior. T A theory believes that alcoholic behavior (games) leads to addiction and that addiction can often be cured.

Two major concepts in T A theory are "games" and "scripts." Games, as previously cited, are defined as a sequence of interactions with one or more people in which the actor has an ulterior motive and some expectation of profit. A script is a person's life-plan that has been assumed during childhood and represents basic decisions the individual has made about himself and others (e.g., "I'm no good and neither is anyone else").

Steiner has outlined three games that he feels alcoholics play. The first of these he has labeled "drunk and proud of it," or D & P. D & P is a three-handed game between the alcoholic and another person who vacillates between two roles, "patsy" and "persecutor." The D & P player is basically interested in getting persecuting parents so angry and frustrated that they show their impotence and foolishness. This relationship starts with a domineering parent or parents and is transferred later in life to spouse, friends, counselors, etc. It is an attempt by the alcoholic to get even with the domineering people in their lives. A typical scenario is when the D & P alcoholic gets drunk, acts out, and then pleads for forgiveness or promises not to do it again. The person (usually a spouse) with whom the game is being played is then forced into two roles: (1) he or she can forgive the D & P player and become a Patsy (it always will happen again); or (2) he or she can become the Persecutor and angrily denounce the behavior. And on and on it goes, with the same game being repeated in many families for years.

The second alcoholic game has been colloquially called "lush." In this game there are four players: the alcoholic (Lush), the Persecutor, the Patsy, and the Rescuer. Lush involves an alcoholic who has been cut off from emotional and (usually) sexual support and who drinks abusively as a response. It is a game because the nondrinking members of the family maintain an appearance of self-righteousness and virtuousness. The family denies any responsibility for the problem and treats the drinker as a scapegoat. The Lush, deprived of warmth or rewards ("strokes") at home, often tries to meet these needs through extramarital affairs and drinking buddies. On the other hand, the underlying guilt feelings of the family (usually the spouse) surface periodically, and this person changes from the persecutor role to that of rescuer. The game is maintained because the love-starved alcoholic settles for the costly strokes obtained when being rescued. However, as long as the alcoholic continues to drink, family members can camouflage their own emotional shortcomings as well as their part of the game. It is important to note that counselors are often a part of the lush game, first playing Patsy and then Persecutor when the alcoholic returns to drinking (in order to be rescued again).

Game three is called "Wino." In this game alcoholics obtain strokes by becoming physically ill and forcing others to literally save their lives and take care of them. Interestingly, the Wino player uses the disease model concept as an excuse to maintain abusive drinking: "I have a disease; therefore I cannot control my drinking, and therefore I cannot really be held responsible for my behavior." To the Wino, the fact that he or she must be at death's door to get aid from those in positions of strength and power implies that others are really not O.K. The Wino operates out of the conviction that he or she is O.K. but the rest of the world is not.

In order to reverse these games and cure the alcoholic, Steiner believes that all those involved in the alcoholic's life must stop playing the game. In this framework the family structure can be seen as the client, as opposed to the alcoholic in isolation. Games take on many additional forms in addition to those outlined here. Although the T A conceptualization of alcoholism is primarily theoretical, it has contributed creatively to the alcoholism field in terms of the analysis and description of interpersonal dynamics within the alcoholic family. Similarly, the view of the alcoholic as "curable" and not diseased has offered a controversial and thought-provoking perception.

Psychodynamic Theory and Alcoholism

Psychodynamic theory explains alcoholism basically as a manifestation of unconscious processes that originated during early stages of the individual's development. These processes are malevolent in that they serve as ineffective and destructive attempts to counter early unresolved conflicts. For example, Blume (1966), after a review of psychodynamic literature, concluded that "oral stage fixation" was a problem for most alcoholics. The result of being fixated (stuck) in the oral stage supposedly accounts for the infantile behavior exhibited by many alcoholics (i.e., narcissism, demanding behavior, passivity, and dependence). The fixation is a result of early deprivation by parents during childhood. Since this dependency and other needs cannot be met by others (until oral fixation is resolved), they lead to anxiety and compensatory needs for control, power, and achievement. For this person, alcohol serves to tranquilize the anxiety as well as create a sense of stength and invulnerability, also known as "false courage."

However, after sobering up from a drinking episode, the alcoholic is flooded with his or her feelings of insecurity, inadequacy, and guilt. Therein lies the motivation to drink again, and a degenerative cycle is established. Because alcoholics can artificially exercise control over their emotional states by drinking, it feeds their grandiose self-images. This need for self-importance is labeled "reactive grandiosity" and is seen as a key dynamic in alcoholics.

The psychodynamic school, like the T A orientation, concedes that alcoholism eventually becomes a physical addiction but holds that it is primarily a symptom and not a disease. Psychoanalysts part company with T A advocates when it comes to treatment, however, seeing alcoholism recovery as a much longer process. The exact treatment strategy of the psychodynamic approach will be outlined in the next chapter. An excellent resource in this area is *Practical Approaches to Alcoholism Psychotherapy* by Zimbler, Wallace, and Blume (1978).

Reinforcement Theories

Reduced to its fundamental elements, operant conditioning simply states that if a behavior is followed by a reward (reinforced), the likelihood that this behavior will occur again is increased. This principle transfers logically to drinking behavior. Consider, for example, the many rewards that follow drinking: relief from tension, euphoria, a sense of well being, increased gregariousness, etc. Alcohol does have a definite effect, usually initially positive, on those who use it.

Most young people sample their first drink of alcohol under parental supervision and consequently enjoy the positive results of drinking (mild euphoria) as opposed to negative results (intoxication and nausea) as an initial experience. This positive first experience is therefore reinforced, which increases the likelihood of subsequent drinking. As additional drinking episodes become similarly rewarded, the bond is further strengthened, and the individual has learned that alcohol consumption is good. According to behaviorists, the longer and more often a behavior is reinforced, the harder the behavior is to stop. This is true even if the behavior is not always reinforced, which may explain why many people continue to drink even though the consequences eventually become aversive.

Another reinforcement system, classical conditioning, involves the occurrence of an object or phenomenon in nature (stimulus) that is reinforcing (such as food or affection) at the same time as a neutral stimulus (bell). If these two stimuli occur together often enough, the previously neutral stimulus will become reinforcing on its own. For example, animals have been taught to salivate at the sound of a bell. The application to alcoholism may be unclear at first, but in our culture many associations between alcohol and/or events are already reinforcing. Adult status, parties, companionship, masculinity, and youthfulness are only a few of the perceived benefits of alcohol use. Such associations are not only a part of our enculturation process but are promoted by liquor distributors who tell us through advertising that liquor is linked with good looks, youth, wealth, etc.

These two processes help to explain why Americans drink so much. We learn from our first drink that alcohol is pleasant, and we associate liquor with a wide variety of enjoyable events.

The use of reinforcement concepts in alcoholism rehabilitation will be elaborated in depth in the following chapter.

Although psychological factors are clearly involved in alcoholism, the following three aspects present problems: (1) the lack of accuracy in measuring psychological factors; (2) the difficulty of establishing a cause-and-effect relationship; and (3) the lack of agreement on operational definitions of psychological factors (e.g., depression, anxiety, etc.).

SOCIOLOGICAL THEORIES OF ALCOHOLISM

The Socialization Process and Alcohol

While there are regional and other sociocultural variations in drinking patterns, the consumption of alcoholic beverages by most adults in American society is normative, social behavior (Barnes, 1977). Thus, drinking behavior by youths seems to be an integral part of the passage into adulthood and is introduced and fostered by the family. Jessor, Graves, Hanson, and Jessor (1968) have elaborated on this process:

> The role of the family as socializer can be seen as primary and pervasive. The family is, after all, the most proximal social system to which patterned exposure occurs; it generally guarantees a continuance exposure extending back in time to the earliest consciousness of social meanings; and it is the single milieu that encompasses at pre-adolescence, the widest range of experience and involvements for the child. Analysis of socialization as it occurs within the family should reveal a significant amount of information about the influence exerted by the culture on the developing child.

It can be assumed that the influence of the family on drinking behavior is great. In the discussion of genetics and alcoholism, the point was made that alcoholism runs in families. However, not only does problem drinking tend to be passed on from generation to generation, but moderate drinking and abstinence are similarly perpetrated along family lines.

The research of Cahalan, Cisin, and Crossley (1969) indicates that, for males in their study, frequent drinking by the father (three times a week or more) was highly correlated with later heavy drinking on the part of the son. Of the males who reported their fathers were frequent drinkers, 35% were heavy drinkers themselves, as opposed to 12% of the men who reported that their fathers never drank or drank less than once a year. Corresponding differences based on the mother's drinking were even more pronounced. In this case, 44% of men who were heavy drinkers had mothers who drank frequently as compared to only 15% of heavy drinkers who had mothers that never drank or drank less than once a year.

The same tendency was true of parents' attitudes toward drinking. Although 28% of the men who reported that their fathers approved of drinking were heavy drinkers themselves, only 12% of the men whose fathers disapproved were heavy drinkers. When the respondents' mothers approved of drinking, 33% of the men drank heavily, but only 15% drank heavily when their mothers disapproved. Women's drinking behaviors are similarly influenced by parental attitudes.

Many additional sociological theories have both general culture-specific applications. In terms of general concepts, three cultural principles are thought to affect the drinking problems of a society. The first is the degree to which a culture induces inner tensions in its members. For example, the Irish peasantry of the nineteenth century suffered from oppression and poverty at the hands of the English. Few personal liberties existed, and life was limited to austerity and hard work. Writings from the period indicate intemperance was a way of life for many, and the words *Irishman* and *drunkard* became synonymous (Bales, 1980). Incidentally, statistics in the United States for hospital admissions for alcoholism currently indicate the Irish to have rates two to three times higher than any other ethnic group.

A second general principle holds that the kind of attitudes a culture holds toward drinking markedly influences the level of consumption and the nature of the consequences. In general, those cultures that have few sanctions against drunkenness have higher rates of alcoholism than those who denounce intoxication. In the first case, American Indians represent a culture that suffers from rampant alcoholism. This group has traditionally tolerated drunken behavior and has often excused violence due to intoxication. It is felt by many tribes that the intoxicated individual is "possessed" during these times, and is not responsible for his or her actions (Hammer, 1965). In the second case, the Jewish culture offers an example of people who use alcohol but denounce intoxication. In virtually every cross-ethnic study of alcoholism rates in the United States, Jews are at the bottom just as the Irish are on the top. Although more than one explanation has been forwarded for this phenomenon, low rates of alcoholism among Jews is thought to be related to the ritualistic manner in which alcohol is consumed. Jews learn to use alcohol in a rational manner from the time they are children, using it primarily for ceremonies and in a family context where intoxication is dissuaded.

The third cultural influence on drinking is the degree to which a society provides suitable substitutes for alcohol use. Unfortunately, other kinds of drug abuse may be substituted. For example, many Moslem cultures regularly use hashish, and the Japanese culture has a high incidence of opium use. Other societal alternatives may include an emphasis on vigorous recreation, higher standards of living, or a just and democratic system of government. However, the amount and kinds of alternatives a society could offer as a suitable alternative to drinking are mostly speculative and unproven.

There are other influences on drinking behavior that can be cited, such as religious affiliation, socioeconomic status, and ethnic identity. The authors' view is that these categories may not in themselves influence drinking but constitute an amalgamation of values that is primarily responsible for the shaping of attitudes and subsequent drinking behavior.

The exact role that socialization and inheritance play, separately or together, in the shaping of an alcoholic is as yet unknown. Is alcoholism learned or inherited? A reasonable and likely possibility is that both processes may be at work, to a larger or lesser degree, depending on circumstances. Defining the conditions under which each is most influential is a continuing challenge in this field.

SUMMARY

The various theoretical hypotheses on the etiology of alcoholism fail to show a definite, single cause. The most reasonable conclusion to draw is that all these theoretical factors contribute to the problem depending on individual circumstances. This book will focus on family influences. The authors, while drawing from the existing theories of alcoholism, have devised a unique perspective of the alcoholic family that constitutes a new approach to intervention, prevention, and treatment strategies. This approach will be described in detail throughout the subsequent chapters.

REFERENCES

Bales, F. Cultural differences in roles of alcoholism. In D. Ward (Ed.), *Alcoholism: Introduction to theory and treatment*. Dubuque, Iowa: Kendall/Hunt, 1980.

Barnes, G.M. The development of adolescent drinking behavior: An evaluative review of the impact of the socialization process within the family. *Adolescence*, 1977, *12* (48), 571-591.

Blume, E.M. Psychoanalytic views of alcoholism: A review. *Quarterly Journal of Studies on Alcohol*, 1966, *27*, 259-299.

Cahalan, D., Cisin, H., & Crossley, H. *American drinking practices*. New Brunswick, N.J.: Journal of Studies on Alcohol, Inc., 1969.

Cruz-Coke, R., & Varela, A. Inheritance of alcoholism. *Lancet*, 1966, *2*, 1282.

Editorial. Alcohol addiction: A biochemical approach. *Lancet*, 1972, *2*, 24-25.

Fialkow, P.J., Thuline, M.C., & Fenster, R.F. Lack of association between cirrhosis of the liver and the common types of colorblindness. *New England Journal of Medicine*, 1966, *275*, 584.

Goodwin, Donald D. Is alcoholism hereditary? *Archives of General Psychiatry,* 1971, *25,* 518-545.

Gorad, S.L., McCourt, W.F., and Cobb, J.C. A communications approach to alcoholism. *Quarterly Journal of Studies on Alcohol,* 1971, *32,* 651-668.

Hammer, J.H. Acculturation stress and the functions of alcohol among forest Potawatomi. *Quarterly Journal of Studies of Alcohol,* 1965, *26,* 1965.

Jellinek, E.M. Phases in the drinking history of alcoholics. *Quarterly Journal of Studies on Alcohol,* 1946, *7,* 1-88.

Jellinek, E.M. Current notes: Phases of alcohol addiction. *Quarterly Journal of Studies on Alcohol,* 1952, *13,* 673-684.

Jellinek, E.M. *The disease concept of alcoholism.* New Haven, Conn.: United Printing Services, Inc., 1960.

Jessor, R., Graves, T., Hanson, R., & Jessor, S. *Personality and deviant behavior—a study of a tri-ethnic community.* New York, N.Y.: Holt, Rinehart & Winston, Inc., 1968.

Kaij, L. *Studies on the etiology and sequels of abuse of alcohol.* Mimeographed. Lund, Sweden: University of Lund, 1960.

Kaij, L. Biases in a Swedish social register of alcoholics. *Social Psychiatry,* 1970, *5,* 216-218.

Kammeier, M.L., Hoffmann, H., & Loper, R.S. Personality characteristics of alcoholics as college freshmen at the time of treatment. *Quarterly Journal of Studies on Alcohol,* 1973, *34,* 390-399.

Lundquist, F. Influence of ethanol on carbohydrate metabolism. *Quarterly Journal of Studies on Alcohol,* 1971, *32,* 1-12.

Partanen, J., Bruun, K., & Markhanen, T. *Inheritance of drinking behavior.* Mimeographed. New Brunswick, N.J.: Rutgers University Center of Alcohol Studies, 1966.

Rogers, D.A., & McClearn, G.E. Alcohol preference in mice. In Bliss (Ed.), *Roots of behavior.* New York, N.Y.: Harper and Row, 1962.

Senior, J.R. Ethanol and liver disease. *Postgraduate Medicine,* 1967, *41,* 65.

Steiner, G.M. *Healing alcoholism.* New York, N.Y.: Grove Press, 1979.

Walton, J.H. Personality as a determinant of the form of alcoholism. *British Journal of Psychiatry,* 1968, *114,* 761-766.

Williams, R.J. *The prevention of alcoholism through nutrition.* New York, N.Y.: Bantam, 1981.

Winokur, G., & Clayton, P.J. Comparison of male and female alcoholics. *Quarterly Journal of Studies on Alcohol,* 1968, *29,* 885-891.

Zimbler, S., Wallace, J., & Blume, S. (Eds.). *Practical approaches to alcoholism psychotherapy.* New York, N.Y.: Plenum Press, 1978.

Chapter 2

Treatment Approaches to Alcoholism

In general, therapeutic approaches to alcoholism very closely follow the various theories of alcoholism etiology that were addressed in Chapter 1. In this chapter, the authors will review several widely recognized models of alcoholism treatment.

ALCOHOLICS ANONYMOUS MODEL

Alcoholics Anonymous (AA) is the most widespread and utilized treatment approach in the field of alcoholism. AA was founded in 1935 by two alcoholics, anonymously named Bill W. and Dr. Bob S. Their idea was to develop a fellowship composed of problem drinkers who would lend each other assistance in conquering their obsession with alcohol. From this beginning, AA has spawned a truly remarkable following that spans geographic, cultural, and socioeconomic lines. Nearly every community in the United States, large or small, has AA meetings on a regular basis. This scope is especially remarkable because AA is composed totally of anonymous volunteers, receives no outside funding, and has no central administration or organized leadership. Over the years, AA has evolved both a set of bylaws, called "traditions," and a relatively uniform procedure of rehabilitation, known as the "twelve steps." In general, AA philosophy holds the following beliefs: (1) alcoholism is an incurable, progressive disease that will result in death without therapeutic intervention; (2) the only remedy for alcoholism is complete abstinence from drinking; (3) once an alcoholic, always an alcoholic—no cure is possible, only remission; and (4) no one can cure his or her own alcoholism without help.

These beliefs form the core of the structure and function of AA. All anyone need do to become a member is have a sincere desire to stop drinking. However, initiation into an AA group usually takes place through "sponsorship," where an experienced member acts as an advocate. Sponsorship may include introducing the new member to the AA group, picking him or her up for the meeting, and in general providing support and advice. Sponsorship is an intergral part of AA recovery, and members believe that being a sponsor is important to their own recovery. In order to get a sponsor, a person can simply call a local AA member and request one. Sponsorship is part of the twelfth (and last) step.

Upon becoming a member, each person learns the philosophy of AA and is given encouragement and support to give up drinking. Other members share their own drinking experiences and describe how they overcame associated problems. This mutual sharing is one of the most effective aspects of AA since it provides practical solutions and alleviates guilt by demonstrating that others have also behaved irrationally while drinking. AA also alleviates guilt by assuring members that their drinking behavior and all the negative consequences associated with it are a manifestation of a disease. However, AA does hold people responsible for their behavior; in other words, it is largely up to them to seek help and maintain their sobriety. In addition to these advantages, AA is helpful in the following ways:

1. AA offers a regular support group composed of individuals who are striving for the same goal—abstinence from alcohol.
2. AA meetings are available daily in most communities and can help alcoholics structure much of their time.
3. Friends and acquaintances are often AA members. This is important because often alcoholics simply do not know many nondrinkers.
4. AA often acts as an important adjunct to professionals who provide psychotherapy to alcoholic clients.
5. AA has no fee and does not discriminate on racial, sexual, or socioeconomic grounds.
6. AA has comprehensive goals, including emotional, behavioral, and spiritual change; the aim is to teach the person a new life style with new values.

Although AA is an effective treatment method for many problem drinkers, there are some limiting factors to AA that the professional counselor should take into account. First, AA is religiously oriented, which may be repugnant to some clients who resist the idea of spiritual surrender. Second, AA has a uniform view of alcoholism, and everyone is indoctrinated into the same basic credo. Research has demonstrated that there are many kinds of problem drinkers, and a complete life style change may be overly rigorous for some who could benefit from lesser modifications in their drinking patterns. And third, AA calls for surrender to God and others as an important first step. This may be confusing for mental health clients who are being helped toward independence and personal responsibility. Counselors should discuss and clarify these issues with clients before referring them to AA.

Finally, it should be pointed out that AA is not a scientific theory but a set of beliefs and procedures that has evolved through years of trial and error. Evaluation research is somewhat difficult to conduct because many AA groups take on unique characteristics and are hard to compare. The anonymous nature of the organization adds to this problem. There is little or no hard data to indicate the effectiveness (success rate) of AA.

Al-Anon

Al-Anon largely incorporates AA principles but focuses on the alcoholic's spouse or significant others. Although Al-Anon often works with family members while the alcoholic is in treatment, in many cases it provides support independent of the alcoholic's actions. Basically, Al-Anon helps those close to an alcoholic face their own problems and see their role in contributing to the family's dysfunction. Participants are encouraged to learn to take care of their own needs and stop revolving their world around the alcoholic's pathology. They are told the alcoholic will not stop drinking until he or she is ready and that many attempts at control (withholding money, hiding liquor, etc.) are counterproductive.

It should be remembered that all family members are negatively influenced by alcoholism, and all contribute to the problems. In the view of the authors, it is equally as important for those in an alcoholic family to receive help as for the alcoholic.

TRANSACTIONAL ANALYSIS MODEL

The Transactional Analysis (TA) treatment model is in marked philosophical contrast to the Alcoholics Anonymous model. TA, as described in Chapter 1, holds that alcoholism is a game or series of destructive interpersonal dynamics and not a disease. TA consequently believes that alcoholism can be "cured," as opposed to being controlled, and that (theoretically) the alcoholic can return to nonproblem drinking.

In his latest book, *Healing Alcoholism,* Steiner (1979) has described his TA approach. First, Steiner believes that alcoholics must sincerely want to seek help for their drinking because many alcoholics initially enter therapy not to be rehabilitated but to involve the counselor in a game. Unless therapists are effective in screening clients requesting help, they may become unwilling participants in the alcoholic game. This assessment involves careful and direct questioning of the person requesting help and "contracting," or committing the client to a specific course of action.

When screening a potential alcoholic client, his or her motives for seeking help should be examined. For example, if potential clients are evasive about having a drinking problem or are being coerced into therapy by family, friends, or the courts, Steiner believes they should be told to delay counseling until they believe a problem exists and they want help. Steiner also avoids diagnoses ("you are an alcoholic") or collaboration with others who want the person to stop drinking. A direct request for help from the person is required. Once a request for help is made, a contract for treatment is specified by the therapist, and this contract must be agreed to by the client without qualifications. More specifically, successful treatment requires alcoholic clients to:

- maintain complete sobriety for a minimum of a year
- attend group therapy sessions regularly every week for two hours during the one-year period
- involve themselves in specific homework including diet and other life style changes addressed to their specific problems
- attend monthly body work sessions (as an example)

The establishment of a mutual informed consent relationship (contract) involves three transactions:

1. the request for treatment from the client,
2. the offer of treatment by the therapist, and
3. an acceptance of treatment by the client.

Also underlying the TA conception of treating alcoholics is the avoidance of counselor responses called "rescues." Below, Steiner (1979) cites ten rules to avoid rescues:

1. When three or more suggestions to an alcoholic have been rejected, you are Rescuing. Instead, offer one or two and wait to see whether they are acceptable. If they are not, stop making suggestions. Don't play "Why don't you . . . Yes, but . . . "
2. It's O.K. to investigate possible therapists for an alcoholic, but never make an appointment for him or her. Any therapist who is willing to make an appointment with an alcoholic through a third person is probably a potential Rescuer and eventual Persecutor.
3. Do not remove liquor, pour liquor down the drain, or look for hidden stashes of liquor in an alcoholic's house, unless you're asked to do so by the alcoholic. Conversely, do not ever buy, serve, mix for, or offer alcohol to an alcoholic.
4. Do not engage in lengthy conversations about alcoholism or a person's alcoholic problem while the person is drunk or drinking; that will be a waste of time and energy and will be completely forgotten by him/her in most cases.

5. Never lend money to a drinking alcoholic. Do not allow a drunk alcoholic to come to your house, or, worse, drink in your house. Instead, in as loving and nurturing a way as possible, ask to see him/her again when he/she is sober.

6. Do not get involved in errands, repair jobs, cleanups, long drives, pickups, or deliveries for an alcoholic who is not actively participating in fighting his alcoholism.

7. When you are relating to an alcoholic, do not commit the common error of seeing only the good and justifying the bad. "He's so wonderful when he's not drunk" is a common mistake people make with respect to alcoholics. The alcoholic is a whole person, and his personality includes both his good part and his bad part. They cannot be separated from each other. Either take the whole person or none at all. If the ledger comes out consistently in the red, it is foolish to look only on the credit side.

8. Do not remain silent on the subject of another's alcoholism. Don't hesitate to express yourself freely on the subject: what you don't like, what you won't stand for, what you think about it, what you want or how it makes you feel. But don't do it with the expectation of creating a change—do it just to be on record. Often your outspoken attitude will be taken seriously and appreciated, though it may not bring about many immediate changes.

9. Be aware of doing anything that you don't want to do for the alcoholic. It is bad enough if you commit any of the above mistakes willingly. But when you add to them the complications of doing them when you would prefer not to, you are compounding your mistake and fostering an eventual persecution.

10. Never believe that an alcoholic is hopeless. Keep your willingness to help ready, offer it often, and make it available whenever you detect a genuine interest and effort on the alcoholic's part. When that happens, don't overreact, but help cautiously and without Rescuing, doing only what you want to do, and no more than your share. (pp. 156, 157)

After the alcoholic client has requested help, has been offered help by the counselor, and has agreed to its terms, the course of therapy involves the frank and thorough examination of the person's games and their payoffs.

This is usually done in both individual and group therapy sessions. Not only do clients explore current behaviors, but they are also helped to identify the root causes of their games, which can often be traced back to early childhood experiences. In childhood, basic decisions about life are made ("I have to be perfect to be O.K."), and life scripts are formed. TA also believes that people mirror qualities learned from their parents (e.g., being critical or accepting), and these early learnings are explored in light of current behaviors and attitudes.

Once these factors have been integrated by the client, new and more healthy ways of getting needs met are explored. Since games involve other people, it is advantageous if other participants (usually the family) are involved in treatment. This is important because others in the alcoholic's life may resist the changes he or she may make because they are also game players and consequently receive their own payoffs. It should be underscored that games are played unconsciously by all involved.

In addition, TA therapists make the point that their approach is not to outwit alcoholics or put them down. In fact, TA emphasizes a true valuing of the individual as well as support and empathy. Essentially, the therapist must avoid becoming a game member since that only serves to prolong and reinforce the alcoholic's self-destructive behaviors. The therapist should be direct and confrontive but in a truly nurturing way.

Psychodynamic Model

Psychodynamic theorists describe several principles for the treatment of alcoholism. First, they believe that all drinking must be terminated if rehabilitation is to be effective. Without detoxification and initial sobriety, it is felt that treatment will be unsuccessful and a power struggle will develop between the client and the therapist. Second, it is important to understand the "transference" that will be established by the client. Transference refers to the attachment of unresolved older feelings in a newer relationship. In this case, the alcoholic client will attach the paradoxical feelings of extreme dependency along with hostility, manipulation, and testing behaviors to the therapist. This leads to the third principle, "countertransference," which the therapist may attach to the client. An understanding of this process is very important because it is easy for a therapist to take the client's resistance personally and become disgusted and discouraged. Instead, the therapist should see clients' behaviors objectively, as a symptom of their pathological condition. It is also underscored that therapists should not see themselves as omnipotent, and they should realize that no one can stop an alcoholic determined to drink.

The fourth principle is that the alcoholic's defenses should not be smashed by heavy confrontation during initial therapy, but should be redirected in a supportive manner. Under this model, insight is not the initial goal of therapy—sobriety is the first goal. For example, Wallace (1978) believes denial can be used to benefit the alcoholic during initial treatment. He points out that rather than make clients face up to all their irrationalities of the past, clients need to preserve some self-worth and save face. Denial can be an effective coping mechanism in order to fend off overwhelming anxiety. Coming to grips with the past, Wallace believes, should come later in the treatment process.

The fifth principle is that therapeutic leverage, or therapist potency, can only come from a clear understanding of the client's developmental past. Not that therapists will bring these issues out, but they need to know what defenses should be left in place (for the present) in order to maximize treatment. The sixth and final principle is the concept of stages. According to psychodynamic theory, three stages are necessary for total recovery, as shown in Table 2-1. Stage one is the client's recognition that "I can't drink." This is an initial stage where a good deal of external control is necessary: detoxification, hospitalization, Antabuse, Alcoholics Anonymous, and family support. In this stage, the alcoholic needs protection against his or her own impulses to drink. The second phase is "I won't drink," or the internalization of controls. At this stage the conflict about drinking is mostly unconscious. Many AA members and other "recovering" alcoholics are at this stage and can function adequately. The third stage is "I don't have to drink" and represents conflict resolution. It is at this point, psychodynamic theorists believe, that insight should be sought, but only after sobriety and stabilization have occurred. They also point out that few alcoholics successfully complete Stage III because their lives are manageable for the most part at Stage II, and the impetus for further change may be diminished. The completion of all three stages is felt to be a relatively long-term process but is needed before the alcoholic can truly be rid of conflict.

Table 2-1 Stages of Treatment

Stages	Patient Status	Treatment
Stage I	"I can't drink" (need for external control)	Alcohol detoxification Directive psychotherapy Antabuse AA Family therapy Al-Anon
Stage II	"I won't drink" (internalized control)	Directive psychotherapy Supportive psychotherapy Consider discontinuing use of Antabuse AA
Stage III	"I don't have to drink" (conflict resolution)	Psychoanalytically oriented psychotherapy

Source: Zimberg, Wallace & Blume. *Practical approaches to alcoholism psychotherapy.* New York: Plenum Press, 1978.

BEHAVIORAL MODELS OF TREATMENT

The principles of operant and classical conditioning were outlined in Chapter 1. How these principles are manifested in specific treatment models will now be described.

Aversive Conditioning Techniques

Nowhere can the classical conditioning model be more clearly demonstrated than in aversive conditioning paradigms. Essentially, a noxious substance is administered to a client at the same time that liquor is consumed. If this procedure is repeated enough times, the liquor will itself become a noxious stimulus, and further alcohol consumption will become impossible. The first example of aversive conditioning to be cited involves the use of nausea-inducing chemicals.

The two chemicals most widely used in aversive conditioning are apomorphine and emetine. This procedure was explored as early as 1941 by Vouegthlin, Lemere, Broz, and O'Hollaren, who reported success rates as high as 60% after one year. The procedure involves the administration of emetine shortly before the sipping of the alcoholic's favorite beverage. This is followed by prolonged vomiting of 45 minutes or more. This sequence is repeated two or three times in a row, every other day for three or four days. In addition, individual and family counseling often accompany the treatment.

A second form of aversive conditioning is electric shock. The treatment format is very similar to the chemical aversion model, but here the client is given painful (but not harmful) shocks via electrodes on the arms as he or she sips a preferred beverage. Often a shock is terminated when the drink is spit out. A variation of this approach is aimed at controlled drinking. The first stage of this process is to teach clients to accurately estimate their blood alcohol levels (BALs) through feedback exercises in which they estimate their BALs. Once different BALs can be discriminated, clients drink to a predetermined level, above which a shock is administered. The goal is to create an aversive experience only after an elevated BAL occurs. Research by Nathon and Bridell (1977), however, indicates this technique is only moderately successful and the effects short lived.

Operant Conditioning

An example of operant conditioning (contingency management) is individualized behavior therapy (IBT), initially developed at Patton State Hospital in 1970. This research represented the first major attempt in the United States to treat alcoholic clients in which the treatment outcome was nonproblem drinking. It was the contention of researchers that diagnosed Gamma alcoholics could learn new drinking responses that were felt (by the client) to be nonabusive. Alcoholics were taught to avoid abusive drinking behaviors such as: (a) ordering a straight drink; (b) gulping versus sipping drinks; (c) ordering a drink within 20 minutes of a previous drink; and (d) ordering more than three drinks in a 90-minute period. Other components of this treatment regime included videotape replays, where drinking antecedents (e.g., anxiety due to social pressure) were analyzed and modified. This technique represents aversive avoidance. Behavior connected to abusive drinking resulted in electric shocks, but new positive behavior was not punished. This is an operant conditioning model in that reinforcement (in this case, lack of shock) is contingent upon the client's behavior.

Work done in Baltimore City Hospitals (Bigelow, Liebson, & Griffiths, 1974) shows that chronic alcoholics moderated their drinking in order to live in an enriched environment (i.e., phone privileges, visitors, regular diet) and to avoid a more austere environment in which these privileges were unavailable. Briefly, it was concluded by researchers that alcoholics could and would voluntarily control their drinking in order to improve their lives in a structured setting. How they would fare in society is another matter.

Assertiveness Training and Systematic Desensitization

Other forms of behavioral techniques can be used without elaborate equipment and in an outpatient setting. Two of these are assertiveness training and systematic desensitization. Assertiveness training is thought to be appropriate for many alcoholics because the expression of anger, resentment, and other forms of confrontation often occurs only during intoxication and is usually destructive. Assertiveness training is aimed at helping an individual better manage interpersonal relationships. Typically, alcoholic clients will describe situations to their therapists in which they were unassertive (accepted a drink when they really did not want one). This scenario is role-played and analyzed, and then new, more assertive responses are rehearsed.

This is followed by a homework session in which the client tries out the new behavior in real life. The next step is to analyze what took place. For example, how did the other person react, and how did the client feel? Following this, other new responses are discussed and practiced, especially focusing on areas of conflict in the client's life. Eventually, the client should be able to generalize new responses (which are more rewarding) in a variety of previously stress-producing situations. This procedure is invaluable for many alcoholic clients who tend to avoid confrontation, feel guilty or ashamed, and then drink as a coping response. Alcoholic clients often avoid confronting marital, work, or social interaction problems, and this avoidance is usually followed by a drinking spree and an explosion of feelings.

Systematic desensitization (Wolpe, 1973) is similar in that stress-producing life situations (which often cue drinking) are the focus of treatment. The general idea behind systematic desensitization is to teach clients to relax while imagining stressful circumstances. The first step in training is deep muscle relaxation, which is accomplished through the contraction and relaxation of muscles. Next, the client and therapist construct a hierarchy of stressfulness, from the least stressful to the most stressful event. Following this, the patient is instructed to imagine being in a low stress situation while fully relaxed. Progression up the scale takes place until the client can imagine the most stressful situation in a relaxed state. Eventually, the client actually enters these situations with reduced anxiety. Because many alcoholics experience anxiety and stress and drink to cope with these states, systematic desensitization, like assertiveness training, is seen as appropriate treatment to offset the immediate impulse to drink in reaction to stress.

Nutritional Approaches

Most detoxification centers and residential treatment facilities include proper nutrition as an integral part of their treatment regimen. It is generally felt that alcoholic clients neglect proper diet and often suffer the effects of malnutrition. But malnutrition has also been forwarded as more than a side effect of alcoholism; Williams (1981) and others consider nutrition to be a contributing factor in its development. According to this theory, people vary greatly in their inherent tolerance and appetite for liquor. Williams feels many are therefore born with a predisposition to alcohol abuse and are at high risk to become alcoholics from birth. He makes two essential points in this regard: (1) alcoholism may be prevented through proper nutrition; and (2) it may also be treated in this manner.

For prevention, Williams describes seven principles to follow. Individuals should: (1) know their unique physiological needs; (2) eat high quality foods; (3) avoid low quality foods (e.g., sugars and starches); (4) exercise; (5) cultivate inner peace through moderation and emotional health; (6) use nutritional supplements (vitamins and minerals); and (7) use glutamine, an amino acid, as a food supplement. For alcoholism treatment, Williams underlines the importance of glutamine. This naturally occurring substance is thought to protect bacterial cells that are important in metabolism of food. Research with laboratory animals has shown rats to lower their voluntary consumption of alcohol by 40% through the use of glutamine. With humans, Williams relies on case histories rather than experimental research but insists that some alcoholics' craving for alcohol can be significantly reduced by adding glutamine to their diets. More on the subject can be found in Williams' book *The Prevention of Alcoholism Through Nutrition*.

Employee Assistance Programs

The Employee Assistance Program (EAP) is not a model of alcoholism treatment but a model for intervention and referral of alcohol abusers at a worksite. These programs have proliferated in recent years as businesses have discovered their financial and humanitarian value. Essentially, an employee whose work has slipped consistently is no longer simply fired. He or she is instead approached by a trained supervisor who offers the worker an option—accept confidential help or face possible job action. Often this comes as an ultimatum. Get help or lose the job.

In the majority of cases, the problems are alcohol related—absenteeism, tardiness, or a decline in performance. The company benefits because a trained employee can be rehabilitated and return to work. Employees obviously benefit because they are forced to accept help (which they otherwise might refuse), and they often keep their jobs. All supervisors are trained and are told not to attempt to diagnose but to base the referral strictly on work performance. The entire procedure is confidential and does not go into the employee's personnel file. Often insurance carriers for the company have a special clause that pays for hospitalization for alcoholism and other problems that interfere with the employee's ability to perform. EAPs also serve the insurance agency because it is less costly to rehabilitate a worker than pay for years of disability. Also, the rate of accidents and injuries is reduced because impaired workers are not allowed to remain on duty.

Typically, the initial referral is made by the EAP coordinator who assesses the nature of the employee's problem and makes a referral to an appropriate rehabilitation agency. Progress is monitored. When the treatment agency, the EAP coordinator, and the employee feel the time is right, he or she returns to the worksite. Upon the employee's return to work, the immediate supervisor monitors work performance. EAP programs in such companies as Kemper Insurance, Eastman Kodak, Consolidated Edison, Dupont, and many, many others, have reported both savings and a high rate of success—up to 80% (Rouse). These results may be due to the high level of motivation created when an individual's job is on the line and the relatively high level of functioning of the population served.

Alcoholism Services

The most available alcoholism service, as mentioned earlier, is Alcoholics Anonymous. Nearly every community has AA groups that meet on a regular basis. AA also functions as an adjunct to many public and private alcoholism treatment centers. Meetings are usually held once a week; however, many communities have several different meetings that make it possible for an individual to attend nearly every day if so desired. Larger communities have a wide variety of AA groups consisting of individuals with homogeneous socioeconomic backgrounds. In some areas, there are AA groups for physicians and priests. It is therefore often possible and desirable to refer a client to a meeting where he or she will find people with similar backgrounds. Information about AA can be obtained from a variety of sources, including local mental health centers, physicians, clergymen, the "personals" section of many newspapers, or General Services Office, Grand Central Station, New York, NY 10017.

Other alcoholism services include public and private rehabilitation facilities, as well as counselors, psychologists, psychiatrists, and other individuals who specialize in alcoholism rehabilitation. Public alcoholism centers are often (but not always) incorporated within a community mental health center and consist of inpatient (hospital) or halfway house residential care (one to three months long), outpatient counseling, and social setting detoxification (one to five days long). These programs can be found through local, state, or federal government departments of health and mental health. Private alcoholism rehabilitation programs offer basically the same range of services as the public ones but are more often "free-standing," which means they are not a part of a larger mental health system. Also, most private programs are affiliated with hospitals administratively and are often housed in hospitals. An additional comment is that most public and private alcoholism programs, as well as AA, provide outreach services and will therefore make home visits if necessary.

SUMMARY

Although not covered in this review, many additional forms of alcoholism treatment do exist. For example, Glasser's reality therapy techniques, gestalt methods, and others have been used in the treatment of alcoholic clients. What the authors have attempted to do, however, is present those models that have addressed themselves *directly* to the treatment of alcoholism and are most widely used.

Evaluation of these various models is difficult because treatment outcome data are either not available (e.g., AA) or are not generally agreed upon by various theoretical orientations. Even programs that do publish outcome results, such as aversive conditioning programs, are subject to question because it can be argued that private programs serve more highly functioning clients than AA, for example. Private facilities require payment, and the clientele usually are (or were recently) employed and/or have health insurance; therefore, lower socioeconomic groups are screened out.

The authors recommend an eclectic approach; the treatment should fit the needs of the client and should be individualized.

Many similarities exist between the models presented. For example, all call for initial abstinence. In this vein, it can be argued that the specific model of treatment may not be as important as the competence of the practitioner and the motivation and readiness of the client. The authors' conclusions are that no one model is universally "true" or appropriate and that all the models presented can be effective, depending on the unique needs of the client.

It is also important to point out that no mention of family therapy approaches was made. Traditionally accepted approaches by and large have not visualized alcoholism treatment in a family context. Rather, the "identified patient" medical model has predominated.

This book was written to offer an alternative, and the authors feel, a superior concept of alcoholism treatment. Obviously, family therapy is not the only "true" effective approach. Many models of treatment can be adopted to focus on the family system (as opposed to the individual) as the client.

REFERENCES

Bigelow, G., Liebson, I.A., & Griffiths, R.R. Alcoholic drinking suppression by a behavioral time out period. *Behavior Research and Therapy,* 1974, *12,* 107-115.

Nathon, P.E., & Bridell, D.W. Behavioral treatment and assessment of alcoholism. In B. Kissin & H. Begleiter (Eds.), *The biology of alcoholism* (Vol. 5). New York, N.Y.: Plenum Press, 1977.

Rouse, Kenneth A. *What to do about the employee with a drinking problem.* Kemper Insurance Companies, public relations, Tongrove, Illinois.

Steiner, C.M. *Healing alcoholism.* New York, N.Y.: Grove Press, 1979.

Voegthlin, W.L., Lemere, F., Broz, W.R., & O'Hollaren, P. Conditioned reflex therapy of chronic alcoholism IV. A preliminary report on the value of reinforcement. *Quarterly Journal of Studies on Alcohol,* 1941, *2,* 505-511.

Wallace, J. Working with the preferred defense structure of the recovering alcoholic. In A. Zimberg, J. Wallace, & S. Blume (Eds.), *Practical approaches to alcoholism psychotherapy.* New York, N.Y.: Plenum Press, 1978.

Williams, R.J. *The prevention of alcoholism through nutrition.* New York, N.Y.: Bantam, 1981.

Wolpe, J. *The practice of behavior therapy* (Ed.), (Vol. 2). New York, N.Y.: Pergamon Press, 1973.

Part II

Etiology

The previous chapters have discussed traditional and contemporary theories of the etiology and treatment of alcoholism. Therapists choose treatment methods based on their views of the cause of alcoholism. In many of the previous theories, the assumption was that drinking problems originated with the drinker, and the treatment was therefore directed toward the individual. However, excessive drinking behavior may lead to disruption of a social system, or it may be a result of a dysfunctional social system such as a family. This drinking behavior may even have a function in the family system that acts and reacts to perpetuate the behavior. Family therapists are acutely aware of the environmental, biological, and interpersonal factors that may lead a family member to abuse alcohol. This family viewpoint focuses on interpersonal relationships and transactions rather than on personal pathology. The therapist works interactionally with the entire family. Rather than involving family members simply to enhance the treatment of the identified patient, the focus is shifted to the family as the patient. Thus, the goal of treatment is an improvement in family functioning and not just sobriety for the alcoholic member. With this approach the therapist works for a healthy family system that has no need for a symptomatic member—a family that communicates freely, both emotionally and cognitively, with each other on every subject and whose members meet their needs in the family.

A large portion of this book is dedicated to understanding the role the family members of an alcoholic play in the onset, progression, treatment, and prevention of alcoholism and problem drinking. The etiology section will address the interlocking relationships of family members as they relate to the drinking behavior of the alcoholic and will examine the part these relationships play in perpetuating this destructive cycle. The roots of alcoholism must be understood not only to aid in choosing the proper treatment method, but also to help prevent alcohol abuse in families, especially those with longstanding histories of alcoholism. This issue will be addressed more fully in Chapter 4.

Chapter 3

Viewing the Family as a Client

The first part of this chapter will discuss the family of origin and the nuclear family and will examine these interlocking relationships in terms of their value for treatment. The second section will cover the overlapping, yet unique, theories of the etiology of family dysfunction as proposed by the communication model, the systems model, the structural model, and the social learning model of family therapy.

THE NUCLEAR FAMILY AND THE FAMILY OF ORIGIN

The nuclear family consists of those individuals with whom the alcoholic is presently living. The husband and wife of this family originated from separate families of origin. These families of origin are the parents, in-laws, and future grandparents of the marital partners. In discussing the family, it is impossible to explain the nuclear family without intertwining it with families of origin in a circular fashion. The nuclear family, in turn, becomes a family of origin for all of the siblings.

The nuclear family begins with the decision of a man and a woman, both from separate social systems with unique values, beliefs, and interactional dynamics, to marry and form a third system, bringing with them parts from their original systems (families of origin). The attraction these two people feel for each other is invariably linked to the marital relationships of their parents or the role they played in the family. The woman, for example, may be looking for someone strong like her father because she is weak like her mother. Or, she may be looking for someone she can dominate and someone who will allow her to maintain her compulsively intense relationship with her mother. The man, on the other hand, may feel weak but defensively appears strong to impress his mate. Because his father was the family authority, the man may wish to recreate this role for himself.

Bowen (1978) believes people with equal levels of differentiation from their parents are attracted to each other. He says, "It is common for young people to get into marriage blaming their parents for past unhappiness, and expecting to find perfect harmony in the marriage" (p. 263). However, people who are overly dependent on their parents and have a low capacity for independent problem solving are often unable to form new attachments in marital relationships.

Framo (1976) believes "the relationship problems that adults have with their spouses and children are reconstructions and elaborations of earlier conflicts from the family of origin" (p. 194).

He states that people perceive their spouses based on their own needs and make demands that are irrational but are needed to fill the voids they experienced in their own families. Mate selections, according to Framo, are "made with exquisite accuracy, and unconscious deals are made—e.g., I will be your conscience if you will act out my impulses" (p. 194). Thus, a wife with a large superego will control her antisocial husband within limits, while he acts out her rebellious needs that she is unable to fulfill. The two personalities become dependent on each other and increasingly intertwined, making it difficult for either to leave regardless of the dysfunction of the relationship. Marital partners enmeshed in these relationships (based on the inability to function as an individual) can manifest dysfunctions leading to superficial relationships, emotional upheaval, and possible drinking behavior (if this drinking model was present in their family of origin). Often these marital partners reach out to each other for identity and fuse into a single entity in the marriage. To achieve some separateness the marital partners must set up emotional distance. One spouse may take the dominant position in the relationship with the remaining spouse adapting to the other and further losing identity. "If this pattern is continued long enough, the adaptive one is vulnerable to some kind of chronic dysfunction, which can be physical illness, emotional illness, or a social dysfunction such as drinking, the use of drugs or irresponsible behavior" (Bowen, 1978, p. 263).

Fogarty (1976) describes marital relationships as having an emotional pursuer and an emotional distancer. Usually the pursuer is the wife and the distancer is the husband, but these roles can be reversed. As the wife works toward emotional closeness, the husband distances. A diagram of this process is shown in Figure 3-1.

In healthy systems these roles are interchangeable with both parties pursuing at times and achieving intimacy. Often the pursuer in one area will be the distancer in another area. If mutual distancing remains over a prolonged period of time, a fixed distance occurs that may place the husband in a peripheral position in the family. This result may be functional for the husband's identity but dysfunctional for the marriage. Often in these cases the wife can become overinvolved with one or several children, passing on the inability to differentiate from the parents. Alcoholism as a coping mechanism can be transmitted from generation to generation.

Figure 3-1 Distance, Pursuit, Closeness, and Overinvolvement

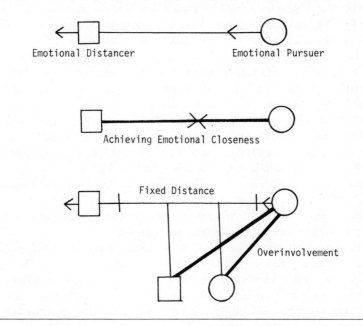

Emotional distancing is frequently seen between every member of an alcoholic family. The discussion in the chapters to follow will deal with overprotective and overinvolved parents as predisposers of alcoholism.

Case History

A case example of marital difficulty resulting from emotional distancing in the wife's family of origin was seen at a child guidance clinic. Judy, aged 33, and Marvin, aged 47, were referred to the center for parenting information and help with their son Chris, aged 4. A large portion of the therapy hours was concerned with Judy's complaints about her husband's behaviors, in addition to withdrawal of love and deterioration of their sexual relationship since the birth of their son. The therapists at this point began to focus on the marital relationship. Judy explained that this was the second marriage for both her and her husband. Her husband had three children by a previous marriage and did not wish to have any in this marriage. Judy had been told that it would be very difficult for her to have children, and she was unable to have children during her first marriage. The assumed marital agreement was marriage for love and companionship—not to raise a family. When Judy became pregnant, she was extremely happy but feared Marvin would feel she had deceived him. After Chris' birth, Judy became very suspicious of Marvin. His work took him on the road five days a week while Judy stayed home and became overinvolved with Chris. She also accused Marvin of not caring for Chris and stated she was working very hard to have a loving family that would be different from the unfeeling family she grew up in.

During a history-taking session the therapist discovered that Judy had never felt loved by her alcoholic father and was jealous of his relationship with her sister. She tearfully admitted, "If he would just put his arms around me once and tell me everything was all right, maybe I could finally believe he cares."

Judy continued to criticize Marvin in the family sessions for minor issues that Marvin would attempt to change. Repeatedly, Marvin assured Judy that he had neither felt trapped nor tricked by Chris' birth and that he really loved her and their son. Judy was unable to believe him and complained about the infrequency of sexual activity. Upon investigation, Marvin explained that Judy's critical remarks during sex had angered him, and he had been avoiding her (setting up the distance). This pattern of criticism was a repetition of the conflict between Judy's mother and father that distanced her father from the family.

As improvements began to occur in the relationship due to the therapy, Judy would continue to find fault and state that she did not believe Marvin loved her. Although Judy protested that she was pursuing intimacy, all of her actions were distancing the relationship. Finally, she demanded to have another baby, knowing that Marvin was opposed to the idea. This demand gave Marvin a further excuse to avoid sexual activity and also provided Judy with further proof of Marvin's lack of love. At this point in the therapy, Marvin became weary of working toward intimacy and refused to attend further sessions.

During Judy's remaining individual sessions, she began to understand that she was unable to feel love from her child or her husband because she had never felt it from her father. Since Judy did not feel worthy of love, she created situations in her marriage to prove to herself that her husband was so angry at her for having a child that he was seeing other women and withholding love from her.

Because Marvin felt frustrated when Judy thwarted all his attempts to show love, he increased his drinking, stayed away from home long periods of time, and eventually left the marriage. Judy moved home with her parents. In this marriage, Judy became the emotional distancer, hoping to gain emotional closeness that she had never felt as a child.

The marital relationship may be functional or dysfunctional depending upon the hopes, fears, and needs of the individuals and their motivations to marry. To a great degree these needs are influenced by the roles these individuals played in their families of origin and the degree of differentiation from these family members. If, as a child, a wife took on caretaking duties in her family to gain self-worth and protect an alcoholic parent, she may seek a husband who needs similar protection, thus maintaining her self-worth as a caretaker. This may be one explanation for the high rate of daughters of alcoholics who marry alcoholics.

Since children have a great need for acceptance and verification, they record and copy their parents' behaviors. Parents often hear themselves repeated. While playing house, Susie yells at Johnnie for coming home late and then turns to her dolls to lecture them on the disarray of their toys. Parents want their children to be like them and carry on their family traditions and positive traits. However, children mirror bad habits as well and may cause negative responses from their parents. Unfortunately, some children learn that negative attention is acceptable if the positive kind is infrequent. If Mommy does not show love, the child may be able to elicit anger, which is better than indifference. Children cannot verify themselves with indifference.

Unfortunately, negative attention sets up inner conflict that cannot be resolved. The more children repeat negative behavior to gain acceptance, the more rejection they receive. Siblings may divide this attention. The oldest child may be the family darling who does no wrong, leaving no room for the second child to outshine this perfectionist. However, there is much negative attention left for a rebellious troublemaker. "Every rebellious child is raging inside over his parent's failure to show him love he desperately needs and wants. What he is angry about is that he does not *feel* loved despite the loving words he/she may hear" (Hoffman, 1979, p. 26). These children have a faulty belief that they can only belong in this family by hurting others as they feel hurt. This revenge cycle teaches passive aggressive ways of dealing with the anger over loss of love.

Jenny is an example of a passive aggressive child. At age four, she accidently dropped and broke her mother's favorite crystal vase that had been a wedding present from her mother's parents. At age 10, Jenny went to a friend's softball game after school and missed dinner with her grandparents, who had driven all day to visit her. Jenny's parents were humiliated and hurt when they could not explain where Jenny was. When Jenny was 14, she ran away from home the day before the family was to attend her grandparents' 50th wedding anniversary. None of these incidents involved direct confrontation with Jenny's parents, but she wanted them to feel the hurt she had felt. She forgot rules, disobeyed at times that would affect her parents the most and would cause further disapproval of her parents' parenting skills from the grandparents. These were not isolated incidents in Jenny's family—they were representative of a pattern that developed when Jenny felt she could not belong to this family without hurting others.

Revenge cycles are present in many families for periods of time. In the alcoholic family, these patterns can become chronic. Alcoholic parents may be modeling these behaviors and may be unable to give these children the love and approval they are asking for by their behavior.

The emotional vacuum just described is further compounded if the parents are unable to love one another and one spouse sees negative mirroring of the other spouse in a child. If the family rule is that spouses do not fight, these children are vulnerable for attack on the negative mirrored behavior. In this situation, the spouse erroneously combats misplaced marital issues with the children. Frequently, this pattern appears in divorced or separated families when one parent is not living with the family and the custodial parent has not settled the marital issues with the other spouse. This pattern is certain to reduce the self-image of the child even further in a downward spiral. The children mirror the parents, and the parents further reject them. Self-destructive patterns like these can continue on to adulthood. Hoffman (1979) believes self-destructive problems of adulthood (such as alcoholism) can be traced to the rebellion of a child who is still holding on to anger with mother and father. These individuals may know they are endangering their lives with drinking but are daring their parents to stop them. Hoffman continues to say:

> This conflict between the intellect and the emotions is the reason most attempts to permanently solve addiction are ineffective. No amount of information or encouragement is powerful enough to counter the force of our angry rebellious child underneath the veneer of our intellect. In the most extreme cases even the fear of untimely death is not a strong enough deterrent. (p. 27)

This inability to love and show love becomes a multigenerational problem. If father and mother did not really love each other, then their children will have difficulty maintaining loving relationships. This is a real problem for many. Hoffman says, "We pursue the love our parents did not know how to give and become unloving in spite of our quest for love" (p. 22). Bowen (1971) says that children are unable to raise their level of differentiation above their parents' level, and Hoffman believes children are unable and do not dare to rise above the emotional giving of their parents.

In healthy families destructive patterns often correct themselves, but in alcoholic families the avoidance of intimacy becomes chronic and predictable.

When the children of alcoholics marry, they often seek others who remind them of the parents that withheld love. The daughter of an alcoholic who marries an alcoholic is saying to her father, "I've not turned my back on you. I've married someone who acts like you. Now, will you love me?" To her mother she says, "I'm a martyr like you. We are alike; please love me." In the case history of Judy and Marvin, Judy copied her parents' emotional distance in her own marriage, even though she said she wanted a marriage different from her mother's. The conflict occurred when she rebelled against the unfeeling patterns of her parents, which caused guilt. Eventually, Judy used this rebellion to recreate emotional distance and continue to beg for parental love.

Many of these needs for acceptance go unspoken during courtship, and as the initial defenses used by each partner fade with time, disillusionment sets in. The fantasized white knight becomes a human being who squeezes the toothpaste tube in the middle and fails to replace the cap. This disillusionment can lead to detachment and can end either in divorce or in a changed perspective that allows growth in the relationship. Feelings of disillusionment may lead to the decision to have a child that will presumably rejuvenate the marriage and change the couple into a family. Unfortunately, this usually divides the couple more by adding a heavy responsibility to an already strained relationship. If the parents' self-esteem is low, they may look to the child to fill this void and prove the family's worth to the community. Many hopes ride with these first children, and at their birth the family becomes a social and psychological unit that is more than just the sum of its parts.

Homeostasis

A common bond or thread runs through family members. Jackson (1957) coined the term *family homeostasis* to define a balancing behavior in families. "This balance or equilibrium shifts in response to changes which occur within the family (illness, aging, death, unemployment) and influential forces from without (economic, political, social)" (Meeks & Kelly, 1970, p. 400). Ewing and Fox (1968) adopted theoretical concepts from Jackson's theory of homeostasis in families. They view the alcoholic marriage as a "homeostatic mechanism" that is "established . . . to resist change over long periods of time. The behavior of each spouse is rigidly controlled by the other. As a result, an effort by one person to alter typical role behavior threatens the family equilibrium and provokes renewed efforts by the spouse to maintain status quo" (p. 87). Alcohol is often a key part in the balance of the alcoholic family.

Wegscheider (1981) draws an analogy between the theory of homeostasis and the operation of a mobile in this excerpt:

A family system resembles a mobile. A mobile is an art form made up of rods and strings upon which are hung various parts. The beauty of the mobile is in the balance and its flexibility. The mobile has a way of responding to changing circumstances such as wind. It changes position but always maintains connections with each part. If one flicks one of the suspended parts, energy, the whole system moves to gradually bring itself to equilibrium. The same thing is true of a family. In a family where there is stress, the whole organism shifts to bring balance, stability, survival. (Wegscheider, 1981, pp. 36-37. Reprinted with permission.)

Wegscheider explains that in the chemically dependent family each person is affected by the chemical abuse of one member and says that "in an attempt to maintain balance, members compulsively repress their feelings and develop survival behaviors and walls of defense to protect them from pain'' (p. 37).

Family balance is often achieved in the alcoholic family with drinking as a central point. When this drinking is removed through treatment, the family is thrown into turmoil as if it were a mobile in a windstorm. Mother is not needed as the overly responsible martyr when Dad returns to take over running the household. Brother has no reason to stay away from home and must reevaluate his relationship with Dad. The family suddenly notices little sister's hyperactive mannerisms. The emotional distance of the marriage may still exist, and the precipitating environment that began the drinking may still exist. Without family intervention, drinking behavior may reoccur; the family may separate; or a new family member may become symptomatic.

Family Roles

The basic principles of homeostasis include predictable roles for family members to act out and a set of rules, both overt and covert, for interaction of these roles. These family roles are diagrammed in Figure 3-2.

Each man and woman who marry has his or her own ideas, values, and notions of appropriate sex roles. They are unique individuals who, given the conglomerate of their life experiences, act and react in a predictable way. Their job is to blend into a single marital unit the values, beliefs, and behaviors they embraced in their own families. In today's American society, many of these marriages attempt to share leadership responsibilities in an equitable manner. This produces a new set of rules different from those of our ancestors, whose families may have been ruled by an autocratic father with mother as second in command and the children in a pecking order under both parents. The women's movement and economic stresses have produced the two-income family and have restructured the "traditional" family diagram.

This dual leadership creates a unique situation not found in most social systems. What corporation could function with two chairpersons? During the 1980 presidential elections there was a flurry of excitement at the Republican National Convention when Ronald Reagan hinted at choosing Gerald Ford as his running mate. The negotiations reportedly fell through when the two men could not agree on the mechanics of a copresidency. Although the concept is difficult to envision—two men running a country with equal power—it is this theory many marital relationships struggle to enact. Continued spoken and unspoken negotiations are required to keep the relationship functional. Money, religion, in-laws, friends, sex, child rearing, and recreation are key issues in these negotiations.

With the addition of a child to this unit, the husband and wife take on a third role. The man must add the new role of father to his other roles as an individual with personal needs and as a husband working out a marital relationship. The

Figure 3-2 Family Roles

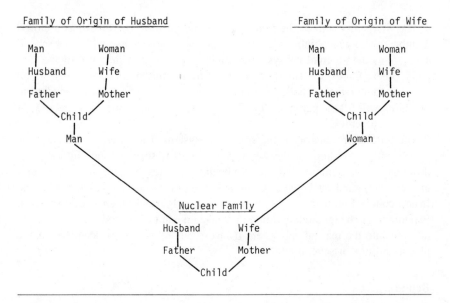

woman also juggles three roles, and further negotiations take place on child rearing and discipline philosophies. Who will punish? How will we discipline? What is the role of the father? Should the mother work?

Family Rules

Decisions are made or not made according to the rules, boundaries, and alliances of family members. Families have rules about the expression of feelings such as love, hurt, or anger. These rules include who can express them, how they are expressed, and how they are received. In an alcoholic family the unspoken rule may be that anger can only be expressed during intoxication or that affection and intimacy can occur only when one or both spouses are drinking. Barnard (1981) believes other areas where rules are formulated for family functioning are: (1) what, when, and how family members may comment on what they see, feel, and think; (2) who can speak to whom and about what; (3) how can a member be different; (4) how can sexuality be expressed; (5) what does it mean to be male or female; and (6) how can a person acquire self-worth and how much is appropriate to possess. These rules are the basis for dyadic and triadic relationships and interactions in the family subsystems that are formed by generation, sex, mutual interest, or duties.

Family Subsystems

The first subsystem in the family is the marital subsystem that has a closed membership in which duties are performed by the husband and wife. The second subsystem, the parental subsystem, usually emerges with the birth of the first child. These duties are usually carried out by the husband and wife, but in an alcoholic family, the alcoholic parent may abdicate his or her role and a grandparent or sibling will fill the parental gap. This may blur the generational boundaries or parentify the child.

The third main category is the sibling subsystem. There may be one or many subsystems depending on the number of children, sexes of the children, age differences, and common interests. In healthy families the subsystems are fluid, and members can flow between them as the overall system changes and balances. In an alcoholic family these systems may become rigid and uncertain of their tasks. Parenting may be ignored; children may take on adult roles; and children may be allowed into the marital subsystem if incestuous relationships occur between a parent and one or several children.

Boundaries

Boundaries exist between each member of the family and between subsystems. These are the rules of interaction and the methods of functioning. Minuchin (1974) defines three types of boundaries: enmeshed, clear, and disengaged. In reality most boundaries fall somewhere on a continuum from the very rigid to the very diffuse, with the clearly defined boundaries falling in the center.

Clear boundaries are found in most healthy relationships that are based on mutual respect. Clear boundaries allow separateness for each member yet maintain closeness. Freedom and flexibility in these relationships promote clear and direct communication patterns.

Enmeshed or rigid boundaries leave no room for flexibility and no room for differences. Sameness and unity are stressed in these relationships and a sense of belonging does occur. However, adolescents, whose job it is to individualize and pull away from their parents in order to find individual identities, become smothered and may turn to alcohol or drugs to reduce this conflict. The fused marital relationship is an example of the loss of self-identity that occurs when the individual personality of each partner is sacrificed for the sake of the marriage.

Disengaged or diffuse boundaries are often seen in alcoholic families and are identified as isolation of the members or isolation of the family from society. The rules in these families are: (1) do not talk about the alcoholism; (2) do not confront drinking behavior; and (3) protect and shelter the alcoholic so that things don't become worse. These rules perpetuate the drinking, and the drinking maintains the need for isolation. Often, marital relationships in these families have arrived at a fixed distance. Similarly, siblings in this situation lack a sense of belonging, and very little love is transmitted to build self-worth. These children may use alcohol to numb the pain of rejection, or they may act out inappropriately to try to get the recognition they want. Misbehavior may escalate to attract others' attention.

Case History

A case example of an alcoholic family shows how both of these maladaptive boundaries can be present in the same family.

Susan, age 34, and John, age 40, were practicing alcoholics and drug abusers before their marriage. They married because they felt sorry for each other, and they became fused in "we-ness" to fight the world. Both spouses lost self-identity, and in order to achieve an individual identity, they pulled back to a fixed distance in their relationship. They set up a covert marital rule that Susan would be the dominant spouse and breadwinner, while John would become adaptive, lose self-identity and become unable to hold a job. Both of these positions reflect the role that each played in his or her family of origin. Susan was the oldest child in her family and felt she had to be perfect to win her mother's love. When she failed to meet her mother's expectations, she felt very guilty and began to drink. John was an adopted only child, who was raised in an overprotective and overdemanding family. He was forced into college against his wishes and paid his parents back with repeated failures, job losses, and drug abuse. His rage at his parents was unresolved and colored his role in the nuclear family.

The disengaged marital relationship did not allow for direct confrontation, and issues between spouses were ignored. When the first child, Denise, was born, the father made a strong alignment with her. Denise was repeatedly compared with her father by members of the family, and when the second daughter was born, she was rejected by the father and aligned with the mother. Wars could now be fought between the enmeshed father-daughter subgroup and the mother-daughter subgroup without having direct marital confrontation. The undercurrent was that "if I confront my spouse directly, things will get worse."

A further dynamic of this family centered around Susan's belief that she would not be an alcoholic if she did not drink before four o'clock in the afternoon. When Denise arrived home from school at three o'clock, using the same figures of speech and mannerisms as her father, she reminded Susan of her issues with John, and Susan would beat Denise. Then, feeling guilty, Susan would begin to drink at four o'clock. Denise blamed herself for these attacks although she never understood them. Susan inflated her guilt and increased her drinking. Denise suffered from her enmeshed relationship with her father and failed to gain her own identity in the family.

Eventually, both parents sought alcoholism treatment and maintained sobriety. However, the marital roles and the emotional distance between the spouses and between Denise and her mother remained. The family balance became unachievable, and the spouses divorced. Family therapy was initiated with this family when Denise became progressively withdrawn.

Denise is now learning to relate to her mother for the first time in family therapy sessions that involve Susan (the custodial parent) and her daughters. Denise is making friends for the first time and has been able to complete her school work, thereby recovering from years of underachievement. Since Denise had been often told that she had no sense, like her father, she had hidden her intelligence to gain acceptance from him. Denise is at high risk to marry an alcoholic if she fails to fully gain the approval from her parents she has longed for. She will be saying, "See, I married someone like you. Now will you accept me?"

Family Values

As family roles, rules, and boundaries begin to develop, so do the values of the nuclear family. These values again are a blend of those values transmitted from the spouses' families of origin. These values may be shared by the couple or be more strongly supported by one spouse or the other. Possible values in families are: athletics, musical ability, money, work, education, power, control, winning, social status, conservatism, or radicalism, to name a few. Conflict can occur when the mother embraces music and education as her strong values and wants her son to become a musical virtuoso, while the father longs for an athlete who is competitive and values winning. In some cases, children make adaptations and combine values to please both parents, but when the values are in direct opposition, the child must choose one or none of the conflicting values. This is a "no win" situation for the child because one of the parents will withhold approval. The children in the family have the option of accepting or rejecting any or all of the family values and are not bound by pure imitation of their parents. However, it is often true that the parent who sees his or her values mirrored in the child will come forth with more approval. Depending on the boundaries and rules of the family, children who choose different values may be allowed this differentiation, or they may defy a family rule that says family members must not be different.

Other conflicts arise when a female child is born in a family that values boys and needs an heir for the family business or when a male child is born to a family that needs a girl for balance or to satisfy a parent's psychological need.

As the family develops, it takes on an overall atmosphere, depending on the amount of conflict involved in balancing of roles, family values, and interaction rules. The interactions produce atmospheres that are friendly, competitive, or cooperative or environments that are hostile, autocratic, or permissive.

Family Constellation

With the addition of other children and the solidification of rules and roles, a family constellation develops. In the average family, some generalities can be made about birth order. First-born children are, for a while, only children. They compare themselves with adults and learn the rules of adult interaction, sometimes becoming pseudoadults. The second-born children come along and dethrone the first born, and competition is set up. When third-born children arrive, they turn the second born into middle children, who often become occupied with making sure things are fair.

The youngest child is usually looked at as the baby and may act cute, weak, or awkward. The youngest child may demand service or act like the family clown. These birth order roles play a part in determining what survival behavior each child adopts to maintain homeostasis when a family becomes dysfunctional. These will be discussed in detail in Chapter 9.

Alliances and Relationships with the Family of Origin

The previous sections covering homeostasis, family roles, family rules, family subsystems, boundaries, family values, and birth order pertained chiefly to the nuclear family, although there were references to the families of origin. This section will deal more directly with relationships between the nuclear family and the families of origin.

In healthy families, alliances form in a horizontal pattern within generations (see Figure 3-3). That is, grandparents have an alliance between themselves; parents have a marital and parental alliance; and the children have special coalitions among themselves. These alliances can become vertical in nature if, for instance, there is a cross-generational alliance between one spouse and his or her parent that takes the place of marital closeness. In the discussion on boundaries, a cross-generational alliance was discussed between one spouse and a child when a fixed distance occurred in the marriage.

"Whenever generational boundaries are consistently violated and members of one generation supply what should be received in another generation, pathology can be expected" (Haley, 1976, p. 39).

These cross-generational alliances disturb the balance of the nuclear family by changing role definitions and pulling members of the family of origin into the dynamics and workings of the nuclear family. Marital issues cannot get resolved if they are only discussed between the wife and her mother. If the maternal grandmother was overprotective of her daughter and is reluctant to allow her to break away and become an independent person, this attachment may continue through their adult lives. If the daughter married and had children because the expectations of society were stronger than the overprotective tie with her mother, she may be

Figure 3-3 Alliances

Paternal
Grandfather ⟵⟶ Grandmother

Maternal
Grandfather ⟵⟶ Grandmother

Husband ⟵⟶ Wife

Father ⟵⟶ Mother

Child ⟵⟶ Child ⟵⟶ Child ⟵⟶ Child

Examples of horizontal, within generation, alliances

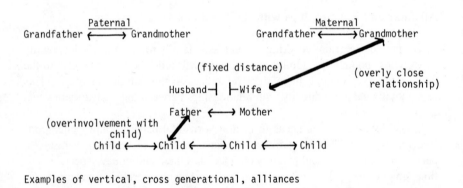

Examples of vertical, cross generational, alliances

very angry with her husband for taking her away from her mother and angry with her children for keeping her in a difficult position. This anger often is not shown directly but is manifested in the same overprotective parenting style with which the mother was raised. The mother's underlying wish to be rid of her husband and children must be repressed and covered with overconcern. Her anxiety and overprotection often produce symptoms in one of the children and may cause an overinvolvement between the parent and child, thus passing on a cross-generational alliance and maladaptive behavior.

As the nuclear family develops as a social system, the spouses define themselves in terms of their relationships with their families of origin. Framo (1976) has identified four categories of relationships with families of origin.

The first category is the overinvolved relationship, which may resemble the enmeshed subsystems in the nuclear family. These families may live close together—maybe even down the street. The people in these families will often talk daily on the telephone. In some families that are forced to move apart, this daily phone contact may continue long distance. These families usually have very little social life outside their own confines and are closed off from the rest of society. The (other) spouse in these relationships may resent the spouse's overinvolvement or may welcome the relationship with a parent substitute. Difficulty occurs in these situations if grandparents give advice on home management, parenting, marital relationships, and areas that are typically roles of the marital and parental subsystems. Self-identity and self-worth as a spouse and parent are sabotaged with messages from the family of origin to the effect that "you are inadequate, and you need our help." What the family of origin may really mean is "we need you to need help so we can busy ourselves with your problems and not look at our own marital difficulties."

The second type of relationship is superficial. It involves infrequent, nonpersonal contact, usually revolving around ceremonies or family rituals. Framo believes that people in these relationships see themselves as having resolved their difficulties with their families in a mature way. They have used space, distance, and time to reduce conflict.

The third pattern occurs when people completely cut themselves off from their families. They proclaim that the absence of contact is the only way to maintain their own sanity and virtually deny the existence of other family members, treating them as if they were already dead. Framo believes that these people have the greatest chance of repeating the irrational patterns of their parents.

The last category is a positive one in which a person establishes an identity within the family of origin before leaving. This differentiation or individuation occurs when families have clear boundaries and parents can solve their own problems without projecting them onto their children or involving their children in the resolution process. These children consequently have no need to stay in the family or to escape its clutches. There is neither an overattachment nor an angry rebellion. These families do have a sense of belonging, but it is balanced with a respect for independence. The parents in this type of family of origin could love their children enough to let them leave. In Transactional Analysis terms, these adult children could relate more in adult-to-adult transactions with their parents than in adult-to-child transactions.

"In general, the more a nuclear family is emotionally cut off from parental families, the higher the incidence of problems and symptoms in the nuclear family" (Bowen, 1978, p. 264).

Carter and McGoldrick (1980) in describing the family life cycle state:

> In outlining the stages of the family life cycle, we have departed from the traditional sociological depiction of the family life cycle as commencing at courtship or marriage and ending with the death of one

spouse. Rather than considering the family to be the operative emotional unit from the cradle to the grave, we see a new family life cycle beginning at the stage of the "unattached young adult," whose adequate or inadequate completion of the primary task of coming to terms with his or her family of origin will most profoundly influence whom, when and how he or she marries and all succeeding stages of the new family life cycle. Adequate completion of this task would require that the young adult separate from the family of origin without cutting off or fleeing reactively to a substitute emotional refuge. (p. 13)

Symptoms

The family roles, rules, boundaries, values, atmosphere, birth order roles, and alliances all combine to constitute the family homeostasis. Meeks and Kelly (1970) state:

Any attempt to shift the family equilibrium either from within (i.e., change in a member) or from without (i.e., input from a therapist) may evoke resistance from the family system which seeks to maintain the status quo (equilibrium). No matter how sick it may appear to the outside observer, the established equilibrium represents that family's attempt to minimize the threats of disruption and pain. (p. 400)

In the alcoholic family, a balance is maintained with the presence of alcohol, and the family may resist any attempts to remove this part of the balance, although they may also ask for the drinking to cease. They believe that change may be worse than the pain they are already suffering. Steinglass (1976) says "the presence or absence of alcohol becomes the single most important variable determining the interactional behavior not only between the identified drinker and other members of the family but among non-drinking members of the family as well" (p. 106).

When families present themselves to a therapist, it is usually due to a symptom in one member resulting from a disturbance in family homeostasis or is a result of the suggestion of someone outside the family. Bowen (1971) defines three areas within the nuclear family in which symptoms are expressed: (1) marital conflict; (2) dysfunction in a spouse; and (3) projection to one or more children. Bowen labels this third area as the family projection process, which he believes exists to some extent in all families. In this process, families project their problems onto their children who become the symptom bearers for the family. The symptom bearer often unconsciously volunteers for this position and may be instrumental in bringing a family into therapy where alcohol abuse or dysfunctional family patterns can be corrected, thus relieving the symptoms in the child. These children have a stake in saving their families and themselves in the symptom bearer role. "Children, and adults as well, will forego their own nature in order to save a parent from going crazy or in order to become the kind of person a parent (or parent representative) can love" (Framo, 1976, p. 207). Children may mirror the behavior of the parent to gain acceptance, but instead they receive rejection. The child's symptoms may be labeled as inappropriate, causing conflict and anxiety in the child.

Family therapy has evolved around the notion of the identified patient or the symptom bearer as the person who expresses a particular dysfunction for the whole family. Therefore, the context of the alcoholic person is reframed as the alcoholic family, with the alcoholic as the identified patient. Steinglass (1976) points out that, uniquely, symptoms occur in the parental subsystem in the alcoholic family. This is in contrast to the majority of dysfunctional families in which children are the symptom bearers.

The alcoholic family may also be unique in the process of triangulation, in which the tension between two people is displaced onto an issue or a substance (e.g., alcohol or drugs) instead of being projected onto the child. Unfortunately, the removal of the substance may result in a worsening of tension or another displacement.

AN OVERVIEW OF FAMILY THERAPY PHILOSOPHY IN TERMS OF ETIOLOGY

This section will review the theories of personality development and causes of dysfunction in the family as viewed by the communication model, the systems model, the structural model and the social learning model of family therapy.

Each theory will be examined in terms of origin of the theory, therapists involved in the theory, basic theoretical concepts of etiology, and relevance to the alcoholic family.

Communication Model

The communication model of family therapy was a pioneering effort in a new field. It was developed in the early 1950 s in Palo Alto, California. Bateson began working with interpersonal communications in schizophrenic families and was joined in developing this theory by Haley, Weakland, and Jackson (Bateson, Jackson, Haley, & Weakland, 1956). Their core belief was that communication between members was the most important factor of family life.

In 1959, Satir (1967) joined this movement and added her own ideas about how the person is influenced by the family and by society as a whole.

These theorists believed that blocked forms of communication in the individual were symptoms of overall dysfunctional communication in the family. They proposed that dysfunctional communication patterns produced family tension that was projected onto one or more family members. (See Figure 3-4.)

Jackson was responsible for developing a theory of *homeostasis* in the family. He believed that a lack of need satisfaction on the part of the family members would lead to an imbalance in family functioning and would produce tension. Jackson (1968) found that healthy family systems would, at this time, seek alternative ways of gaining need satisfaction, but dysfunctional families, because of their lack of adequate problem-solving techniques, would project this tension onto a family member who would become the symptom bearer for the family. Ironically, both of these methods reduce family tension and restore homeostasis (see Figure 3-4). Jackson referred to this process as the homeostatic mechanism. He says this homeostatic mechanism is found at times in all families, but when it is in constant motion, it will produce disturbed individual members whom he refers to as "scapegoats."

If alcohol is a central force in this balance and it is removed without helping the family to find new alternatives, the system may break up (divorce), or a new symptom bearer may emerge to maintain tension reduction.

While working with Bateson, Haley, and Weakland, Jackson (1960) developed the theory of the "double bind" and later related it to clinical work. The double bind is a communication pattern involving a victim or scapegoat and a message sender. The sender gives two messages at the same time. Often one is verbal, while the other is nonverbal. In order for these messages to be defined as a double bind, they must be conflicting and be repeatedly sent over a long period of time. One message must carry a negative connotation or punishment message (which may seem life threatening), while the other is more abstract and contradictory. The victims are trapped in this pattern by their need for love and approval. This trap is similar to what Hoffman (1979) refers to when a child mirrors the parent's negative behavior for approval but receives rejection or "negative love" instead.

Children can feel frustrated and angry with their parents when they receive these double bind messages. A case history involves Bobby, who was unable to express his anger to his mother when he felt frustration. The mother would say in therapy sessions that she wanted Bobby to show his anger and not bottle it up. She had done this in her family, and it had caused her pain. At home, however, when Bobby would get angry, the mother would send him to his room until he could calm down and show his anger nicely. Bobby was confused and could not figure out how to please his mother. As much as he would try, he found it impossible to express anger nicely. When Bobby confronted her with this dilemma, she named off several occasions when this was not the case. His mother had denied Bobby's feelings and further frustrated him by not allowing him to show the anger she had previously demanded he express.

Figure 3-4 Patterns Explained by the Communication Model

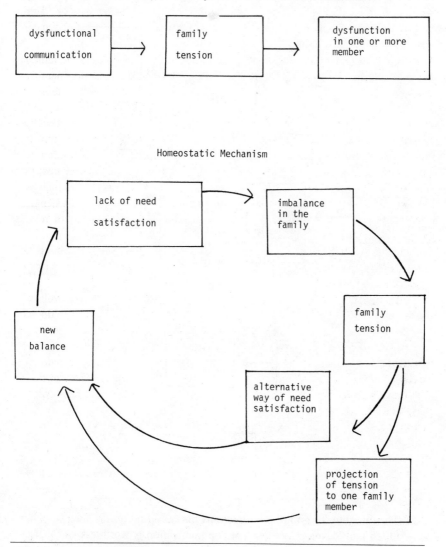

If these double bind patterns of communication continue over prolonged periods, the victims have several ways of responding (see Figure 3-5):

1. They can continue to repeat the behaviors that elicited the double bind responses to try to find their meaning, which will lead to frustration and possible escape to drugs and alcohol.

Figure 3-5 Reactions to the Double Bind

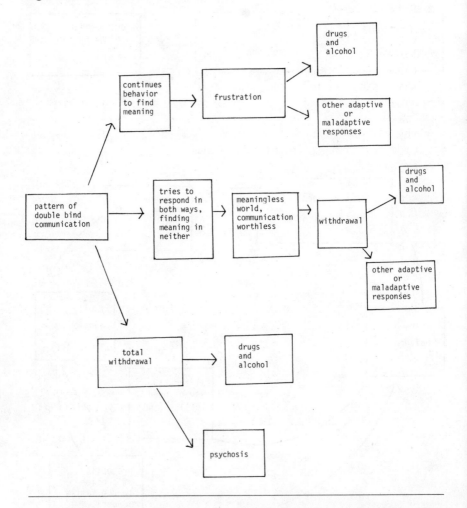

2. They may try to go in both directions but may find no meaning in either. Often they develop a belief that communication is worthless and that the world is a meaningless place. This process may lead to withdrawal from the environment and possible drug and alcohol abuse.
3. They can completely withdraw from the relationship and turn to alcohol and drugs or retreat with pyschotic behaviors as in schizophrenic families. "Double binds are present in all families, but more so in families of substance abusers than in 'normal' or 'neurotic' ones" (Kaufman, 1979, p. 269).

Another therapist from the communication model, Haley (1976) has developed a philosophy involving personal alliances in the family. In the healthy family, he noticed mutually satisfying and need fulfilling relationships. In the dysfunctional family, he found confused communication patterns and shifting alliances. Haley hypothesized that confused, out-of-order communication patterns can lead to misinterpretations, assumptions, guessing, and misunderstanding between family members. If children cannot interpret what their parents' needs and wishes are, they certainly cannot fulfill them. Haley also found that cross-generational alliances produced confused communication and misunderstanding in the power hierarchy of the family. He believed that change in communication patterns and alliances in the family would change the overall functioning of the family and reduce symptoms in the symptom bearer.

Satir (1967) similarly has continued to develop the communication model with her theories of conjoint family therapy. She refers to the symptom bearer as the *identified patient* (I.P.), and to the symptoms as *pain*. She states that individual pain is a symptom of pain that is present in the larger system of the family and the society the family lives in. This pain is seen as having a purpose in the interworkings of the family process.

Like others involved in the communication model, Satir sees communication as a key factor in functional and dysfunctional relationships. Homeostasis is more valuable to a family than an individual member's well-being.

Satir also states that parents bring their faulty patterns of communication to the marriage from their families of origin and that children learn these patterns (a multigenerational process).

In terms of etiology, Satir believes that dysfunctional people have not learned how to effectively interact with others. They either lack a model of appropriate communications in their family or they have been sheltered and spared responsibility for interpersonal relationships.

Alcohol treatment centers often focus on teaching of interpersonal skills when it becomes clear that their patients have not developed such skills as beginning conversations, giving compliments, joining a group of peers, finding a job, or expressing feelings. Goldstein has similarly been successful in teaching these social skills to alcoholics using behavior modification techniques described in his book, *Structured Learning Therapy* (1976).

Satir further finds that dysfunction occurs due to people's inaccurate perception of interactions and their unwillingness to accept differences in others as well as themselves. Walsh (1980) states:

> Parents who depreciate a child because of the development of different characteristics or behaviors, are creating the basis for self-doubt and insecurity. As he grows, any display of differentness on the part of others can be perceived as threatening to (an) already weak self-concept.

He may feel, "If this person is right, and I believe differently, I am wrong and less of a person." This attitude can lead to a rigid approach to the world or a rejection of others through withdrawal. (p. 13)

Satir further developed four basic role types that family members typically adopt when dealing with crises in the family:

1. The placater is a person who reduces tension by smoothing things over. The person may be a martyr, a role often played by the alcoholic's spouse. This role parallels Bowen's adaptive spouse who allows the partner to become dominant and risks losing self-identity. The placater would avoid confrontation of abusive drinking behavior and deny personal emotions.
2. The blamer role is often played by people with low self-esteem who attack to keep the focus off themselves. The alcoholic plays this role by blaming others and insisting that his or her drinking behavior was caused by the spouse's nagging or the children's misbehavior.
3. The irrelevant role is played by people in the family who avoid conflict by changing the subject, responding inappropriately, distracting others, or having temper tantrums.
4. The super-responsible role is characterized by ultrareasonable communication. These people act calm, cool, and collected but internally they feel vulnerable.

In summary, the communication model of family therapy relies heavily on identifying faulty communication patterns in a system that produces tension, disturbing the homeostasis and producing symptomatic problems for an identified patient. Dysfunctional behavior, including alcohol abuse, can result from: (1) a lack of appropriate problem-solving techniques; (2) a chronic double bind communication pattern; (3) unclear and cross-generational alliances; (4) a lack of interpersonal skills; and (5) an inability to accept differences and fixed role behaviors in the family. It should also be stressed that these behaviors are transmitted across generational boundaries.

Systems Model

The systems model of family therapy was developed in the early 1950 s at the same time as the communication model. It was largely devised by Bowen (1978) at Georgetown University in Washington, D.C. Ackerman, Boszormenyi-Nagy, Zuk and Paul also work in this model with some variations.

Bowen's theory was developed during his work with schizophrenic families. He began seeing distinctions in affective states and cognitive processes that led to his "scale of differentiation." This early work was based on psychoanalytic theory and applied to an approach that defined the family as a system operated by the same principles as other systems, such as societies, corporations, or institutions. Bowen further believed that a person's current behavior was caused by a transference process that inappropriately applied past history and behaviors to present situations. Bowen's initial focus was on the mother-daughter relationship, which fostered his theory of the *family projection process*. When he began to add grandparents to his sessions, he developed his theories on *multigenerational transmission*.

Bowen, like Jackson, also arrived at a theory of homeostasis in his observations of families who exhibited a feeling of oneness. He further found varying degrees of this oneness (in families who seemed overly dependent on one another) and labeled it "stuck togetherness." In these families, he observed that uniqueness was discouraged, much as Satir had discovered.

Bowen noticed that this "stuck togetherness" was the family's defense against crisis or tension. They would pull together when they felt stress and isolate themselves from outside influences to restore balance. This system was described as a delicate balance; a change in one member would affect all other members. If self-destructive behaviors, such as substance abuse, helped maintain balance, the family would tolerate them.

In this system, the smallest unit (consisting of three people) was called the *triangle*. Bowen felt that dyads (two people) who could not handle stress would bring a third person into play to stabilize the unit. In states of calm, there are two comfortable sides of the triangle and one in conflict. Over a period of time, these roles become fixed. When conflict occurs between the two comfortable members, they project conflict onto the third, who develops symptoms in a family projection process. A familiar example is the mother, father, and child triangle. When conflict occurs in the marriage, tension rises in the mother and is projected onto the child who will accept it to maintain the family oneness. In this case, the father may be the adaptive spouse who gives up his identity for the sake of the marriage and supports the other spouse's needs as well as her projection to the child. This father may also withdraw from the conflict by working long hours, drinking with his buddies in the local tavern, or finding endless chores out in the garage.

The child selected for this projection is often the one closest to the mother. It may be the oldest boy or girl (depending on the gender valued by the family), the only child, a child born during a crisis, or one born with a defect. When this child leaves the family, another will take its place until the children have all left, and then the projection is passed on to those outside the family. The therapist can be a prime target. If the therapist accepts this projection, the tension in the family will be reduced, but the system will remain unchanged.

The teenager who leaves this family will create a pseudoindependence based on anxiety that will be transmitted to the marital relationship in a multigenerational process. Therefore, the patterns of the family of origin will be repeated in the nuclear family.

Families with a high degree of "stuck togetherness" produce children who become distancers in an attempt to gain self-identity. They may: (1) become rebellious adolescents or withdraw destructively; (2) gain physical distance by moving away from home; or (3) emotionally distance themselves, which will also create physical distance. These children never differentiate themselves from their parents and are consequently unable to become problem solvers in crisis situations. Some of these children may become substance abusers who say, "I can't take pressure or I can't cope; I'm an alcoholic." The question is, does the alcohol cause the inability to cope or does the lack of problem-solving skills cause drinking and avoidance?

Bowen has devised a scale for determining self-differentiation in family members. (See Figure 3-6.) This scale ranges from 0 to 100. The range from 0 to 25 contains those who are dominated by their emotions. These people live from day to day, unable to make decisions or form opinions. Essentially, they lack a self; their only feeling of self-worth comes from others. The two rules of behavior for these people are: (1) "Does it make me feel good?"; or (2) "Will others approve of me?"

Moving up the scale, differentiation is added to this profile to create people who begin to use intellectual processes in decision making and who gain personal opinions. The upper half of the scale reflects goal-orientation and includes those who can respond with rational principles and have less need to be defensive. They have achieved a self with a high degree of differentiation from their families. These people are able to achieve intimate relationships and are problem solvers.

In Bowen's words, self-differentiation "is the degree to which the person has a 'solid self' or solidly held principles by which he lives his life. This is in contrast to a 'pseudoself' made up of inconsistent life principles that can be corrupted by coercion for the gain of the moment. The 'differentiation of self' is roughly equivalent to the concept of emotional maturity" (Bowen, 1978, p. 263). This rating is based on the amount of a person's differentiation from his or her parents, the type of relationship that exists with the parents, and the quality of emotional separation from the parents in young adulthood.

Bowen states that people with similar scores tend to be attracted to one another, and they pass on similar degrees of differentiation to their children. The child with the lowest degree of differentiation is at highest risk for the family projection process and later problems.

The following case example of a family demonstrates several of the principles of the systems theory. The family was seen at a child guidance clinic when their daughter (I.P.) refused to attend school even when she was physically carried there. She would continually run out of the building and return home. Although the school tried its traditional methods of working with a school phobia, they had

Figure 3-6 Bowen's Scale of Differentiation

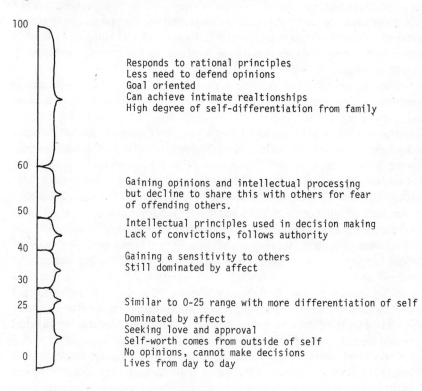

100

Responds to rational principles
Less need to defend opinions
Goal oriented
Can achieve intimate realtionships
High degree of self-differentiation from family

60

50

Gaining opinions and intellectual processing
but decline to share this with others for fear
of offending others.

Intellectual principles used in decision making
Lack of convictions, follows authority

40

Gaining a sensitivity to others
Still dominated by affect

30

25

Similar to 0-25 range with more differentiation of self

Dominated by affect
Seeking love and approval
Self-worth comes from outside of self
No opinions, cannot make decisions
Lives from day to day

0

no success and, therefore, made a referral for family therapy. During the evaluation sessions, which included a family history, the therapist learned that the mother and the maternal grandmother were excessively close. They talked for hours every day—even long distance during the time the family had been transferred halfway across the United States. Upon further questioning, it was learned that this mother-daughter alliance had gone on for many generations in the past in the mother's family.

The identified patient, Sally, eight years old, was the youngest of three children. Her sister was 14 and her brother 10. When the mother was pregnant with Sally, her mother (the maternal grandmother) and her sister were killed in a car wreck. The mother formed a strong attachment to Sally, probably as a replacement for the alliance with her mother (Sally's grandmother). This was seen as a passing on of a family intergenerational pattern and possibly as a repression of anger toward her children and husband for taking her away from her mother. She may have wished they would all disappear so she could return to the safety of her family of origin. However, this unconscious wish caused anxiety for the mother, and as a result she felt her children needed constant protection. This protection became a more rigid pattern when a neighborhood girl was struck and killed by a car while riding her bicycle. This vivid reminder showed that bad things really can happen to family members.

As the family talked about their daily behavior, patterns of overprotection emerged. The mother would not let the children ride with their father to a town 50 miles away because she feared they would all be killed. Whenever one of the children was out of the house, the mother would worry and often shared this worry with Sally. She would ask Sally to run and make sure father was all right or check on the other children. Mother also disclosed that she had agoraphobia and often would have to run out of stores and rush home because of a panic attack.

Although the marital couple insisted they were happy, they agreed that they never went out without the children and that the mother did most of the parenting because the father was usually busy in the garage or drinking at the local bar. The mother stated that during the previous summer she had begun to worry about what would happen when her children grew up and left home. She felt she and her husband no longer ''knew each other.'' In response to this worry they planned a three-day trip for the two of them to rejuvenate their marriage. Following her mother's habit of excessive worrying when a family member was out of the house, Sally cried for three days and refused to participate in activities that her aunt had planned for her while her parents were away.

In later family sessions, Sally talked about her mother's constant threats to leave home. Several times, the mother had gotten in the car after screaming that she was going to drive off a bridge, and she did not return for several hours. Another time, she packed a suitcase and looked in the want ads for apartments to rent. Her mother's behavior terrified Sally, and she feared that if she let her mother out of her sight she might not return. The mother felt this was ridiculous and said she had never meant to leave. She just wanted the children to see how their behavior upset her and she was using these threats to communicate her unhappiness to her husband. Sally continued to strengthen the mother-daughter alliance by picking up her mother's phobic behaviors. Sally would not go into her room alone, would not go down into the basement, and began to refuse to leave the house for any reason.

This is an example of the family projection process in which the marital couple had reached fixed distance. The mother was the dominant spouse, and the father adapted to her power and satisfied her need to control while giving up his own need fulfillment. He was withdrawn from parental duties and was spending most of his time at a bar. The mother's tension about the loss of a marital partner had been projected onto Sally, who produced symptoms that reinforced the mother-daughter alliance. For Sally these symptoms were an attempt to keep the family together.

The mother was very uncomfortable when the focus of therapy was not on Sally, and between sessions she took Sally to psychiatrists in an attempt to reinforce the notion of a "sick child," as well as get approval for the family projection process. The therapist made a contract with the family, who agreed to stop seeing other therapists for four weeks. Sessions were started with the marital couple only.

Sally came to the first marital session and was left in the lobby. When she decided she would no longer be the focus of therapy and her parents were getting the help she felt they needed, she returned to school. By the third marital session, Sally was in school full time and had returned to her other activities outside the home.

The father's drinking behavior was reduced significantly when he was given an equal share of the parenting responsibilities, and the marital couple began planning social engagements without the children.

In summary, the system theorists believe that dysfunctional behavior in the nuclear family should be looked at in terms of the lack of differentiation of family members, repression of individuality, and the inability of spouses to differentiate from their parents' past behaviors.

Structural Model

In the mid-1960 s the structural model was developed by Minuchin, (1974) who believed that change could be brought about in the individual by altering the source of the person's behaviors—the structure of the family. Minuchin was concerned with environmental factors and found the family to be the interpreter of societal values, rules, and behaviors. Children, he felt, learn either functional or dysfunctional behaviors in the family through observing and interpreting the family structure.

The *family structure* is defined as transactions that are unique to a family: levels of authority, power structure, and mutual expectations. The structure is created with the marriage and the agreement of the spouses to satisfy each other's needs. The evolution of spousal functions creates the core of the nuclear family. The structure changes when the first child is born and parental functions are negotiated. With this child rides the potential for family growth or possible destruction. If the family cannot clearly differentiate the spousal and parental functions, dysfunction in the family may occur. This theory is similar to Bowen's concepts of the family projection process and cross-generational alliances.

Within the family structure, Minuchin defines *subsystems* as one or more family members who share something in common: generation, sex, interests, or family duties. He defines boundaries as the rules of the subsystems that are either rigid, diffuse, or clear. Dysfunction occurs with rigid boundaries that create isolation and discourage family communication, or with diffuse boundaries that do not clearly define areas of authority or responsibility. These diffuse boundaries discourage individual responsibility and promote random and confused problem solving.

The fourth concept in Minuchin's structural model categorizes the family's methods of experiencing stress:

1. Stress can be caused in one family member by someone outside of the family, such as the father's boss. This stress is transmitted to the wife, who in turn is angry with the children, who kick the dog or spank the doll.
2. Stress may be caused in the entire family by an outside force, such as economic change or a move to a new location that would affect everyone.
3. Stress can be caused by life crisis transitions, such as the birth of a child, a child attending school for the first time, adolescence, adolescents leaving home (particularly the last child), or mid-life crises, such as the mother's return to the workforce (which may occur simultaneously with the adolescence of the children).
4. Stress may result from the presence of a chronically ill person in the family.

In summary, Minuchin feels that dysfunction in a family occurs when there are unclear levels of authority and power, expectations are misunderstood, there is confusion as to the functions of subgroups, or rigid or diffuse boundaries exist in the family. Further, he has identified four major areas of stress a family must deal with according to the defined structure of the family.

Social Learning Model

The social learning model of family therapy emerged in the mid-1970s largely through the efforts of Patterson at the Oregon Research Institute in Eugene, Oregon (Patterson, 1971).

This theory is based on the principles of behaviorism and behavior modification, many of which were developed by Skinner and then applied to the family unit. Patterson states that all behaviors of family members, whether functional or dysfunctional, are learned through correct or faulty training of individual family members by other family members. Children are taught how to behave by their parents, siblings, and other relatives, and conversely, children teach parents and others about themselves with their reactions to the parents' teaching. Problems occur in the family when individuals cannot discriminate between teaching positive and negative behaviors and when parents unknowingly teach negative behaviors. This theory is similar to Hoffman's idea of negative love that children receive through mirroring parents' negative habits while in search of love and approval.

Patterson, like other family theorists, believes in looking to the families of origin to understand the patterns of behavior in the nuclear family. He believes that individuals' present behaviors are determined by the reactions they received from their families in the past. These behaviors become predictable and repetitive and are seen as fixed patterns, similar to the Satir role patterns, that can be observed and changed by the family. These learned behaviors can be unlearned by changing the response pattern to the undesired behaviors, while new replacement behaviors can be conditioned to substitute for dysfunctional behaviors.

The main principle used by Patterson is that reinforcement will increase the probability that desired behaviors will be repeated, and nonreinforcement will decrease the probability or cause extinction of the behavior. There are four types of reinforcers:

1. Positive reinforcement is a reward for appropriate behavior. These rewards can be material, such as paychecks, candy, or desired gifts; social, such as kisses, hugs, or verbal praise; or intrinsic, such as self-worth and positive internal feelings. The first two are external reinforcers and require a second person. The third is internal and is a solitary process. An important consideration is for the second person to know what type of reinforcement will motivate the individual. Therapists use these reinforcers in a hierarchical method beginning with material reinforcers, but moving to social and then to intrinsic reinforcers as soon as possible.

The recovering alcoholic who obtains money from a job, receives love and approval from the family, and begins to gain intrinsic self-worth from sobriety is responding to positive reinforcers. However, if drinking behavior is rewarded by a reduction of personal tension and escape from responsibility, reduced guilt, a diminished demand from the spouse and children, and a reduction of family tension, the drinking behavior is being reinforced.

2. Negative reinforcement occurs when some unwanted experience is removed. For example, if a child cries and refuses to comply with a request, parents negatively reinforce crying if they withdraw the request. If responsibility and pressure are withdrawn because the family reduces demands when the alcoholic drinks, the behavior is negatively reinforced.

3. Punishment is any aversive stimulus in the person's environment, such as hitting or yelling. Therapists avoid punishment because of a carryover to positive behaviors and a chance that children will imitate punishing behaviors. Children learn that if a person is not pleased with someone's behavior he or she can hit that person, and if individuals are not pleased with their own behavior they can be self-destructive.

This theory may be useful in understanding why people continue to drink when they are aware of the self-destructive nature of alcohol. Research has also shown that parents who were physically abused themselves tend to abuse their children.

4. Nonreinforcement is the removal of a positive reinforcer such as praise and attention or the removal of the person from the reinforcing environment. The removal of a child from a group interaction to an isolated timeout chair is a nonreinforcer.

In summary, the social learning theory looks at the dysfunctional behavior as learned behavior that is taught by others, especially family members. This behavior can be unlearned and replaced with functional behavior by using operant conditioning and reinforcement techniques.

REFERENCES

Barnard, C.P. *Families alcoholism and therapy*. Springfield, Ill.: Charles C. Thomas, 1981.

Bateson, G., Jackson, D., Haley, J., & Weakland, J.   Toward a theory of schizophrenia, *Behavioral Science*, 1956, *1*, 251-264.

Bowen, M.   Family therapy and family group therapy.   In H. Kaplan & B. Sadock (Eds.), *Comprehensive Group Psychotherapy*. Baltimore: Williams & Wilkins, 1971.

Bowen, M. Alcoholism as viewed through family systems theory and family psychotherapy. *Annals of the New York Academy of Science*, 1974, *233*, 115-22.

Bowen, M. Alcoholism and the family. In *Family therapy in clinical practice*. New York: Jason Aronson, 1978.

Carter, E., & McGoldrick, M. *The family life cycle: A framework for family therapy*. New York: Gardner Press, 1980.

Ewing, I.A. & Fox, R.E. Family therapy of alcoholism. In Messerman (Ed.), *Current psychiatric therapies*. New York: Grune & Stratton, 1968.

Fogarty, T. Marital crisis. In P. Guerin (Ed.), *Family therapy: Theory and practice*. New York: Gardner Press, 1976.

Framo, J.L. Family of origin as a therapeutic resource for adults in marital and family therapy: You can and should go home again. *Family Process*, 1976, *15*, 193-209.

Goldstein, A.P. *Structured learning therapy*. New York: Academic Press, 1976.

Haley, J. *Problem solving therapy*. New York: Harper and Row, 1976.

Hoffman, B. *No one is to blame, getting a loving divorce from your parents*. Palo Alto, Calif.: Science and Behavior Books, 1979.

Jackson, D.D. The question of family homeostasis. *Psychiatric Quarterly Supplement*, 1957, *31*, 79-90.

Jackson, D. *Communication, Family and Marriage*. Palo Alto: Science and Behavior, 1968.

Jackson, D.D. (Ed.) *The etiology of schizophrenia*. New York: Basic Books, 1960.

Kaufman, E. The application of the basic principles of family therapy to the treatment of drug and alcohol abusers. In E. Kaufman & P. Kaufman (Eds.), *Family therapy of drug and alcohol abuse*. New York: Gardner Press, 1979.

Meeks, D. & Kelly, C. Family therapy with the families of recovering alcoholics. *Quarterly Journal of Studies on Alcoholism*, 1970, *31*, 2, 399-413.

Minuchin, S. *Families and family therapy*. Cambridge, Mass.: Harvard University Press, 1974.

Patterson, G. *Families*. Champaign, Ill.: Research Press, 1971.

Satir, V. *Conjoint family therapy*. Palo Alto, Calif.: Science and Behavior Books, 1967.

Steinglass, P. Experimenting with family treatment approaches to alcoholism, 1950-1975, a review. *Family Process*, 1976, *15*, 97-123.

Walsh, W.M. *A primer in family therapy*. Springfield, Ill.: Charles C. Thomas, 1980.

Wegscheider, S. From the family trap to family freedom. *Alcoholism*, 1981, 36-39.

Chapter 4

Physiological, Sociological, and Psychological Influences on the Family

This chapter will present the three primary theoretical models of the etiology of alcoholism—physiological, sociological, and psychological—and will describe the relationship of these models to the family. In each of these areas, the major research will be covered and a framework will be provided for a central theory of etiology that includes the critical influences of the family. This chapter should give the reader a clear understanding of the role the family plays in development of alcoholism.

At the end of each major section, several questions will be presented that the reader may use to determine whether an individual is at high, low, or medium risk for alcoholism. By asking these questions and completing the chart in Figure 4-1, it will be possible to determine the alcoholism risk factor for an individual.

Although the physiological and sociological models of etiology have a solid basis in empirical research, alcoholism treatment personnel have little control over these genetic and cultural factors. However, a knowledge of these areas is important both for the treatment specialist and the prevention worker.

PHYSIOLOGICAL THEORIES OF ETIOLOGY AND THE FAMILY

This section will examine the physiological/genetic factors of alcoholism etiology and their relationship to the family, particularly the family of origin. Is alcoholism hereditary? If so, what factors are inherited? What makes a person physically at high risk for alcoholism? Some of the major studies in this area have already been presented in the overview in Chapter 1. They will be reviewed briefly here with a focus on the role the family plays in the development of a high or low risk level for alcoholism.

Figure 4-1 Risk Factor Chart

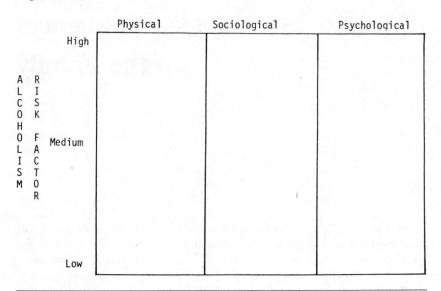

Family Studies

It is apparent that children of alcoholics have more problems with alcohol than children from families with nonalcoholic parents. Without exception, every family study of alcoholism, no matter what the country of origin, has shown much higher rates of alcoholism among the relatives of alcoholics than in the population in general (Goodwin, 1971a). In a recent review of the literature, Cotton (1979) found that all 39 of the studies reviewed revealed that the rates of alcoholism were substantially higher in relatives of alcoholics than in relatives of nonalcoholics, even when nonalcoholics were psychiatric patients.

Twin Studies

Others in the field have approached the problem of genetics by studying pairs of twins. These studies compared the degree of similarity, or concordance, in alcohol consumption between identical twins (monozygotic or one-egg twins) and fraternal twins (dizygotic or two-egg twins). Monozygotic (MZ) twins have 100% genetic likeness, but dizygotic (DZ) twins have only about 50% genetic likeness and are no more similar than any brother and sister. This idea assumes that MZ and DZ twins differ mainly in genetic makeup and that the environment is the same for both sets of twins.

Two major studies have been reported using this technique. The first was by Kaij (1960) of Sweden, who identified 174 male pairs of twins in which at least one partner was registered at a temperance board because of a legal conviction for drunkenness or other alcohol abuse. He interviewed 90% of the subjects and established zygosity by a blood test. The concordance rate for alcohol abuse in the MZ group was 54% as compared to 28% for the DZ group and the difference was statistically significant. He also noted that the more severe the drinking problem in the first identified twin, the higher the concordance rate. In an interesting follow-up, he discovered that the social and brain function deterioration aspects of alcohol abuse correlated more closely with zygosity than did the amount and frequency of alcohol intake.

In a somewhat different approach, the Finnish group of Partanen, Bruun, and Markkanen (1966) studied 133 MZ pairs and 471 DZ pairs, 28 to 37 years of age. This nonalcoholic population did show more concordance with regard to frequency and amount of drinking among MZ twins than among DZ twins. However, there was no report of heritability for the presence of "addictive" symptoms or drinking consequences (i.e., arrest for drunkenness).

It would appear that in both these studies inherited traits passed on by families (parents) played a contributing role in drinking behavior. However, these studies have been faulted because of the greater physical resemblance between MZ twins than DZ twins. This is thought to be a pertinent factor because identical twins are often treated more similarly (i.e., similar clothing) than fraternal twins, and therefore their life experiences are more alike.

Adoption Studies

Another family method used to separate nature from nurture is the adoption study. Some see this method as the most productive way to approach the problem. Goodwin (1973) and his collaborators went to Denmark to take advantage of a pool of 15,000 known adoptees, most of whom were separated from their biological nuclear families at birth or during early childhood and were raised by nonrelatives. It would be very difficult to attempt such a study in the United States because of the lack of access to adoption records.

The experimental group in Denmark consisted of 55 male adoptees who had at least one biological parent who had been hospitalized primarily for alcoholism. Each had been separated from the parents in the first six weeks of life, had no subsequent contact with his or her biological parents, and was adopted by nonrelatives. A control group used for comparison consisted of 78 adopted males who met the same criteria except that they had no biological alcoholic parents. The groups were matched for adult age and approximate age at adoption. The mean age in both groups at the time they were interviewed was 30, with a range of 25 to 45. All adoptees were interviewed by a Danish psychiatrist who did not know to which group they belonged. The information obtained included demographic factors, information on adoptive parents, psychopathology in adoptees, drinking practices and problems, and a variety of life experiences. Of the 55 subjects with alcoholic parents, 10 were classified as alcoholic, at a rate nearly four times that of the controls. Almost without exception, this group had more drinking problems than the controls. Differences were significant in five types of problems, including hallucinations, inability to control drinking, morning drinking, amnesia, and tremor. Goodwin's conclusions were that severe forms of alcohol abuse may have a genetic predisposition, but that heavy drinking itself, even when problems resulted from the drinking, reflected predominantly nongenetic factors. A later follow-up study by Goodwin (1974) also suggested a relationship between the severity of alcoholism and increased tendencies toward alcohol problems in offspring.

Half-Sibling Studies

In another variant of family genetic research, Schuckit, Goodwin, and Winakur (1972) studied 60 male and 9 female subjects who were diagnosed as primary alcoholics and who also had half-siblings. A number of detailed analyses were done on these subjects. Using this approach, the incidence of alcoholism was measured in children who had biological alcoholic parents but were raised in foster homes with no alcoholic parent figures. Conversely, the alcoholism outcome was determined for children without biological alcoholic parents who were raised in homes with an alcoholic parent. In this study, of the 32 alcoholic half-siblings and the 32 nonalcoholic half-siblings, 62% of the former and only 19% of the latter had at least one alcoholic biological parent, clearly indicating a strong genetic relationship. The rates of alcoholic and nonalcoholic half-siblings who lived with an alcoholic parent figure were almost identical, suggesting a stronger relationship with hereditary than with environmental factors.

Drew, Moon, and Buchanan (1981) graphically reported the situation as shown in Figure 4-2.

Does this research prove conclusively that alcoholism is inherited? No, there are some definite problems with the studies just cited. Even though alcoholism may run in families, this tendency does not constitute proof of inheritance. Many things run in families, such as language, eating habits, and occupations, but these are sociocultural factors and are not due to heredity. Although there are many studies linking alcoholism to heredity, none have demonstrated heredity to be more than a contributing factor in the etiology of alcoholism.

An authority in the area of alcoholism and heredity, Goodwin (1981) feels this type of research is plagued with difficulties. For example, the sources of information may be faulty, or conflicting stories may be reported to researchers. Problems with definitions (particularly in the field of alcoholism) are also significant, as are

Figure 4-2 Drinking Habits of Children Compared with the Drinking Habits of Their Parents

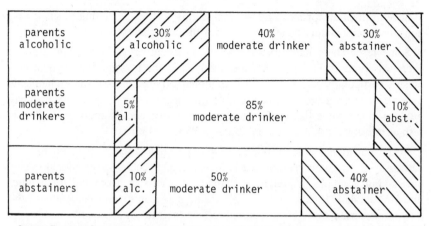

Source: Reprinted from *Alcoholism: A Handbook* by L.R.H. Drew, J.R. Moon, and F.H. Buchanan with permission of Wm. Heinemann Ltd., © July 29, 1981.

many other inherent methodological problems. As Goodwin points out, these problems must be acknowledged and improvements made. However, the apparent consistency of results across studies is encouraging, and the volume of work done in this area should not be ignored. Indeed, studies of families are not the only evidence of genetic factors in alcoholism. Several other methods have been developed to examine this issue.

Animal Studies

Although some feel that alcoholism is a human condition and animal research is irrelevant, this type of research continues to provide useful information about the hereditary determinants of alcoholism. For example, it has been shown that different strains of mice and rats will seek out and ingest different amounts of alcohol. And, if members of nondrinking strains and members of heavy drinking strains mate, they produce moderate drinking offspring with intermediate alcohol intake. This suggests that voluntary alcohol consumption was "regulated by numerous genes" (Goodwin, 1971a). The primary reason that research is conducted with animals is that experimental manipulations can be carried out on animals that would be detrimental or unwise for man, such as the mating procedure in the experiment mentioned above. It is clear that these experiments have produced strains of animals that have different responsiveness to alcohol. It is entirely possible that such hereditary factors exist in man and that they are passed on from family to family.

Other Physiological Studies of Alcoholism Etiology

Several theories appear to be relevant to this section, including biochemical, nutritional, and endocrine system theories of alcoholism.

Some researchers have focused on the biochemistry of the brain. Certain chemicals produced in the brain are involved in the transmission of neuroimpulses, particularly those related to emotional expression, and these chemicals may affect alcohol intake. According to one of these hypotheses, alcohol may produce a morphine-like substance in the brain of certain individuals that is responsible for alcohol addiction (Davis & Walsh, 1970).

In the nutritional area, Williams (1959) postulates that alcoholism may be caused by a metabolic pattern that is inherited and results in nutritional deficiencies. For example, a glutamine deficiency results in a craving for another nutrient, alcohol. In certain cases, glutamine has been given to alcoholics, and they have subsequently been reported to lose their taste for liquor.

Another major physiological theory, the endocrine theory, postulates that alcoholism is caused by a dysfunction of the endocrine system. Experimental clinical evidence, however, does not provide a great deal of support for this theory. The available information suggests that heavy drinking may be the cause rather than the result of these endocrine dysfunctions.

The above discussion presents only a sample of the evidence that physiological and genetic factors contribute to alcoholism. The reader who is interested in a detailed review should consult McClearn (1970) and Lindsey, Loehlin, Monosevitz, and Thiessen (1971).

Although heredity has never been demonstrated to explain alcoholism in total, it is clearly one of the many contributing factors. If people can inherit brown eyes from their parents, they may also inherit the way alcohol is metabolized by their body. The genetic endowment a person receives may only set down a predisposition to alcoholism, but the final outcome may depend on a combination of physiological, sociological, and psychological factors. However, some people clearly are at a higher physical risk for alcoholism than others, and this trait may be passed on from family to family. A genetic involvement does not mean the condition is hopeless. Genetically influenced diabetes can be modified by injections of insulin; genetically influenced myopia can be modified by lenses; and future alcoholism can be modified by intervention and prevention techniques. Like so many pathologies, the earlier the predictions of future alcohol problems can be made, the better the chance of effective prevention.

Who is at high risk and who is at low risk physically for alcoholism? By asking the following questions, an approximate risk factor for the physiological area can be determined:

1. Do you have a parent or grandparent who was or is alcoholic?
2. If you have started drinking, are you or were you able to drink larger amounts of alcohol than most of your friends with fewer physical consequences (i.e., hangover)?
3. Did you drink large amounts of alcohol from the first time you started drinking?

The rationale for the first question is obvious. If the client has a parent or grandparent who is alcoholic, he or she has a better than average chance of being physically at high risk. However, there are a few problems with this first question. For example, if none of the relatives drink, there is no way to know if they would have had alcohol problems had they drank. The other possibility is that there are conflicting views on the grandparent's or parent's status. To the teetotaler, the person who has two drinks every day might be considered a problem drinker. However, to an alcoholic, a person who drinks a fifth of liquor a day might seem quite normal. Despite these problems, the first question will be easy to answer for most people. If alcoholic aunts or uncles exist, the client would be at least at medium physical risk.

The second question is for those who have started to drink, and it is an excellent indicator of a high physical risk factor. The rationale for this question comes from the authors' personal experience with alcoholics. Of the hundreds of alcoholics the authors interviewed in the past 11 years, a significant number fit the description detailed in question two. Some people believe that alcoholics are in an endless search for good feelings, without the negative consequences that were present when they first began drinking. However, for most alcoholics, early drinking experiences were mainly pleasant.

The third question has the same rationale as the second. Many alcoholics claim they became alcoholic with their first drink. A person who answers yes to question three should be considered at high physical risk for alcoholism.

The risk factors in each of the three theoretical models can change. However, the physical risk factors are less likely to change than either the sociological or psychological factors. Physical risk does increase slightly with age since the body's ability to metabolize alcohol deteriorates as a person ages. For example, people over age 65 would need much less alcohol to gain the same effect they received at age 25. Similarly, a physical injury or disease can change the physical risk factor. A person with a liver ailment might become at higher physical risk for alcoholism. Abusing the body with alcohol or drugs can raise the physical risk factor. People who drink heavily for many years may increase their risk.

Who would be a low risk? People who answer no to all three questions, people who almost always get sick when they drink too much (unless they are in the advanced stages of alcoholism), and people who never drink alcohol would all have a low risk for alcoholism.

SOCIOCULTURAL THEORIES OF ETIOLOGY AND THE FAMILY

In the previous section, biological or physiological characteristics that make a person a high risk for alcoholism were presented. This section examines the sociological or sociocultural factors that influence alcoholism. Generally, a person's physical capacity to handle alcohol is inherited from parents or grandparents. Social attitudes toward alcohol use also result from family orientation.

The family has multiple ways of influencing drinking behavior. As with physiological risk factors, parents again are the major contributors to the development of high risk factors for their children in the sociocultural area. Some of the major sociological theories will be examined and questions will be provided to determine whether an individual is at low, high, or medium risk on the risk factor chart. (See Figure 4-1.)

Social factors determine not only whether people will drink, but also how people will view themselves after drinking. In a recent review of a 33-year prospective study of alcoholism, Vaillant and Milofsky (1982) found data suggesting that ethnicity (South European) and the number of alcoholic relatives accounted for most of the variance in adult alcoholism. Other social factors, such as age, sex, religion, socioeconomic class, and family background, have been studied to help explain the diversity in alcoholism rates among different groups of people. Tarter and Schneider (1976) have identified 14 variables that impact on an individual's decision to start, continue, or stop drinking. These are: (1) childhood exposure to alcohol and drinking models; (2) the quantity of alcohol that is considered to be appropriate or excessive; (3) drinking customs; (4) type of alcoholic beverage used; (5) levels of inhibition considered safe; (6) symbolic meaning of alcohol; (7) attitude toward public intoxication; (8) the social group associated with drinking; (9) activities associated with drinking; (10) the amount of pressure exerted upon the individual to drink and continue drinking; (11) use of alcohol in social or private context; (12) the individual's mobility in changing drinking reference groups; (13) the permanence of; and (14) the social rewards or punishments for drinking.

The importance of these social variables has largely been discounted by the majority of people in the field of alcoholism rehabilitation. This is due in part to the incompatibility of these theories with the predominantly accepted "disease model" of alcoholism.

One author who has rejected this disease model, primarily due to conclusions based on his research, is Cahalan (1970). In a national survey published in 1970, he concluded that social environment, to a large extent, determines whether an individual will or will not drink. Social/psychological variables also determine the level of drinking maintained. Variables cited by Cahalan include: (1) an attitude favorable to drinking; (2) the amount and type of environmental support for heavy drinking; (3) the individual's impulsiveness and his or her desire for conformity or nonconformity; (4) the degree of the individual's alienation and maladjustment; (5) the individual's expectations for success; and (6) the looseness of social control. To become a problem drinker, Cahalan says, a person must permit heavy drinking under at least some circumstances. The social variables of age, sex, ethnicity, and social position will influence the probability of drinking as a dominant response.

Loss of control occurs when the reinforcing effects of alcohol become stronger than the negative effects of the physiological and psychological conditions that follow the termination of drinking. This loss of drinking control is commonly assumed to be caused by alcohol's effect on the brain. The area of the brain that controls inhibition is said to be temporarily inoperative. On the other hand, MacAndrew and Edgerton (1969) have come to a different conclusion. By surveying evidence from many diverse societies provided by anthropologists, historians, missionaries, explorers, and other observers, they show that in many parts of the world drinking is followed by either no change in behavior or a wide variety of changes. The drunken "misconduct" that does take place occurs within socially defined limits.

On this basis, drunken behavior cannot be explained simply as a result of alcohol's effect on the brain. Instead, these changes in behavior can be explained on the basis of social definitions of drunkenness as a state of reduced responsibility or of "time out." MacAndrew and Edgerton (1969) argue that excuses are of great importance in all social systems and that drunkenness is one such excuse.

The author's personal experiences have corroborated somewhat the findings of MacAndrew. The author spent five of the last ten years in such countries as England, Holland, Germany, Greece, and Spain and traveled extensively throughout the rest of Europe. The drinking habits of at least eight separate cultures (all different from one another and all very different from the United States) were observed at first hand. European people, in general, seem to have a healthier attitude about drinking than people in the United States. Although drinking seemed to be more thoroughly integrated into social custom and routine, drunkenness was far less acceptable.

Myerson (1940) has used the term *social ambivalence* in reference to American cultural attitudes toward drinking. He believes that this ambivalence limits the development of more stable attitudes toward drinking as shown in certain other cultures. He further states that this ambivalence restricts the meaning of drinking to hedonism and insulates drinking practices from social control. Drinking becomes an extreme and uncontrolled form of behavior for many people.

Some observations based on personal experience verify this view. During the five years the author spent in Europe, most people observed drunk in public places were American tourists or American military personnel. Stolnick (1958) found alcoholic complications in students from abstinent backgrounds. He states: "Total abstinence, teaching which imposes and implants a repugnance to drinking and inebriety, tends to identify the act of drinking with personal and social disorganization. This inadvertently suggests inebriety as a pattern of drinking and encourages the behavior it most deplores.''

Stolnick is suggesting that people who become alienated from their abstinence background may use excessive drinking to express their frustration with early familial, religious, and community teachings. Problem drinking is a symbol of revolt against early family values that became overly rigid during adulthood. Again, the author's personal experience confirms this idea since an estimated 30% of more than 500 people personally seen in treatment during the past 11 years came from homes where at least one parent had a strong religious and moralistic bias against alcohol.

Some people believe that if drinking was more thoroughly integrated into American social custom and routine, these competing attitudes (abstinence and hedonism) would be neutralized along with alcoholism. To substantiate this position, they refer to the low alcoholism rate among Jews (Lolli, Serianni, Golden & Luzzatto-Fegiz, 1958) and among Italians, (Pittman & Snyder, 1962) and the high rate among Irish and Scandinavian groups (Pittman & Snyder, 1962). They point to the high integration of drinking into the Jewish subculture and the negative status drunkenness has for Jews. They also indicate that drinking plays a significant part in Jewish family ritual. In contrast, the Irish male's drinking is disassociated from the church and is also not part of the family's social routine. For Jews, drinking is integrated into the subculture, but for the Irish, it is the subject of ambivalence (Pittman, 1968).

Hedonism and utilitarianism are terms coined by Bales (1946) to describe what he sees as the major functions that drinking may serve, other than for religious and ceremonial purposes. Bales proposed that a society that produces acute inner tensions (such as the suppression of aggression, guilt, and sexual tension) and that condones the use of alcohol to relieve those tensions is susceptible to high rates of alcoholism. Bales also listed the collective attitudes toward alcohol that influence drinking practices as follows: (1) abstinence; (2) ritual use connected with religious rites; (3) convivial drinking in a social setting; and (4) utilitarian—the use of drinking for personal, self-interested reasons. These reasons for drinking were thought by Bales to cause most drinking problems for a society.

Bales has also cited the degree to which the culture offers alternatives for the release of tension as a significant variable in drinking practices. If there are few alternative means for tension release, more drunkenness will occur.

Since tension is a societal factor in alcoholism, Cloward (1959) focuses on the difference between the socially desirable aspirations instilled in an individual and the opportunity that society affords the person to achieve such aspirations. He feels that if the means to meet these goals are not available, the person is likely to retreat into alcoholism.

Many other sociocultural theories exist. Merton (1957) postulates that anomie or normlessness is brought about by a dysfunction between goals shared by persons in the same society and the means for achieving them. Deviant behavior (such as alcoholism) results from the strain between perceived goals and the means available to meet them. Similarly, Horman (1979), in a more recent statement, has identified alienation and the depression, nonspecific anxiety, and rebellion that stem from it as key causes of the recent increase in adolescent drinking in this country. Bacon (1974) believes that alcoholism occurs in any society that combines a lack of indulgence of children with demanding attitudes toward achievement and negative attitudes toward dependent behavior in adults. The low rate of alcoholism among Italians would seem to support this theory, but Bacon ignores the much higher rate of alcoholism among the French, despite the similarity of cultures.

In terms of the family, O'Connor (1975) has identified eight characteristics that correlate with a low incidence of alcoholism. These factors are: (1) children are exposed early to alcohol in family or religious situations; (2) the parents present an example of moderate drinking; (3) the beverages most commonly used contain large amounts of nonalcoholic components; (4) the beverages are viewed mainly as a food and are usually served with meals; (5) no moral importance is attached to drinking; (6) drinking is not viewed as proof of adulthood or virility; (7) abstinence, but not excessive drinking or intoxication, is considered socially acceptable; and (8) there is virtually complete agreement among group members on standards of drinking behavior.

There are additional sociocultural theories that will not be covered due to practical limitations although there are many questions yet to be answered in this area. For example, why do Native Americans have such a high rate of alcoholism? Is it because they have been drinking a relatively short period of time compared to other groups (i.e., 300 years compared to 3,000 years for Jews)? Is it because they are caught between two cultures? Or is it a combination of these factors and more? More research will be conducted in this area in the future, but the purpose, for now, has been to establish that the sociocultural area is an important factor in the etiology of alcoholism. For some interesting and informative readings on the cultural factors in alcoholism see *Journal of Studies on Alcohol,* January, 1981 Supplement No. 9. The sociological view, along with the physiological and psychological views, are all necessary for a comprehensive theory of alcoholism etiology. It is important for the reader to keep in mind the important role the family plays in each of these areas.

For the sociological area there are five questions that can help establish a client's risk factor. In this format, each question is worth one point. A score of zero is low risk; a score of one or two is medium and a score of three to five is high risk. The questions are:

1. (Do) Did one or both of your parents have strong religious or moral views against drinking alcohol?

      yes +1   no +0

2. Are either of your parents alcoholic?

      yes +1   no +0

3. Do you come from an ethnic background that has a reputation for a high rate of alcoholism?

      yes +1   no +0

4. Do you consider your friends to be heavy drinkers?

      yes +1   no +0

5. Does your social status match your concept of where you feel you should be in society?

      yes +0   no +1

Just as in the last section on physiological factors, a high risk score in the sociological area does not mean a person is or will become an alcoholic. Many people have high risk scores in this area but never experience drinking problems, and they will be discussed in Chapter 5. For now, this score is to be used with the other two risk scores shown on the chart in Figure 4-1.

The rationale for the questions comes from various researchers and from personal experience. The first question is derived from a combination of the research of Stolnick (1958), mentioned earlier in the chapter, and the authors' personal experiences. Question two was used in the last section and will be used again for different reasons. In the last section, the reasons were biological and genetic, but this time they are sociological. A person growing up in an alcoholic home experiences alcoholism as a model for adjustment. By using the question twice in determining risk factors, both nature and nurture, environment and heredity, are accounted for. The psychological ramifications will be discussed in the next section.

The third question is open to some interpretation. There are some groups that are generally accepted as having high rates of alcoholism (i.e., Native Americans and Irish Catholics). However, in some other groups the distinction is not clear. Many Southern Baptists, for example, do not drink at all, and they are not only low risk, but no risk. However, those Southern Baptists who do drink have a higher rate of alcoholism than the population in general. If you cannot determine an answer to this question, ask as many people as you can who you do not know and who are not from your client's ethnic group and go with the consensus.

Question four is also open to some interpretation. If a client drinks a case and a half of beer a day and his or her friends only drink a case, the client might not consider them heavy drinkers. However, if a client drinks a case and a half a day, put the book down and refer him or her to the nearest treatment center—and take the friends along. Seriously, opinions vary as to what constitutes heavy drinking.

For example, people from the East and West coasts drink somewhat more than those in other parts of the country. When asking this question, the regional norm should be taken into consideration. Three drinks a day might seem normal in New York or San Francisco, but that amount may be considered excessive in Iowa.

In some cases, clients may have reached the point in their drinking where they no longer have friends and only drink alone. In that case, forget about the questions and give them checkmarks in the high risk category.

The fifth and final question might be the most difficult to answer objectively. Some people of very low social status in this country may feel as if that's where they belong. On the other hand, some high status people do not feel comfortable and would prefer to be in a lower position. These dynamics are difficult to understand, and cognitive dissonance and association theories complicate the matter (for a discussion of these see a recent social psychology text). In order to determine a risk factor if the question is too difficult for the client to answer, the question "are you happy with your life?" can be substituted. (Yes = +0 No = +1). However, many alcoholics may answer "yes, I'm happy," during sobriety and "no, I'm not happy" when drunk.

Sociological theories of the etiology of alcoholism are not foolproof. Even the low rates of alcoholism for Jews have recently become suspect (Blume, 1978). However, they do fill in some pieces of the puzzle, and the next section on psychological theories of etiology will fill in the puzzle even more. Finally, Chapter 5 will address some important questions about the treatment and prevention of alcoholism.

PSYCHOLOGICAL THEORIES OF ETIOLOGY AND THE FAMILY

The previous two sections have discussed the sociological and physiological theories of the etiology of alcoholism. Although these areas are important, the most important area, in terms of treatment and prevention, appears to be the psychological area. Some say it is the personality of the individual that has more to do with the way he or she deals with the environment than any other factor. This section will examine the psychological causes for alcoholism and will, as in the two previous sections, show a relationship between the family and high psychological risk for alcoholism. The original research in the psychological area of alcoholism attempted to answer the question, "What causes people to become dependent on alcohol?" This question proved much too broad, and an alternate question took its place, "How do alcoholics differ from the population in general?"

A review of the literature on personality traits associated with alcoholism suggests that chronic alcoholics may indeed have a distinct personality type. Characteristics such as dependency, denial, depression, superficial sociability, emotional instability, suspiciousness, low tolerance for frustration, impulsivity, self-devaluation, and chronic anxiety occur with high frequency among alcoholics. Gross and Adler (1970) reported that 266 male alcoholics tested on the 16 PF personality inventory showed traits that differentiated them from the general population, with significant differences on 12 of the 16 personality traits on the 16 PF. Jones (1968) identified adult problem drinkers as being uncontrolled, impulsive, and rebellious.

The problem with these studies is that they leave several important questions unanswered. For example, does excessive drinking cause these personality traits, or do the personality traits cause the drinking? Furthermore, a considerable number of problem drinkers do not possess these traits, and many people who do have these traits are not problem drinkers. In another study, Robins (1966) found that, as adults, alcoholics closely resembled sociopaths even though nonalcoholic sociopaths may have many of the same personality characteristics. Robins also found evidence that the childhoods of alcoholics resembled the childhoods of sociopaths. The difference between the two groups may lie in the sociological and physiological areas of risk. The sociopath becomes the person who shows up as high risk in the psychological area but low risk in the other two areas. Again, for a complete picture of the individual, all of the risk areas must be considered.

Alcoholism is apparently caused not by a single factor, but by many complicated interrelated factors. Seven factors have been identified that differentiate those who abuse alcohol from those who do not. These seven basic characteristics are present in successful people and absent in people who tend to fail. These characteristics show the difference between the low risk person and the high risk person in the psychological area of the etiology of alcoholism, and they all involve the family. Not limited to alcoholism, these factors also predict success in a variety of other areas.

As presented by Glenn (1981) at a prevention seminar, the characteristics of high risk people are:

1. Low identification with viable role models, which refers to a person's self-concept and reference group (family). Persons who are vulnerable in this area see themselves as different from people whose attitudes, values, and behaviors allow them to function and "survive" in their total environment. For instance, a child might not relate to his or her family and may reject their values.
2. Low identification with and responsibility for "family" process. In this instance, people do not identify strongly with things greater than themselves (e.g., relationships with other people, groups, mankind, or God). They also do not see how this behavior affects others. This process refers to shared investments in outcomes, shared responsibility for achieving outcomes, and accountability to others.

3. High faith in "miracle" solutions to problems. This area involves the skills and attitudes necessary to work through problems and includes the belief that problems can be solved through application of personal resources. When these skills are poorly developed, people believe that problems have been escaped when they cannot feel them (involving the use of drugs and alcohol, for example). These individuals do not believe that there is any way to affect the present or future—things just happen. (The role parents play in fostering this attitude will be discussed later in this section.)
4. Inadequate intrapersonal skills. This area includes the skills of self-discipline, self-control, and self-assessment. Weakness in these areas shows up as inability to cope with personal stresses and tensions, dishonesty with self, denial of self, and the inability to defer gratification.
5. Inadequate interpersonal skills. These skills involve communication, cooperation, negotiation, empathy, listening, and sharing. Poor performance in this area shows up as dishonesty with others, a lack of empathetic awareness, resistance to feedback, unwillingness to share feelings, or the inability to give or receive love or help.
6. Inadequate systemic skills. This area involves the ability to respond to the limits inherent in a situation (responsibility) and the ability to constructively adapt behavior to a situation in order to get needs met (adaptability). Irresponsibility, refusal to accept consequences of behavior, and scapegoating are all expressed when there is a weakness in this area.
7. Inadequate judgmental skills. This area includes the ability to recognize, understand, and apply appropriate meanings to relationships. Weaknesses in judgment are expressed as crises in sexual, natural, consumer, and drug and alcohol environments and as repetitive self-destructive behavior.

So the person who is successful in life and is unlikely to abuse alcohol or drugs has well-developed skills in these areas.

Successful individuals also tend to identify with viable role models and take responsibility within the family. They have problem-solving abilities and strong intrapersonal and interpersonal skills. They are skilled at working within "the system" and have good judgmental skills. The remainder of this section will look at the role of the family in thwarting the development of these traits in the individual.

The parents play the most important part in a child's early development. In the authors' experience, there have been four major identifiable parent types. Each alcoholic almost always has one or both parents in one or more of the categories. This theory has been presented by the authors to perhaps 1,000 alcoholics, who were students or workshop participants. Only one person indicated that the parents did not fit this scheme. The theory has had virtually unanimous support. However, many people who are not alcoholic also have parents who fit into one or more of these categories. In these cases, the other two risk categories become useful. The four parent types are: (1) alcoholic; (2) teetotaler; (3) overdemanding; and (4) overprotective.

The Alcoholic Parent

Alcoholic parents foster alcoholism in their offspring in many ways. Probably, the single most important factor is modeling. Children learn acceptable behavior by watching those around them. If a parent deals with problems through alcohol, the child learns that drinking is an option.

Even if the child is initially repulsed by parental drinking behavior, abusive drinking becomes a possibility for him or her. A child may say to himself, "I will never drink like Daddy," only to find himself later in life doing just that. Some people feel that sons become alcoholic to say to their parents, "See, I love you; I'm just like you." Many daughters of alcoholics marry alcoholics. They essentially are saying, "See Daddy, I love you. I married someone just like you" (Hoffman, 1979). Both of these reactions come from feelings of being unloved and neglected as children and, perhaps, from guilt about a parent's drinking. A child often feels responsible for a parent's drinking or for a poor relationship between parents. The child may reason that "if only I had been good or if only I had kept my room clean, Daddy would not have hit Mommy." Unfortunately, treatment for the alcoholic often heightens the guilt experienced by children. The child may hate Daddy because of his drinking behavior. When the child hears that Daddy didn't mean it and that Daddy has a disease, the child may feel guilty for hating a "sick" person who "couldn't help it." Unless the family is treated concurrently with the alcoholic, the children may not be better off than they were before the parent's treatment. They may worry constantly about what will happen when Daddy gets sick again, or they may continue to feel guilty about hating a sick person.

In addition, the alcoholic parent is in no position to promote general mental health and development in his or her children. It is understandable that alcoholics, in their uncomfortable, guilt-ridden, and anesthetized state, are unable to establish a loving and meaningful relationship with their children. The alcoholic is usually self-centered and self-occupied. Children similarly cannot turn to the spouse of the alcoholic for attention, since he or she is often too overcome with anger, frustration, and futility to be of any comfort.

Many other factors account for the psychological trauma that leads children of alcoholics to become alcoholics themselves. The disruption of important family rituals (e.g., holidays, dinnertime, weekends, or vacations) due to drinking has serious implications. In families where rituals were maintained in spite of alcoholism, recurrence of alcoholism in children was low, compared to high alcoholism rates in children from families that did not maintain rituals (Wolin, Bennett, Noonan, & Teitelbaum, 1977).

Whatever the reason, children of alcoholics often are weak in major areas of psychological functioning, and they often have very poor self-images. These problems will not necessarily be resolved just because a parent has entered treatment. The entire family also needs treatment.

The Teetotaler Parent

The next parent type that shows up often among the parents of alcoholics is the teetotaler. The term *teetotaler* in this context is not implied to mean merely a person who has chosen not to drink. In this instance, teetotaler refers to a person who chooses not to drink and condemns those who make a different choice. For some reason, usually moral or religious, the teetotaler feels that any drinking is immoral and indecent. The contrast to a teetotaler is a person who merely chooses not to drink but does not condemn the drinking of others. The last section presented the teetotaler parent in the sociological perspective; here, the teetotaler parent will be addressed in terms of the psychological outcome on the children.

The psychological effects on a child who grows up in a home in which one or both parents are teetotalers or one parent is a teetotaler and the other parent is alcoholic are rarely positive.

One of the problems with parents who have a rigid stance against alcohol is that they also tend to have a rigid, moralistic approach to life. Problems are presented to children with right and wrong, black and white answers. The children grow up with the words *shouldn't* or *should* ringing in their ears. They learn that parents, teachers, ministers, and others in positions of authority have all the right answers and that there is a right and a wrong position on every issue. They become intolerant of any but their own viewpoints. When they are presented with life problems that do not have right and wrong answers, their rigid stance only causes difficulties. Living in a world of gray with only a black and white rule book can be a trying experience (e.g., Archie Bunker). This approach to life is similarly detrimental for people associated with this person.

In short, the teetotaler parent gives the child a set of rules and expectations that is inconsistent with basic human needs and impossible to live by. In turn, the child has the perfect opportunity to graphically show contempt for these rules by abusing alcohol, usually during adolescence or early adulthood. Basically, the individual says to his or her parents, "How dare you give me rules that are impossible to live by. I reject your rules, and I reject you as my parent. To make sure you understand this, I will abuse alcohol to the point that you cannot ignore it. I will become alcoholic." To complicate matters, this person usually has a low self-image due to guilt about not being able to live up to the parents' expectations. This last example crosses into the "overdemanding parent" type. However, it is not unusual for one parent type to show the tendencies of another. The over-demanding parent, for example, comes in several forms.

The Overdemanding Parent

The most common type of overdemanding parents make it quite clear to the child what it is they expect, but these expectations are generally unrealistic. It is not uncommon for a child to excel in one area (e.g., math, sports, spelling, or social skills), but very few excel in all areas. Many do not excel in any area. Often, when the parents ask a great deal from their children, they are living vicariously through them. These parents may be heard to say something like "By damn, I never had a chance to go to college, so you're going to go." Parents who choose career fields for their children often fit into this category. "You're going to be a doctor!" It's only natural for parents to want the best for their children, and no parent wants his or her child to make the same mistakes he or she did. Such overdemanding parents often do not cause serious psychological problems unless their expectations are extreme.

The overdemanding parent likely to have a son or daughter with a problem models a high degree of success. These parents inadvertently place high expecta-tions on their offspring even if their only wish for their children is that they be happy. The parents' own achievement level makes it impossible for their children to develop a positive self-image when comparing themselves with parents who are extremely successful. Often, these parents achieve this success at the expense of the family. Children find it hard to feel good about themselves when parents seem to care more about their career than about the children. This is often a tragic situation because the parents may truly believe they are working extra hard so the family can benefit financially and otherwise.

This phenomenon is not limited to children and parents. Brothers and sisters may compare themselves with one another; often, there is a brother-to-brother or sister-to-sister competition. But family rivalry does not stop there. Mom can compare herself with Dad or Dad with Mom—the dynamics and the results are the same. When people compare themselves with someone they see as "better," they will perceive themselves as less than they want to be or should be, and their self-image will suffer as a consequence. Alcoholism and drug abuse are not always the solution for these people; sometimes they inadvertently choose to commit suicide or become mentally ill. The large number of sons and daughters of movie stars who have these problems graphically shows these dynamics at work. Similar-ly, an example of brother-to-brother rivalry is shown in the relationship of Jimmy and Billy Carter. Examples of husband and wife conflict involving alcoholism can be seen in Betty and Jerry Ford and Joan and Edward Kennedy. Of course, many other factors are also involved. Human behavior is complex, and there are very few behaviors that are simple to justify or explain. There may be hundreds of reasons why people become alcoholic, but the ones mentioned here seem to be very important, based on research and personal experience. The one person, mentioned earlier in the section, whose parents did not fit into any of these categories described her parents this way, "My parents were not alcoholic; they drank moderately. They were not teetotalers, and they were not overly protective or overly demanding." "In fact," she said, "they were perfect parents." Someone in the class pointed out that it must have been hard to live up to "perfect parents," and she got the point.

Overly Protective Parents

The final parent type is overly protective. The dynamics here are complex, but the outcome is simple. The child never gets a chance to develop a sense of self-worth and a positive self-image. After a childhood and adolescence of being "taken care of" it is very difficult to handle life's problems because there has been no chance to practice.

Two of the possible dynamics here include, first, the parent or parents who are overinvested in their children. Too much of their self-worth and ego needs are met through the children. Second, the parent or parents may be suffering from a reaction formation. The parents may have some doubts in their minds if they even really like their children. This thought is so unacceptable that they react by showing their children, as well as the rest of the world, how much they care through their overprotective behavior. Again, children in these families have no chance to grow up and develop coping skills or self-worth.

The common element among all of these parent types is that their children do not develop a positive sense of self-worth. In many cases, children are not exposed to a sufficient number of life's problems to prove to themselves that they can succeed or can fail without falling apart. They fail to learn to adjust to their environment when necessary and very often have low interpersonal communication skills. This is not an indictment of parents. Parents do not cause alcoholism, although they do have a hand in its development. But blaming parents for alcoholism is an exercise in futility. If someone must bear the blame it should be the cultural system that fails to teach how to parent effectively.

There are six questions that determine high, medium, and low risk for alcoholism in the psychological area. A positive answer to any item could indicate a high psychological risk for alcoholism. But, as in the last section, number values have been assigned to answers. To be high risk on this scale requires a score of five to six. Medium risk is three to four, and low risk is one to two. The questions are:

1. Did you have a parent who was alcoholic or chemically dependent?
   yes   +1   no   +0

2. Were one or both of your parents teetotalers as described in this section?

    yes   +1   no   +0

3. In your opinion, were your parents overly protective of you?

    yes   +1   no   +0

4. Were your parents, in your opinion, overdemanding of you, in words or deeds?

    yes   +1   no   +0

5. Do you have something to do in life that makes you feel worthwhile? (e.g., a job, a hobby)

    yes   +1   no   +0

6. Do you have someone who loves you and someone you love?

    yes   +0   no   +1

Although the first two questions were used in the last section on sociological reasons for alcoholism, they are also used here because of psychological ramifications. Questions three and four address overly protective and demanding parent types. It is possible to score one point for each type. For example, the person who had an overprotective mother and an overdemanding father would score a point for each. The final two questions come from the writings of William Glasser (founder of the Reality Therapy Institute) who believes that successful people must have someone who loves them and someone they love, as well as something they feel is worthwhile to do.

In an abbreviated version of this process, simply ask "how do you rate yourself compared to others?" The risk factor is inverse to self-image. Exhibit 4-1 presents an example.

Now that the importance of each of the three risk areas has been established, it is time to determine what all this means in terms of the treatment and prevention of alcoholism. What good does it do to know that alcoholism is caused by many factors all falling into either physiological, sociological or psychological areas? These and other questions will be answered in Chapter 5.

Exhibit 4-1 Self-Image and Psychological Risk

	Psychological Risk	Self-Image
High	_____	Low
Medium	_____	Medium
Low	_____	High

REFERENCES

Bacon, M.K. The dependency-conflict hypothesis and the frequency of drunkenness. *Quarterly Journal of Studies on Alcohol,* 1974, *35,* 863-876.

Bales, R. Cultural differences in rates of alcoholism. *Quarterly Journal of Studies on Alcohol.* 1946, *6,* 480-499.

Blane, H.T. *The personality of the alcoholic: Guises of dependence.* New York: Harper & Row, 1968.

Blume, S. Jews shown not to be immune to alcoholism. NIAAA Information and Feature Service, HEW, September 20, 1978.

Cahalan, D. *Problem drinkers: A national survey.* San Francisco: Jossey-Bass, 1970.

Chafetz, M.E., Blane, H.T., & Hill, M.J. *Frontiers of alcoholism.* New York: Science House, 1970.

Cloward, R. Illegitimate means, anomie and deviate behavior. *American Sociological Review,* 1959, *24,* 164-176.

Cotton, N.S. The familial incidence of alcoholism: A review. *Journal of Studies on Alcohol,* 1979, *46*(1).

Cruz-Coke, R., & Varela, A. Inheritance of alcoholism. *Lancet,* 1966, *2,* 1282.

Davis, V.E., & Walsch, M.J. Alcohol amines, and alkaloids: A possible biochemical basis for alcohol addiction. *Science* 1970, *167,* 1005-1007.

Drew, L.R.H., Moon, J.R., & Buchanan, F.H. *Alcoholism: A handbook.* Melbourne, Australia: Heinemann Health Books, 1974.

Glenn, S. *Directions for the 80's.* Paper presented at the Nebraska Prevention Center, Omaha, February, 1981.

Goodwin, D.W. Is alcoholism hereditary? *Archives of General Psychiatry.* 1971, *25,* 518-545.(a)

Goodwin, D.W. Is alcoholism hereditary? A review and critique. *Archives of General Psychiatry,* 1971, *25,* 545-549.(b)

Goodwin, D.W. Drinking problems in adopted and nonadopted sons of alcoholics. Report submitted to the National Institute on Alcohol Abuse and Alcoholism, January 15, 1974.

Goodwin, D.W. Family studies on alcoholism. *Journal of Studies on Alcohol,* 1981, *42*(1).

Goodwin, D.W., Schlosinger, F., Hermansen, L., Guze, S.B., & Winaker, G. Alcoholism problems in adoptees reared apart from alcoholic biological parents. *Archives of General Psychiatry,* 1973, *28,* 238-243.

Goss, F.W. & Carpenter, L. Alcoholic personality: Reality or fiction. *Psychological Reports,* 1971, *28,* 375-378.

Gross, W.F. & Adler, L.O. Aspects of alcoholics' self-concepts as measured by the Tennessee self-concept scale. *Psychological Reports,* 1970, *27,* 431-434.

Hoffman, B. *No one is to blame.* Palo Alto, California: Dutton & Co., 1979.

Horman, R.E. The impact of sociological systems on teenage alcohol abuse in youth alcohol and social policy. In Blane, H.T. & Chafetz, M.E. (Eds). New York: Plenum Press, 1979.

Hurwitz, J.I. & Lelos, D.A. Multilevel interpersonal profile of employed alcoholics. *Quarterly Journal of Studies on Alcohol,* 1968, *29,* 64-76.

Jones, M.C. Review of studies in the field of alcohol using psychometric methods. *Encyclopedia of Alcohol Problems.* Stanford Institute for the Study of Human Problems, 1962, 336-343.

Jones, M.C. Personality correlates and antecedents of drinking patterns in adult males. *Journal of Consulting and Clinical Psychology,* 1968, *32,* 2-12.

Kaij, L. Studies on the etiology and sequels of abuse of alcohol. Lund, Sweden: Department of Psychiatry, University of Lund, 1960.

Lindsey, G., Loehlin, J., Monosevitz, M., & Thiessen, P. Annual Review of Psychology, 1971, 22, 39.

Lolli, G.S., Serianni, E., Golden, G., & Luzzatto-Fegiz, P. Alcohol in Italian culture. Glencoe, Ill.: Free Press, 1958.

MacAndrew, C. & Edgerton, R.B. Drunken comportment: A social explanation. Chicago: Aldins Publishing Co., 1969.

McClearn, G.E. Annual Review of Genetics, 1970, 4, 437.

Merton, R.K. Social theory and social structure. New York: Free Press, 1957.

Myerson, A. Alcohol: A study of social ambivalence. Quarterly Journal of Studies on Alcohol, 1940, 1, 1940.

O'Connor, J., Social and Cultural Factors Influencing Drinking, Irish Journal of Medical Science, June, 1975, 65-71.

Partanen, J., Bruun, K., & Markkanen, T. Inheritance of drinking behavior. New Brunswick, N.J.: Rutgers Center for Alcohol Studies, 1966.

Pittman, D.J. Drinking and alcoholism in American Society. In R.J. Catanzaro (Ed.), Alcoholism: The total treatment approach. Springfield, Ill.: Charles C. Thomas, 1968.

Pittman, D.G. & Snyder, C.R. (Eds.). Society, culture and drinking patterns. New York: Wiley, 1962.

Robins, L.N. Deviant children grown up; a sociological and psychiatric study of sociopathic personality. Baltimore: Williams and Wilkins, 1966.

Schuckit, M., Goodwin, D.W., & Winakur, G. Life history research in psychopathology. Minneapolis, Minn.: University of Minnesota Press, 1972.

Smart, R.G. Future time perspectives in alcoholics and social drinkers. Journal of Abnormal Psychology, 1968, 73, 81-83.

Stein, L.I., Niles, D., & Ludwig, A.M. The loss of control phenomenon in alcoholics. Quarterly Journal of Studies on Alcohol. 1968, 29, 598-603.

Stolnick, J.H. Religious affiliation and drinking behavior. Quarterly Journal of Studies on Alcohol. 1958, 19, 452-470.

Tarter, R.E. & Schneider, D.V. Models and theories of alcoholism'' in Tarter, R.E., Sugleman, A.A., (Eds.). Alcoholism: Interdisciplinary approaches to an enduring problem: Reading. Mass.: Addison-Wesley Publishing Co., Inc., 1976.

Vaillant, G.E. and Milofsky, E.S. The Etiology of Alcoholism: A prospective viewpoint, American Psychologist, 37, No. 5, May, 1982, 494-503.

Williams, R.J. Biochemical individuality and cellular nutrition: Prime factors in alcoholism. Quarterly Journal of Studies on Alcohol, 1959, 20, 452-463.

Wolin, S., Bennett, L., Noonan, D., & Teitelbaum, M. Families at risk: The intergenerational recurrence of alcoholism. NIAAA Grant #2 R01 AA 01 454, Study conducted from 1974-1977.

Chapter 5

The Relevance of Etiology for Treatment and Prevention

Designing a treatment or prevention program for alcoholism without a thorough understanding of the etiology is like taking a trip without a map. You may or may not arrive at your destination, and if you do arrive, you may not be sure whether you took the shortest route. The fields of mental health and medicine often recognize an illness or a disease before its cause is discovered or a treatment is developed. Very rarely, an effective treatment is developed before the cause is known. In the field of medicine, the cause of an illness is often limited to a single factor, such as a germ, a virus, a genetic predisposition, or perhaps a vitamin deficiency. In mental health, illnesses are often multicausal. Depression, for example, can have many causes. Conditions with several causal factors are often perplexing to treatment personnel, and several things can happen.

Often treatment approaches are developed for each theory of cause. Cancer, for example, is often treated with chemotherapy, radiation therapy, or surgery. Since doctors are often unsure of the outcome of any of these treatments, they are often used in combination. This multimodality treatment is often used for conditions whose causes are unclear.

Another approach is to find something by trial and error that relieves the major symptoms and then use that approach on everyone. The problem here is that, upon scientific investigation, many of these approaches prove to be counterproductive. For example, for many years milk or dairy products were taken by people with ulcers in an attempt to reduce acid in the stomach. Recent findings indicate that, long after the antacid effect of milk wears off, the calcium left in the stomach causes an increase in the acidity levels and makes the use of milk counterproductive. However, because milk seems to reduce pain, many people will continue to use it for ulcers.

Although the actual causes of alcoholism are unknown, most experts agree that there are many causes, not just one. Research and observation lead to the conclusion that there are three main factors to be considered regarding the etiology of alcoholism—physiological, sociological, and psychological factors. Knowledge about the causes of alcoholism must be used to bridge the gap between research, treatment, and prevention.

The accepted line of thinking in the alcoholism field is that alcoholism is a disease. Although the cause is unknown and the disease is incurable, it can be arrested if the alcoholic stops drinking. According to this concept, the most effective way for the alcoholic to give up drinking is through the fellowship of Alcoholics Anonymous.

This model of alcoholism poses some interesting problems. For example, the only people who can be accepted for treatment and who can successfully complete it are those willing to give up alcohol completely for the rest of their lives. What if Masters and Johnson ran a sex clinic and required, as a criterion for admission, that clients abstain from sex altogether? The implication would be that sex is the problem, and if people abstain from sex they will have no difficulties with it. Many people believe that alcohol is the problem and that, if the client gives up drinking, the problem will be resolved. Unfortunately, in most cases, this is not true. In fact, it is possible for an individual to have lifelong alcohol-related problems even if that person doesn't drink. Many children of alcoholics suffer their entire lives because of the parents' alcoholism. People can have alcohol problems without drinking just as they can have sex problems without having sex.

When alcohol consumption is seen as the major concern in treatment, the issue of denial becomes a problem. Denial is considered a primary symptom of alcoholism, and a good part of many treatment programs is spent in breaking down the alcoholic's denial. The irony here is that almost anyone can be considered an alcoholic when asked if drinking causes a problem. If people say "yes," they are alcoholic, and if they say "no," they are denying alcoholism. With this philosophy, it is not difficult to keep inpatient alcoholism treatment beds full. However, because of this approach to diagnosis and treatment, many early cases of problem drinking are unidentified. People who could return to nonproblem drinking are never given a chance to reach this goal. If they do reach it, the alcoholism rehabilitation community may simply discount this successful effort by considering the person a nonalcoholic or may predict that problem drinking will, in time, return.

Of course, in some cases, denial is a serious issue for the alcoholic in treatment. However, the denial that exists among those who work in the field of alcoholism is a far more serious problem. Practitioners deny that they know enough about the causes of alcoholism to plan successful treatment programs for problem drinkers who refuse to take a vow of lifetime abstinence. They also deny that there are many different types of alcoholism and that some may respond to different treatment approaches, not just AA. Similarly, they deny that alcoholism is not truly a disease but a complicated condition caused by physiological, sociological, and psychological factors. Finally, alcoholism treatment personnel may deny that the family should be treated, not just educated, and that alcoholism can be prevented, not just treated.

Treating all alcoholics and all alcoholism the same is like prescribing castor oil for all stomachaches. Although some stomach problems will respond and improve, many will not. Almost a million people have responded to AA and have improved, but if there are ten million alcoholics in the U.S., nine million are not responding to AA, or total abstinence. Put another way, only one out of ten alcoholics is being helped through AA.

If the standard procedure for a stomachache was exploratory surgery, many people would put off seeking help for their stomachaches until they could not function because of the pain. Many people put off seeking help for their alcohol problems because they see the treatment (total abstinence) as worse than the pain. Treatment programs tend to promote this attitude because of the two major premises underlying the therapeutic approach to alcoholism. According to the first premise, excessive drinking is maladaptive. The second premise holds that there are ultimate causes that lead to alcoholism. These concepts have caused therapists to use uniform treatment techniques for all alcoholics and to focus attention on the maladaptive behavior. Such attempts often lead to short-term improvement, but relapse is likely in the long term, leading to frustration for both the alcoholic and the therapist.

The focus should be on the adaptive consequences that reinforce drinking. People drink inappropriately or behave inappropriately under the influence of alcohol for definite reasons. For the purposes of treatment and prevention, it is important to determine how this behavior serves an adaptive function in the family. Therapy should then be structured around helping the alcoholic to manifest these behaviors while sober, as well as to learn alternative behaviors. In many cases, these results are most effectively achieved through family therapy.

AA is a wonderful program for those who accept it, but many people who need treatment may find AA unacceptable. Some sample cases will be presented to show why AA works for some alcoholics and not for others. These sample cases will indicate how an understanding of etiology can help determine a treatment approach.

Suppose Individual A, a person in treatment, has answered high and low risk questions in the way shown in Figure 5-1. The treatment task involves moving the person down on the risk chart where possible. Not much can be done in the physiological area, except to prescribe Antabuse and medical aid. In this hypothetical case, the individual has refused this form of treatment, and so the two other risk levels must be reduced.

For this person, AA can reduce both risk levels. In the sociological area, AA removes this person from a circle of friends who abuse alcohol and places him or her among friends, fellow AA members, who all have a desire to quit drinking. This moves the person from a high to a low risk level in the sociological area.

Figure 5-1 Alcoholism Risk Factors for Individual A

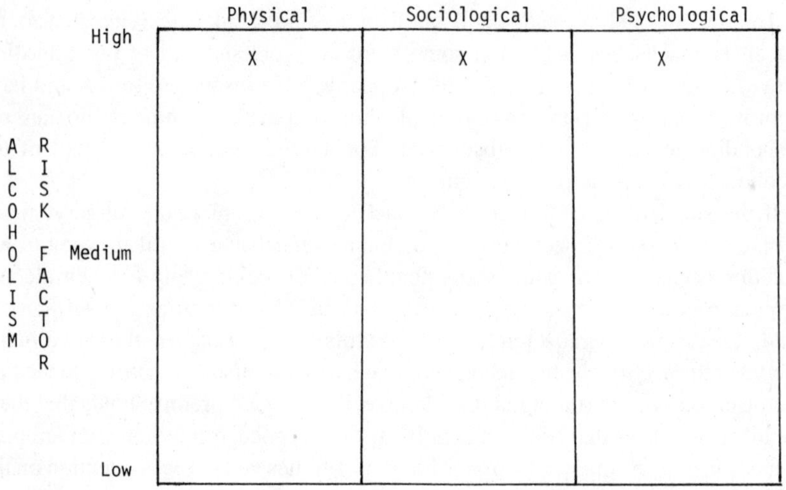

			Physical	Sociological	Psychological
		High			
			X	X	X
A	R				
L	I				
C	S				
O	K				
H					
O	F	Medium			
L	A				
I	C				
S	T				
M	O				
	R				
		Low			

In the psychological risk area, the person's self-image must be improved. The individual needs someone to love and someone who loves him, and he must feel he has something worthwhile to do. From the moment the person walks into the AA meeting, the feeling that "I'm not alone with this problem " begins to improve his self-image. Later, as this person becomes more involved in the program and experiences successes, he feels even better about himself. When the AA sponsor becomes available 24 hours a day, the individual has a chance to develop some positive relationships. The final push toward a genuine feeling of self-worth comes when the individual begins to do 12-step work and helps others with their alcohol problems. Many recovering alcoholics find this activity so rewarding that they become full-time alcoholism counselors, sometimes at a salary scale lower than their previous employment.

The results of Individual A's contact with AA are shown in Figure 5-2. All effective treatment and prevention programs will generally bring about the results illustrated in Figure 5-2. However, these risk levels cannot be changed in a matter of minutes. Permanent changes take a great deal of effort on the part of the individual.

In some cases, AA may be antithetical to rehabilitation. The individual in such a case may have a profile similar to Individual B in Figure 5-3.

This person is from a social subgroup that drinks a great deal. He or she has self-esteem that could be improved but could also be worse. Therefore, this person would be approximately in the middle of the psychological risk area. Suppose this person received a citation for driving under the influence of alcohol, and part of the

Figure 5-2 Effect of AA on Alcoholism Risk Factors for Individual A

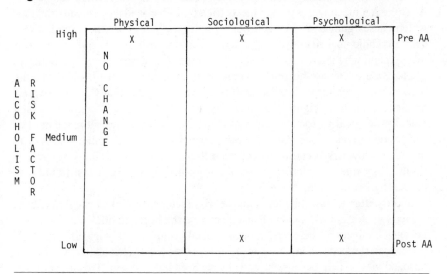

Figure 5-3 Alcoholism Risk Factors for Individual B

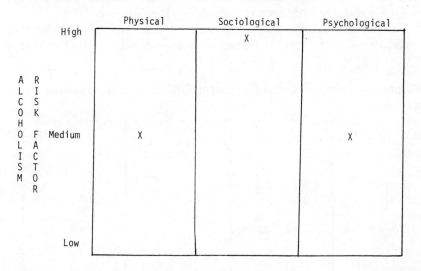

court's recommendation included participation in AA. At the first meeting, this person sees no one with whom to identify. Most members are older, and the individual drinking histories that are recounted by the members sound nothing like this person's drinking pattern. As a result, this person's self-image begins to drop, and he or she may think "Can my drinking really be as bad as these people's?" After the AA meeting this person meets friends at a bar, and they end up drinking, which causes guilt and more self-doubt. After the AA experience, the individual's psychological risk level may increase as shown in Figure 5-4. This result may explain why many people do not return to AA and many never go initially.

There are other case histories that are interesting and provide insights into the dynamics of alcoholism. The risk profile of a woman, Individual C, is shown prior to her alcoholism in Figure 5-5. Since her father was alcoholic, she was at high risk physiologically. Socially, she was at medium risk because, although most of her friends drank, none abused alcohol openly. Psychologically, she was at medium to low risk because of her high self-esteem that came almost solely as a result of her role as a mother. Most of her positive self-image came from being needed by her children.

Shortly after her last child left home her risk factor chart looked like Figure 5-6.

Her sociological risk factor changed because she began to drink alone and was no longer subject to the controls of her social group. Psychologically, her self-image deteriorated when she was no longer needed by her children, and her husband was no help because he had always been independent. Treatment for her involved altering her environment to help make her feel needed. In this case, the goal was accomplished when she became an alcoholism counselor. If this problem had not been solved, her treatment would have been unsuccessful.

This example indicates that there are two distinct types of alcoholics. For simplicity's sake, they will be referred to as Type A and Type B. The Type A

Figure 5-4 Effect of AA on Alcoholism Risk Factors for Individual B

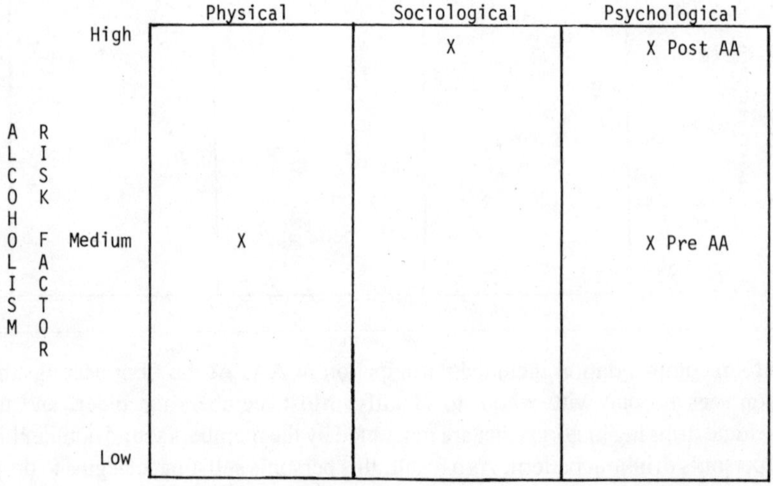

		Physical	Sociological	Psychological
	High		X	X Post AA
A R L I C S O K H O F L A I C S T M O R	Medium	X		X Pre AA
	Low			

Figure 5-5 Alcoholism Risk Factors for Individual C

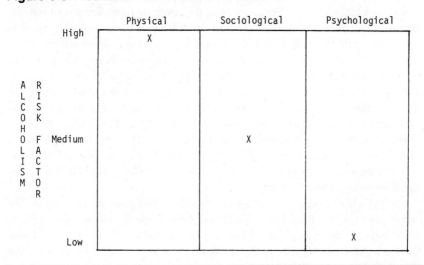

Figure 5-6 Alcoholism Risk Factors for Individual C after Children Left Home

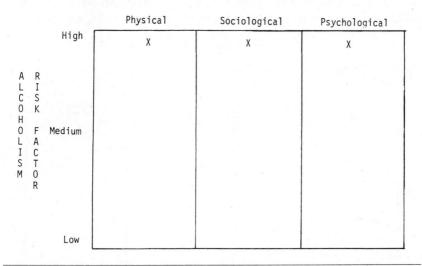

alcoholic never had a positive self-image due to a family background that restricted this person's psychological development. Such a person may sometimes say "I was alcoholic from my first drink." The profile of a Type A alcoholic is shown in Figure 5-7.

Adolescents often fall into this category. They never develop a positive self-image, and alcohol helps them cope with the resulting pain. Treatment initially focuses on building their self-image from scratch and is often more difficult than working with the Type B alcoholic, who at one time had a positive self-image. In order to determine why the Type A alcoholic's self-image is so poor, it is often useful to examine the role this person played in his or her family of origin. Sometimes, if clients understand how they were controlled by a situation, they can break the hold of the past. A person may say, ''I am no longer going to let my overdemanding mother or overprotective father make me feel bad about myself.'' This is a significant beginning for successful treatment. However, if the client is an adolescent and must return to the family, it is imperative that the entire family receive treatment. In fact, there are very few cases in which family therapy is not called for with alcoholic clients.

The Type B alcoholics, at one time in their lives, had positive self-images. The role of the treatment person is to reestablish these alcoholics' sense of worth. The following is a case example of a Type B alcoholic. Originally from a small town, this man played football in high school and was popular with his peers. Even though there was drinking in his high school, he did not partake because the coach said anyone caught drinking would be kicked off the team. In college, he also had a positive self-image because of his achievements in sports and he was at low risk for alcoholism in all areas. When he left college, he joined the Air Force and went to pilot training. He began to drink but with no significant problems. During his

Figure 5-7 Profile of a Type A Alcoholic

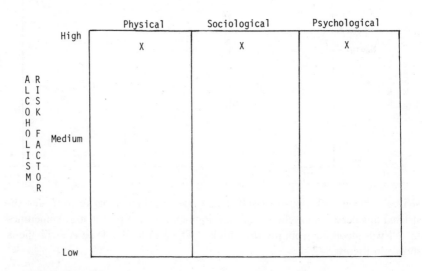

ten-year career in the Air Force, he became a major, a fighter pilot, a husband, and the father of two children. All experiences kept his self-image high, although he did eventually drink regularly, as is the custom among many military personnel. He subsequently left the Air Force, hoping for a job that would provide more time with his family. The job market was not what he expected, and the only position he could obtain was as a traveling salesman. He spent four nights each week on the road, and he made less money than he had as a pilot. After six months or so, he began a pattern of sitting in his motel room each night watching television, in addition to visiting the bar for a few drinks. His sales were not good, and he started drinking more to cope with discouragement. This routine caused him to get a later start in the morning and sell less. Soon he quit earlier each day and drank more. This evolving pattern, as well as family problems, caused him to go from feeling generally good about himself to feelings of depression and despair. He felt guilty about his drinking, yet it continued unabated. For this person, treatment should include a reevaluation of his employment and therapy for his family problems. Abstinence from alcohol (at least for a period of time, maybe for life) should be suggested. In this case, the job change put this person in a high-risk category sociologically and psychologically, and this factor should be taken into consideration in his treatment.

Although there are thousands of reasons people become alcoholic, they all fit into the three areas covered in the etiology chapters. First, a person's body may handle alcohol so that it becomes easy to become addicted. This information should be used in prevention work to identify high risk individuals in this area. After that has been done, the prevention task involves keeping these and other people at low risk levels in the other two areas. The role that society plays in the etiology of alcoholism can no longer be ignored. No major public health problem has ever been prevented by treating only the individual who has contracted it. Schools, public policies, and, most importantly, individual families all play a part in both the sociological and psychological risk development for the individual. In the family, the individual develops values condoning alcohol abuse and fails to learn that there is an acceptable and an unacceptable way to use alcohol. Most importantly, the family teaches the individual to feel good or bad about himself or herself.

If this model of etiology is correct, the key to both prevention and treatment is understanding the family. The family is the natural place for parents to gain feelings of self-worth by helping the system grow and develop and move in a positive direction. If the parents are doing this, the children develop positive feelings of self-worth as well. They learn to help each other and to exist in harmony with their environment. Many alcoholics can regain a sense of positive self-worth and a positive attitude from AA, but AA does not and should not replace the family as the primary source for the fulfillment of the basic needs of being loved and needed. If the AA member is meeting those needs both in the family and in AA, fine. But if only AA meets those needs something is wrong; the family is not functioning effectively.

The remainder of this book will address the methods, problems, and advantages of treating and preventing alcoholism through a family approach. The key to alcoholism treatment is understanding and working with the family.

REFERENCE

Davis, D., Berenson, D., Steinglass, P., & Davis, S. Adaptive consequences of drinking. *Psychiatry*, 1974, *37*, 209-215.

Part III

Treatment

Part II covered theories of etiology of alcoholism. Although many factors contribute to the development of abusive drinking, there is no single cause for alcoholism. Family system theorists focus on "what happened, how it happened, and when and where it happened" during the treatment process, without concern for why it happened (Bowen, 1978, p. 261). Every member of the family plays a part in its dysfunction.

Part III will focus on treatment of the alcoholic family. It will present family therapy techniques that may be unfamiliar to the alcohol counselor and will include techniques for family therapists who are inexperienced in working with alcoholic families. Many alcoholic families receive no treatment, and family treatment personnel tend not to deal with alcohol problems. In the United States, nine million adults and their families are affected by alcoholism, and numerous other families have at least some alcohol-related problems. Alcohol has become the drug of choice for teenagers, making it difficult for family therapists to ignore this maladaptive side of family functioning.

Although physiological, psychological, and social factors lead to the development of self-destructive drinking patterns, they should not be viewed by the family therapist as causal. Berenson (1976) believes that looking for the ultimate cause for alcoholism makes the therapist incapable of effectively treating alcohol problems. He states that, "At the same time, he/she must be willing to allow clients to accept cause-and-effect thinking, such as the disease model of alcoholism, if that will assist them in helping to resolve their drinking problem. The therapist must therefore not commit himself to any causative notion of alcoholism but act as if he/she had one" (Berenson, 1976, p. 285).

The focus of treatment, therefore, should be on the aspect of the system that perpetuates the drinking behavior. This factor is unique in each family and should be evaluated without any preconceived notion about typical behavior patterns.

Bailey (1963) estimated that 15-20% of the cases seen at family service agencies are alcohol related, and if therapists were motivated to look further for symptoms of alcohol abuse, the figures could be greater. Steinglass (1976) says that there are several reasons counselors avoid alcohol-related issues in therapy: (1) they are concerned about their own drinking behavior and are reluctant to diagnose others; (2) they are used to dealing with symptoms in children and not in the parental subsystems; and (3) they are afraid of confronting and experiencing intoxicated behavior. Berenson (1976) also states that a lack of knowledge of alcoholism causes avoidance of therapy with alcoholic families. This avoidance is further perpetuated by the doctrine that only those who have experienced alcoholism can understand it or help others.

Alcohol counselors avoid family therapy for several reasons as well: (1) they may not have training in family therapy; (2) they may believe that it is opposed to Alcoholics Anonymous; (3) they may see it as incompatible with the disease concept of alcoholism; (4) they may be unsupported in their efforts to use family therapy by their employers; and (5) due to the large amount of inpatient treatment of alcoholism, the family may be unavailable or unwilling to participate. The family may scapegoat the alcoholic to wash their hands of the problem.

Part III should provide solutions to some of these dilemmas and encourage both family therapists and alcohol counselors to consider a family approach to the treatment of alcoholism and problem drinking.

REFERENCES

Bailey, M.B. The family agency's role in treating the wife of an alcoholic, *Social Casework,* 1963, *44,* 273-279.

Berenson, D.   Alcohol and the family system   in P. Guerin (Ed.) *Family Therapy: Theory and Practice.* New York: Gardner Press, 1976.

Bowen, M. *Family therapy in clinical practice.* New York: Jason Aronson, 1978.

Steinglass, P. Experimenting with family treatment approaches to alcoholism 1950-1975, a review. *Family Process, 15,* 1976, 97-123.

Chapter 6

The Diagnosis of the Alcoholic Family

This chapter will cover three different processes involved in family evaluation: (1) observations by the therapist; (2) reports from the family; and (3) assessment of the family structure by the therapist. The diagnosis should determine if a family is a candidate for therapy and should have as its outcome a treatment plan that involves every family member. This plan should include goals for treatment and an evaluation of the potential for change within family structures. Diagnoses are not conducted to label individual pathology.

Clarken, Frances, and Moodie (1979), in reviewing family therapy literature, have listed instances when family evaluation is essential. First of all, family evaluation may be needed to understand such situations as the following: (1) the identified patient is a child or adolescent; (2) the problem is sexual difficulty; (3) the family or marital problem is serious enough to jeopardize relationships, job stability, health, or parenting ability; (4) the family is experiencing a developmental or accidental crisis; or (5) the family defines the problem as a family problem. Second, whenever psychiatric hospitalization is considered, family evaluation is essential in order to gain historical information and discover the influences of the family on the illness, as well as to develop family involvement in treatment. Third, family diagnosis is important when family treatment is found necessary due to such factors as obvious family interactions around the problem, failure of other therapies, the number of family members affected by the problem (a parent and child in the same family may both be alcoholic), and when secondary gains of symptoms are linked to family pathology.

On the other hand, family evaluation should not be done when a family member insists on a private session in order not to reveal a valid family secret that would jeopardize another family member (i.e., an adolescent who has just left home). But even when the family is divorcing without hope of reconciliation, family evaluation can be done with the custodial parent and children. However, when repetitive intrapsychic conflicts occur outside of the family structure, individual treatment may be more beneficial. Family treatment is also contraindicated when a client has a history of sabotaging treatment alliances or when a patient has extreme schizoid or paranoid pathology.

The therapist may come in contact with alcoholic families that require family evaluation in a number of ways.

First, the symptom bearer may be a child in a family in which one or both parents have drinking problems. However, these problems may be hidden from the therapist, and the child may experience the pain of the family dysfunction. Although these alcoholic families appear to be much like other dysfunctional families, certain clues may expose a hidden drinking problem. Therapists should inquire about drinking patterns and complete a drinking history of the spouses if the following conditions exist: (1) a pattern of alcoholism is evident in either family of origin; (2) the children are protecting their parents; (3) there is a role reversal with a child appearing in a parental role; (4) denial or isolation is a family pattern; (5) there is a report of physical abuse or incest; (6) there is obvious scapegoating of the child; or (7) parents have an irrational fear of teenage alcohol and drug abuse. It is possible that the presenting problem in the child is alcohol and/or drug abuse. Although these symptoms may not be caused by alcoholism in the family, they can alert therapists to the possibility that abusive drinking may have caused symptoms in the child.

Some families view drinking behavior as incidental to other family problems. Berenson (1976) believes these families occasionally have a history of alcoholism that is characterized by slight or infrequent behavior changes when drinking. The relationship between the spouses is symmetrical on the surface, with a feeling of "we-ness." Also, in this type of family the amounts and patterns of drinking are variable; alcohol problems tend to be secondary and will recede if other problems are resolved.

The third type of family seeks therapy with alcohol as the major presenting problem. This family is organized around alcohol and its meaning in the family; the drinking behavior has become part of the family structure. The drinker may or may not be physically addicted. Berenson (1976) says the members of these families agree that alcohol is a problem, and there may be intense conflict about it. In addition, alcohol consumption in these families increases the severity of other problems. Behavior changes during intoxication are generally intense and common, and the relationship between the spouses fluctuates and is immersed in overt conflict. This type of family is not always distinguishable from the second type by the amount of drinking, but by the behavior change in the drinker, the quality of the spouses' relationship, and the longer history and duration of the problem.

The fourth way an alcoholic family appears for therapy is during a period of aftercare. One or both spouses in this category may have completed inpatient or outpatient (individual) alcoholism treatment, and the family homeostasis may be out of balance. The marital relationship could be threatened, or a new symptom bearer could emerge. Family therapy may be viewed here as a prevention of further difficulties or as a second stage of treatment. Families may resist treatment if they feel the alcoholic member has a special relationship with the therapist, and alcoholics may resist having their families scapegoat them in front of their therapists. If family therapy will be conducted by a therapist other than the alcoholism treatment person, cotherapy may be indicated (especially if the alcohol treatment is continuing simultaneously). This is also a good way to involve alcoholism counselors in family therapy and educate family therapists about alcohol problems.

It is important to remember that families often change categories or fall somewhere in between these categories. A family whose presenting problem is incest may see a serious alcohol problem as secondary.

Families in category three and possibly category one, in which drinking continues to be a major issue, must be treated in a different manner than families in the other categories. The drinking behavior becomes the primary issue. The cooling off of emotional tensions and separation of the enmeshed spouses must precede other family work. All families in conflict tend to search for blame, either within or outside the family. In general, the family evaluation process is entered with one of four orientations: (1) there is nothing wrong with any of us, but nothing is right in the family; (2) there is a problem with someone in the family; (3) there is a problem with everyone, according to everyone else; and (4) nothing is wrong with the family or any member, but someone outside of the family believes there is and sent us here. This general framework may color family responses to the evaluation and diagnosis process. Motivation and receptivity to family therapy can be reviewed with reference to the events that lead up to the initial contact with the therapist. In other words, was the family coerced into therapy? Were they responding to symptoms in a child? Was there a family developmental crisis, such as a death, a birth, a midlife crisis, a divorce, or a change in a member of the family from drinking behavior to sobriety?

In beginning a family evaluation, care should be taken to not develop a therapeutic alliance with the family representative who calls for the appointment. Demographic information and a brief statement of the problem are all that is necessary. This information should later be shared with the rest of the family so that special secrets do not exist between the therapist and one family member.

Also, the family should be involved in treatment as soon as possible and before the alcoholic is further scapegoated and labeled as the problem. Therapists disagree as to the feasibility of working with a drinking alcoholic or problem drinker. Berenson and Steinglass often find the key to understanding consequences and behavior patterns built around drinking by observing drunken behavior. "Drunken behavior, therefore, can be seen as a clue that will help to resolve the problem, rather than being a problem that must be rigorously suppressed" (Berenson, 1976, p. 288). Berenson also states that in the family where alcohol is a chronic problem, the drinking behavior must stop before family change can occur. However, in other families where drinking is less chronic, family therapy techniques may change the system enough to reduce or eliminate excessive drinking. Other therapists insist on sobriety or at least an absence of drinking prior to the family sessions. Kaufman (1979) states that "most therapeutic changes in dysfunctional families cannot be initiated until the regular use of chemicals is interrupted" (p. 255). However, if individual work has occurred with the alcoholic it may increase his or her drive for recovery but increase resistance to treatment in the spouse. The issue of sobriety appears to be a matter of therapist preference and depends on the pattern of drinking behavior in the family. However, if the therapist takes a rigid stand on sobriety for all families, some who could have been helped may be lost.

The evaluation of the family may be limited in time, with a recommendation for family therapy accompanied by a treatment plan. On the other hand, evaluation may be part of the ongoing process of therapy and may represent a continuously changing view of the family as information and observations lead to a more complex diagnosis than is possible in an initial assessment. Therapists not only gather information for an evaluation, but also help the family experience abusive drinking behavior as a family problem.

OBSERVATIONS OF BEHAVIORS

Observations of behaviors are done in the here and now. Family therapists must have all of their senses tuned to the behaviors and actions of the families they are evaluating. There are verbal and nonverbal clues in family functioning patterns in every interaction. From the onset of contact with the family, therapists begin to formulate impressions. If it is possible to see the family enter the clinic, the therapist should note such behaviors as who is walking next to whom, who announces to the receptionist the arrival of the family, where they sit in the waiting room, how the children are controlled, and who fills out application forms.

When the family enters the therapy room, particular attention should be paid to the way the seating arrangement problem is solved. It is useful to have a sofa or combination of chairs that provide for close seating of the marital couple so that they may choose to sit together or obviously sit far apart. If the spouses sit together, note whether one spouse begins to lean away from the other, pulling the other spouse with him or her. This clue is often useful in determining which spouse is the least satisfied with the marital relationship. When extra chairs are provided, more combinations are possible, and distancing can be observed more accurately. If the office is small and seating is limited, some of the observations will be contaminated by the limitations of the environment. Sometimes children tend to move during the interview toward a parent or sibling. They may insist on being between the spouses or jump in the mother's lap if the anxiety level rises.

Communications

As soon as a family member begins to speak, the therapist is experiencing the content of the message and the process of the communication. The way the family communicates is important for evaluating alliances, boundaries, and family roles. For the therapist, observing the process may be more valuable than the content. Who does the most talking? Who speaks for whom? Does a child defocus the conversation if anxiety is high? How do the parents communicate? Does nonverbal behavior contradict the verbal message? Are the children in any double binds? Is anyone reading someone else's mind? Do the family members take turns, interrupt, or all talk at the same time? Family communication patterns are very important in therapy and often reflect the very structure of the family, as well as the areas of difficulty and the resources of the family.

Family Roles

In observing communication patterns, family role behaviors begin to emerge. "One of the most common ways for a family to reduce stress is to assign specific roles to individual members to have them acted out in the conflict situation" (Walsh, 1980, p. 13). Chapter 3 defines Satir's (Bandler, Grinder, & Satir, 1976) four basic role models: placating, blaming, irrelevant, and superresponsible. Similarly, Wegscheider (1979) has developed role categories for the alcoholic family that he calls survival roles. These are emotional masks that are worn by family members to cover their true feelings in an effort to maintain a family's balance. As a crisis develops in the family system or anxiety about drinking becomes high, each member clings to his or her respective role tightly to brave the storm.

Wegscheider describes the person in the family who is projecting low self-worth and is unable to deal with crises (because of defensive behavior) as the victim. Victims feel shame, inadequacy, guilt, pain, loneliness, and fear, but they wear masks of anger, aggression, denial, perfectionism, charm, blame, and manipulation that are similar to Satir's blaming role. "The victim believes that if his or her pain were allowed to emerge full force, the balance of the family system would be destroyed catastrophically" (Wegscheider, 1979, p. 33). "In the family with alcoholism, family members soon learn they cannot expect the usual behavior from the alcoholic person in terms of family roles. To compensate, non-alcoholic members shift their role performance in an effort to keep the family functioning" (Hanson & Estes, 1977, p. 71).

The person who is the closest to the victim cannot escape this process. Wegscheider calls this role the protector. The protector is angry, but, like other roles, does not show this openly. To keep stability, the protector manipulates the victim and derives a sense of importance by keeping the victim in need of protection. It is difficult for the protector to change this behavior or see it as dysfunctional. The protector sees the demand of this role to be superresponsible. He or she is passive and powerless and deserves rewards such as excessive eating or control of family functioning and money. If these roles exist in the parental subsystem, this didactic relationship will seek a third side to the hypothetical triangle, possibly one of the children. This child will work to give dignity and meaning to the family by achieving and putting the needs of others above his or her own. Wegscheider labels this role the "caretaker." It has also been called the "family hero," and the "fixer" by other authors. A special achiever mask is worn by this person, but he or she never reaches personal success. These people have a special role, yet they never feel important or never feel the closeness they wish from their families. The children often continue this pattern throughout their lives, sometimes entering the helping professions in order to perpetuate this role.

The other children also develop roles to save the family. The "scapegoat" volunteers to be "the problem" and may get the family into therapy. A child may also pull out of the family and allow family members not to worry about him or her. The youngest child often plays the "irrelevant" role and defocuses by becoming a comic. "For the sake of balance in the family, the system needs to have someone fulfill each role. So in small families one person may have to play several roles alternately" (Wegscheider, 1979, p. 34). These roles are not the focus of therapy, but they provide a perspective for viewing the family interaction that causes maladaptive behavior in every member.

Family Sculpting

As the family role pattern begins to emerge, triangles, alliances, and emotional relationships begin to appear. The technique of family sculpting is a way of observing these patterns more clearly and is useful with families who are skilled in verbal manipulation and who resist the traditional interview process. Family sculpting was developed by Papp (Papp, Silverstein, & Center, 1973) to demonstrate to families the systems concept and the role of each member in the evolution, maintenance, and resolution of family problems. It is a useful technique to help the family experience the "familiness" of the problem.

To do this, one of the family members assists the therapist(s) in arranging and shifting family members in a tableau of emotional relationships. The therapist may recognize a family member who makes a good family sculptor. "Adolescents usually make excellent sculptors because of their insight into family truths, and their natural relish in manipulating their elders. Latency children are also good natural sculptors, though what they produce may be somewhat idealized and stereotyped" (Simon, 1972, p. 51). When the sculpture is complete, according to one member, all others are asked to report their perspective and their feelings at being placed in their position. Marital difficulties often are portrayed with children being placed between the parents. Often the children are attached to mother, while the father is alone in a corner of the room. People can be placed at the top of chairs to indicate an authoritarian position or power. They may be under tables to represent a protected position or unawareness. Members may face toward the family or look away. When a sculpture has been achieved that everyone agrees represents the family's current position, goal setting can begin. The next step is approached by asking each person where he or she would like to be and asking him or her to experience that position. The emphasis of sculpting is to gather information about individual family perceptions, to activate silent members, and to increase emotional intensity. This often allows the family to experience their reactions to the moment. Care should be taken not to overinterpret the sculpture or believe it is a true picture of the family. ''Some sculptors represent their ideal family, others are the fulfilling of a special wish; others are a deception, with some family-political purpose.'' (Simon, 1972, p. 55)

Family Puppet Interview

A technique that uses the drama of family sculpting but further removes the family from the direct experience of their problems is the family puppet interview. Families who are unskilled in putting thoughts and feelings into words or who manipulate others with intellectualization can use the puppet drama to cut through defenses and examine family dynamics in a nonthreatening way. This technique is most useful for families with children aged five to twelve who may find it difficult to talk to the therapist directly about family problems. The therapist who uses this technique can observe decision making, family patterns, and symbolic communications that help members experience the familiness of the problem.

To begin the interview, the therapist explains the process and rationale for using puppets as a family activity and as an aid to the children. Twenty or more puppets are made available with a stage to further shelter an anxious or resistive family. The puppets are an assortment of real life people of all ages, including role characters, policemen and doctors, or fantasy figures like princesses, kings, queens, fairies, or witches and devils. Animals can take on both tame (dogs and cats) and ferocious (lions and alligators) characteristics that are also effective. Each family member is asked to select one puppet and introduce it, making a statement about what it represents. The therapist at this point should observe which puppets are selected and rejected, as well as who makes the decisions and for whom. Family members may select a puppet to represent themselves and how they wish to be or fear to be, for example, or to represent someone else.

The family is then asked to make up an original story to act out with their puppets. This process should be observed, and the therapist should not take part at this stage. Roles, alliances, and subgroups should be observed. Who takes the roles of organizer, dominator, disciplinarian, scapegoat, victim, or pacifier?

The therapist can set up the drama by announcing the play and calling for the action to start. If the family begins to narrate the story, the therapist can ask to be shown by the puppets how that would look. If the family becomes stuck without a solution, as families in real life do, the therapist can help them explore alternatives.

At the conclusion of the play, the therapist can make use of the established puppet roles by engaging in dialogue with the puppets and encouraging them to speak to one another. Themes and conflicts can be further explored and clarified. Often the issue that brought the family into therapy will be played out.

At the end of the drama, a discussion is held to connect the experience with real life happenings. Family members are asked to think of a title for the play and talk about the moral of the story or the lesson learned. Each member is asked to pick the character he or she would most like to be and least like to be. Finally, the family members are asked if this play was in any way like their own family or experiences they have had. They are encouraged to talk further after the session.

The family puppet interview provides many opportunities to observe the visible as well as the covert way that family members communicate with each other. "The puppet choices, the conflicts expressed in the fantasy, the post-play discussion when members are invited to associate the story with real life, and the inquiry about the relationship of the story to the family's functioning all give important clues about the family and the available ego strength for confronting problems" (Irwin & Malloy, 1975, p. 190).

Structured Task Performance

Another technique that elicits observable diagnostic information and does not rely totally on verbal reports involves the assignment of tasks for the family to complete during the assessment period. Minuchin, Montalbo, Guerney, Rosman, and Schumer (1967) devised a number of tasks that family members were asked to carry out while the therapist observed family interaction patterns. For example, families were asked to plan a menu using their favorite foods or decide how they would spend 10 dollars.

Watzlawick (1966) developed a structured family interview that was based on the assumption that human behavior is patterned. In the interview, solutions to tasks are requested by the therapist, and observations are made to discover patterns of behavior in the family.

Watzlawick begins the interview by asking each member individually what he or she sees as the family's problems. These responses remain confidential. This process defocuses the attention from the identified patient and allows each member to feel his or her input is valued. The family members are then assembled in one room and are told that there are discrepancies in their perceptions of problems and that they should discuss these and come to consensus on their main problem. This procedure also allows early observation of family communication patterns. The second assignment is for the family to plan something they could do together within a five-minute time limit. The importance of this assignment is not what the family plans but whether or not they can make a decision in the time allotted and how it was done.

The third task focuses on the parents and asks them to explain how the couple met and got together. Patterns of marital interaction, methods for handling discrepancies, and current patterns of interaction become apparent.

The fourth item begins with the parents discussing the meaning of the proverb, "A rolling stone gathers no moss." After five minutes the children are returned to the room, and the parents teach the children the meaning of the proverb. Watzlawick has listed 16 possible interpretation patterns and 10 typical responses to this proverb. Marital communication patterns can be observed, as well as teaching patterns. If disagreement occurs in the parental subgroup, children are often pulled into the argument, which points out coalitions and decision making by the children.

The fifth task is entitled "Blame." The seating arrangement for this task is with the father to the left of the therapist, followed by the mother, and oldest to youngest child. Each person is asked to write on a card the main fault of the person on their left, excluding the therapist. No identifying marks or names are included. The therapist collects the cards and adds two cards to the pile that say "too weak" and "too good" to stimulate controversy. The therapist then reads each card asking the family to make a forced choice as to whom each statement applies. "Each family member is thus forced to blame somebody, and by so doing implies automatically that in his opinion this criticism was levelled by the person sitting on the right of the victim" (Watzlawick, 1966, p. 263). This task provides data on scapegoating, self-blame, and favoritism.

This interview can be done in one hour. It gives the therapist a wealth of information about the process of family interaction and allows the family to experience the family philosophy.

Family Art Evaluation

The family art evaluation was developed by Kwiatkowska (1967) at the National Institute of Mental Health. The use of art media in the family interview allows for an alternate mode of expression for families who are defensive, manipulative with words, or are unskilled in verbal expression. Alcoholic families are often described with these adjectives. The initial model of the family art interview takes two to three hours and includes six drawings. This process has been adapted, shortened, or modified by many other family and art therapists

(Bing, 1970; Landgarten, 1981; Rubin & Magnussen, 1974; Sherr & Hicks, 1973). In art evaluation, the family is assembled in a room with easels set in a semicircle. Since many people become anxious when asked to create artwork, it is necessary for the therapist to reduce initial resistance by assuring the family that the quality of the artwork is not the focus and that only the process of family interactions will be important.

Initially, the family is asked to make a free picture—a drawing of anything they wish. Kwiatkowska found that family members introduce themselves in this drawing or illustrate the family problem. Second, the family members are asked to draw a picture of the family. These portraits may show isolation of family members or a close togetherness. The third drawing is an abstract composition of the family. This is the most difficult assignment, and it stirs discussion among family members about symbols used for each member. In the fourth task, family members make scribbles on paper with their eyes closed. They must then find something in the scribble that will help them make a composition by ignoring or adding lines. The next assignment is a joint family scribble. Each person again makes a scribble, and the family decides which one they will use to complete as a picture. In this effort, the entire family works on one composition. The final work is, again, a free drawing that may express feelings about the process of the art evaluation. At the completion of each piece of artwork, the family members are asked to give their pictures a title and to then sign and date them.

It is extremely helpful to have a cotherapist or observer (Kwiatkowska's term) to observe the wealth of verbal and nonverbal behavior elicited by this process. Similar observations can be made in the art evaluation as in any task assignment, but in addition, symbolic art productions confront the family with expressions that cannot be denied.

Rubin and Magnussen (1974) adopted four of these techniques and established a two-hour art evaluation session at the Pittsburgh Child Guidance Center. Families were first asked to make individual pictures from a scribble and title them. Next they were asked to make family portraits and view and discuss these simultaneously. Finally they were to create a joint family mural and free drawings if time allowed. Rubin and Magnussen found, "family members could communicate maximal information about individual and family characteristics with minimal stress" (p. 190). Observations of behavior that correlated with the content of the drawings strengthened diagnostic impressions.

Landgarten (1981) adapted similar techniques to develop her initial family interview. She asks each member to draw his or her initials on the page and then make a composition or design and give it a title. This is similar to the scribble technique, but Landgarten feels it is less threatening to deal with a familiar symbol. The second assignment calls for the family to divide up into two teams to make a nonverbal, mutual drawing. Each person selects a different color so that each contribution can later be evaluated. No talking is allowed, and the family must decide what they will draw and how it will get done without words. The third task is a verbal family task-oriented art product. Each member is given a different color of plasticene clay or construction paper and must decide on an artistic product to create. Therapists can observe decision making processes, such as who the leader is, how the artwork gets started, who initiates communication, who is ignored, and how much discussion occurs. In addition, it can be determined if the family members work in teams, individually, or at the same time. How is the space of the room used? Who chooses the title? Who writes it down? When the family members are finished they are asked to state how their perceptions of the experience can be matched with the actual happenings.

Bing (1970) uses an art evaluation technique in part of a structural family interview. She uses Watzlawick's tasks and adds a conjoint family drawing at the end of the session when the family feels less threatened by an art assignment.

Each family member is asked to choose a colored marker that he or she will use throughout the drawing to color code exactly what each person has drawn. The instructions are as follows:

> I'd like for you as a family to draw a picture as you see yourselves now as a family. You can draw the picture any way you want to, but I'd like to encourage you to be as creative and original as you can in representing yourselves as a unique family. You can draw the persons any size and place them in any position on the paper. They may be drawn touching each other, or separately. You can draw yourselves or each other, whichever way you think best describes your family. (Bing, 1970, p. 176. Reprinted by permission.)

Bing observes specific processes to allow comparison to other families: (1) the organizing role; (2) the sequence of who draws first, second, and so on; (3) the relative size of the person represented, which depends in part on who drew whom, and in what order; (4) choice of which family member was drawn by whom; (5) isolation of persons; and (6) specific content and unusual themes. Bing found that families in which nearly all family members draw themselves rather than someone else are less cohesive than families where people draw mostly each other.

A conjoint family drawing was used in the case of Sally (case history in Chapter 3). When the task of a family portrait was presented to this family, they became quite anxious and resorted to the stress coping roles. To ease the anxiety, Sally, the identified patient, jumped up and began drawing the mother safe in her kitchen. She then drew the withdrawn father under the car, working in the garage. After some time, the mother drew Sally in the picture, sitting at her desk in school. The mother stated that she wished Sally could go to school and be happy. This drew attention to the presenting problem and the notion of the "sick" child. The teenage girl drew herself going to the show alone, without her mother worrying—a wish that put the focus back on the mother. Finally, the middle boy got up and drew the whole family together watching television, the ultimate wish of family unity. Sally had continued to draw members of the family all over the page, causing confusion, with each member of the family represented more than once. The father never drew anything or gave any input into the process (see Figure 6-1).

In alcoholic families it is interesting to have each member draw his or her perception of the family without looking at the others. Often common themes will occur when the family views the drawings together.

In another case, an art evaluation was done on a family who came to a child guidance center to work on issues of parenting and adding a new family member. Jean, age 34, had been a practicing alcoholic and drug addict for 20 years before going through inpatient alcohol treatment. When her first child was born, she was a member of a Hell's Angels group and did not wish to parent her daughter, Joan. Joan was given to the paternal grandparents to raise, and Jean was denied permission to see her. When Jean's son was born, she kept him with her. Jean divorced her alcoholic husband, remarried, and had a third child, a son. Some years later she divorced her second husband.

Figure 6-1 Conjoint Family Portrait

At the time of the evaluation, Jean was living with her fiancè. Joan, age 16, had left her grandparents and came to live with her mother for the first time in her life. When the family was asked to draw family portraits, an unmistakable theme of isolation became apparent. The mother's (Jean) family drawing (Figure 6-2) used compartments to divide the family. She was at the Holiday Inn working, while Joan was shown in a room of the house watching television. A messy kitchen and livingroom separated her from her mother. This untidy house was the source of arguments between the mother and daughter. The two boys were pictured playing ball, but they had a tree between them. Mother's fiancè was drawn in another square representing his job, which took him out of town during the week. Joan's picture (Figure 6-3) showed all of the family in a neat row divided by a line separating her and her boyfriend from the rest. She saw herself as the only one who was isolated. The teenage boy (Bob) (Figure 6-4) drew lines between each member of the family except between himself and his brother. However, he placed his brother's friend between them. The youngest boy (Tim) (Figure 6-5) drew family members as being busy doing something on their own. The teenagers were involved with their respective boyfriends and girlfriends; the mother was leaving; and the mother's fiancè was taking his parrot inside the house, while the boy's

Figure 6-2 Jean's Family Drawing

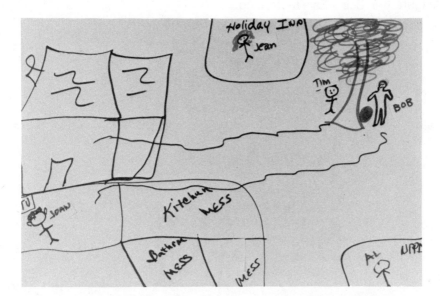

Figure 6-3 Joan's Family Drawing

Figure 6-4 Bob's Family Drawing

Figure 6-5 Tim's Family Drawing

friend was playing with someone else. There was little emotional connectedness in this family.

Family art evaluation offers direct observations of family behavior, as well as graphic creations full of visual symbols that can be useful in family therapy. It further provides a record of the evaluation process that can be referred to later or can be compared with similar compositions at the completion of therapy. The therapist should use caution in interpreting the artwork and should place more value on the process of its production and the interaction patterns of the family than the pictorial content.

The purpose of directly observing family behavior is to gain information about family patterns that may be largely outside of the family's awareness and thus could not be obtained by questioning. In forcing situations where the family must solve problems and interact with each other, behavior patterns, structure, boundaries, and alliances can be noted. The therapist's observations are not shared with the family at the time of the evaluation. Rather, they are stored with the therapist for future reference and matched with other information to formulate treatment plans. The family could not tolerate dealing with other than the presenting problem at that time. Although they are aware of some of the dynamics, they may not wish to have these pointed out.

FAMILY REPORTS

The two categories of direct observations and family reports are not mutually exclusive. Whenever a family is relating an historical report, there is observable behavior and emotion, and whenever a task is being observed, there is a content element present that gives historical information about the family.

Family reports give information of then-and-there behaviors that may provide information about family interaction outside of the therapy setting. Reports can come from the family or from outside sources, such as in-laws, neighbors, teachers, ministers, or previous mental health records. If the family was referred for therapy by someone in the community, this person's report can be valuable. Often families with drinking problems are connected to various public and private agencies, such as alcohol treatment centers, Alcoholics Anonymous, Al-Anon, Alateen, welfare agencies, child protective services, juvenile court, public schools, day care centers, child guidance centers, or public health nurses and physicians. These people play a large part in the social existence of the family and should not be overlooked by the therapist due to the impact they may exert on the family and the therapy. If a release of information can be obtained from the family, it is helpful to consult with other community members who are involved, so that a uniform approach can be developed. Families are also adept at using gossip to get two service providers fighting with each other over treatment planning while they conveniently slide out of therapy or out of the focus. If many agencies are involved with a family, it is helpful to have periodic conferences, which include the family, to set goals and communicate clearly and directly.

Personal Reports

In initial interview processes, it is helpful to get personal reports from all family members about their current family situation and their past history. Personal reports include information such as job histories, educational histories of both parents, drinking histories of the spouses and families of origin, and educational histories of the children (including number of schools attended, academic abilities, behavior problems, and special skills and abilities).

Satir (1967) initiates her conjoint family therapy with a family life chronology. She begins by asking the family as a whole what their perceptions of the problem are. Then she asks the spouses how they met, when they decided to marry, and what attracted them to each other. She divides the spouses to look at their respective families of origin and asks each spouse how he or she viewed his or her parents, siblings, and family life. Following this, a comparison of the past histories of the spouses is made, including how they met. Then the spouses are asked about their expectations of marriage.

This structured interview gives comfort to the family who sees the therapist as being in charge. It gives the therapist information about the families of origin of both spouses and points out strengths of the marital relationship while also giving observations of current difficulties. Continuing in the chronology, she asks about the early married life of the spouses and connects it to past functioning in the families of origin. She explores the married couple's expectations of parenting and links this with the rearing styles of their parents. Turning to the children, she asks about his or her views of the parents. Satir finally addresses the family as a whole, stressing the need for clear communication and gives a note of hope for the family with closing remarks.

Family Genogram

Another form of taking a life chronology involves making a structural diagram of a family's three-generational relationship system called a *genogram*. It is generally accepted that alcoholism can be a three-generational problem. The genogram is a visual diagram of this process.

Guerin (1976) uses the following symbols to illustrate the relationship graph.

> Once the names and ages of each person, the dates of marriages, deaths, divorces and of births are filled in, other pertinent facts about the relationship process can be gathered, including the family's physical location, frequency and type of contact, emotional cutoffs, toxic issues, nodal events, and open/closed relationship index. (p. 452) (See Figures 6-6 and 6-7.)

It is useful to note the physical location of the families of origin to determine if either spouse is using physical distance to avoid emotional issues. Questioning can include the type and frequency of contact. This may demonstrate if the family is cohesive—remaining close to the original location of the family of origin—or explosive—with family members tending to move far away from one another. Information about the frequency of phone contacts is important, as well as insights into communications roles, such as the "family switchboard," who keeps everyone connected and informed. Places and times of family gatherings can point to ritualistic visitation patterns. Notations can be made about each member's personality, occupation, and quality of interpersonal relationships. Information can also be gathered to determine both the emotional pursuers and distancers. Family issues that cause conflict or disruption should be noted. Religion, educational level, an early death of a child or parent, serious physical illness, death of an only child, marriages due to pregnancy, and alcohol abuse can also be discovered. Dates of marriage, death, and divorce can be included, as well as ages of family

Figure 6-6 Genogram Symbols Used by Phillip Guerin

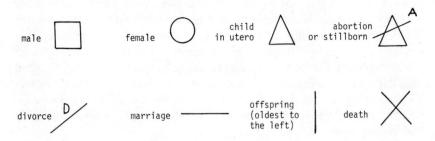

Source: Reprinted from *Family Therapy: Theory and Practice* edited by Phillip Guerin with permission of Gardner Press, © 1976.

Figure 6-7 Genogram Symbols Used by Murray Bowen

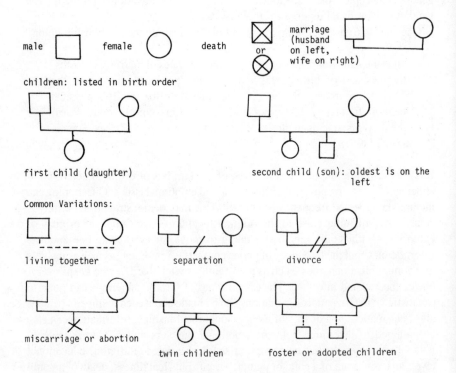

Source: Reprinted from *The Family Lifecycle: A Framework For Family Therapy* by Elizabeth Carter and Monica McGoldrick with permission of Murray Bowen, © 1980.

members shown inside of the symbols. Patterns of intergenerational alcoholism can be traced. Often alcoholism will skip a generation in the blood line but occur in a spouse of a child from an alcoholic family and then reoccur in their children. Figure 6-8 is a genogram of a family with alternating alcoholism and nondrinking patterns. The etiology section addresses the parenting style of the teetotaler, which produces children with alcohol problems. In this family, the nondrinkers appear moralistic, and the alcoholic parent produced nondrinking moralistic children whose offspring then became alcoholic.

The genogram can be useful in connecting current crises to unresolved issues in the families of origin. The genogram in Figure 6-9 shows a family who requested therapy after their daughter attempted suicide with an overdose of medication.

This history-taking session was uneventful until a comment was made by the mother, Sharon, that when she was 10 years old her mother took a job outside the home, and she had never forgiven her for that. It had taken her 23 years to get enough courage to tell her parents how much this hurt her. Sharon had felt that her mother saw money as more important than her, and Sharon vowed never to convey this to her children. Sharon and her daughter had repeated arguments over issues involving money. Everytime her daughter would ask for something special and Sharon would have to turn her down, Sharon felt in a bind. On one hand, she was not able to give her children all they wanted, and on the other hand, she was angry at her daughter for making her sound just like her mother who, as Sharon perceived her, was always preoccupied with money. As hard as Sharon tried not to choose money over her children, the limitation of money and her daughter's demands set up this situation. The daughter interpreted her mother's irritation as a rejection and felt unloved by her family. This issue of money handling was unresolved by the spouses, and although Sharon was uncomfortable handling the money, her husband was unable to accept this responsibility.

Genograms are useful for gaining a clear picture of the extended family and also may provide the family with insights into unconscious behavior patterns.

Family Photographs

An interesting variation of history taking is an analysis of selected pictures from the past. Family members are asked to select a set number of photographs they feel say something important. Each member has a turn telling why he or she chose the photographs, what meaning the photographs have for him or her, and his or her feelings about the pictures.

The therapist can observe many important behaviors, such as which pictures were shown first and last, who in the family was left out, how quickly or slowly they are presented, how much interest or anxiety is aroused, and how much joking and laughing accompanies the presentation. Pictures can be observed for closeness and distance of each family member to others and the general atmosphere of the

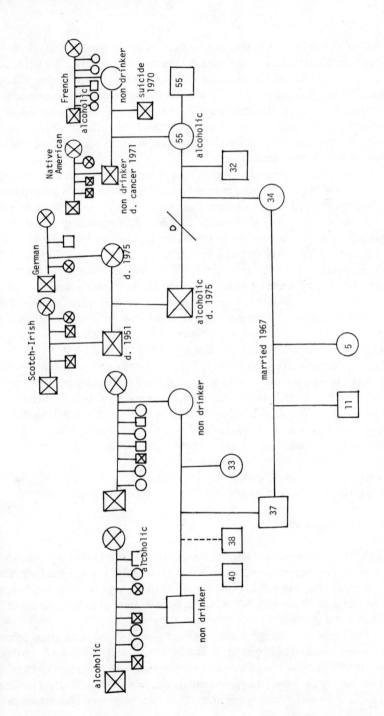

Figure 6-8 Genogram

Figure 6-9 Genogram

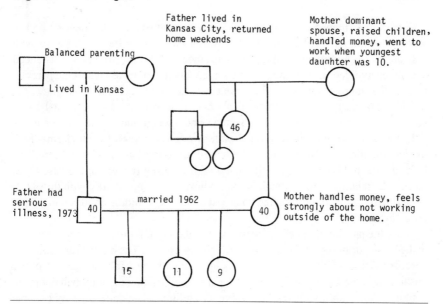

photographs. "Usually, alignments, splits, role behaviors, boundaries, communication processes, and family structures are thrown into sharp relief in this process" (Anderson & Malloy, 1976, p. 262).

The purpose of these reports is to gain additional information from outside the family and from the family itself that will support the observations of current behavior. Evaluations usually contain components of both processes. "The choice of a particular method for evaluating a family depends upon the ideology of the therapist and the state of the family when it enters therapy" (Guerin, 1976, p. 450). Therapists should choose techniques that are compatible with their personal styles. They should pick the method that would get the most information from the family while causing family members the least amount of stress. The therapist should be sensitive to the needs of the family and willing to listen to their pleas for help with a crisis. They may need a cooling off period before being given assignments that might seem unrelated to their immediate needs.

THERAPIST ASSESSMENT OF FAMILY STRUCTURE

At the completion of the evaluation process, the therapist will have impressions about the family structure, communication patterns, boundaries, alliances, triangles, subgroups, and intergenerational patterns. Role patterns will become apparent, and levels of involvement between family members can be assessed.

Family Relationships

A cognitive map can be formed to delineate the overinvolvement or under-involvement in each subgroup. Table 6-1 is a rating scale for relationships with indications for treatment planning. For instance, if marital partners are distanced and underinvolved, if one parent is in charge while the other abdicates the parental role, and if there is an overinvolvement between a mother and a daughter, the relationship chart would look like Table 6-1. Involvement is rated on a 1 to 10 scale, with 1 representing no involvement and 10 extreme overinvolvement.

In the alcoholic family, a typical pattern might consist of an underinvolved marital relationship (except around the issue of drinking), an unbalanced parenting load, an alcoholic spouse underinvolved with children (except in the case of an incestuous relationship), a nonalcoholic spouse in a strong alliance with the oldest child (the fixer), an overprotected youngest child, and a middle child isolated from all members.

Often the pattern of underinvolvement or isolation of family members occurs as in the family drawings in Figure 6-2 through Figure 6-5. The mother may abdicate her role as a parent because of her preoccupation with the drinking behavior of her husband and the daughter may become parentified (taking on adult behaviors) to help maintain stability and protect the other children. The daughter may become angry at her mother for not being more loving to her father, causing distance between mother and daughter. This daughter then becomes overly concerned with the father and may begin to believe that she can cure alcoholism with love. Eventually, she may seek an alcoholic to marry and cure. Drinking behavior itself sets up isolation in the alcoholic family. The father drinks away from home by himself or with his friends and returns home to nurse his hangover in private. The mother drinks at home but isolates herself to hide this fact. If both parents drink together, they shut out the children, and both become underinvolved. These children may become symptomatic to gain attention or decide that their needs are unimportant. The focus for these children becomes the problems of the parents and others outside of the family. If this rigid role behavior continues, these children

Table 6-1 Relationship Chart

Relationship	Score	Therapy Goal
Husband-Wife	2	increase involvement
Father-Mother	2	mutual parenting responsibility
Father-Son	4	slight increase
Father-Daughter	1	increase involvement
Mother-Daughter	9	decrease involvement
Mother-Son	2	increase involvement
Brother-Sister	2	increase sibling support

may marry alcoholics or go into helping professions to perpetuate this pattern. They have difficulty caring for themselves or achieving emotional closeness when they believe their needs are unimportant.

Families with longstanding chronic drinking problems may not show isolation in the marital couple. They are often violently overinvolved around the issues of drinking, and their personal identities may have meshed into a "we-ness" that Bowen (1978) refers to when people lack a sense of differentiation. If this intense emotional involvement can be cooled off, Berenson (1976) has found that isolation may then occur, and the second stage of therapy may involve reducing this isolation.

Mapping

Minuchin (1974) developed a process of making a therapeutic map of the family structure. The map is a working hypothesis of family interactions and leads to possible restructuring techniques and therapy goals. This map can be graphed on paper and revised during the therapy process. It might be shared with the family or it may exist only in the therapist's head.

The therapist is looking for information in six areas to construct the map: (1) the family structure as a whole and its transactional patterns; (2) the system's flexibility and capacity for change; (3) internal relationships, i.e., enmeshed or disengaged; (4) sources of stress and support available; (5) developmental stages of the family; and (6) how individuals' symptoms are used or reinforced.

Minuchin uses symbols in his mapping to indicate clear, diffuse, or rigid boundaries. He also maps affiliation, overinvolvement, conflict, coalitions, and detouring. He uses letter symbols for mother, father, children, boy, girl, therapist, and adolescent. These symbols are used to graph parental, marital, and sibling subsystems or the entire family. These diagrams can become complicated but can be a useful shorthand for charting family structure and goals for change. See Minuchin (1974) for a complete list of mapping symbols.

Adaptive Consequences

In evaluating an alcoholic family, the therapist must not only look for the maladaptive consequences of the drinking behavior, but also must define the adaptive consequences of drinking. Davis, Berenson, Steinglass, and Davis (1974) describe this process: "Postulate that alcohol abuse has adaptive consequences that are reinforcing enough to maintain the drinking behavior, regardless of its causative factors. These adaptive consequences may operate on different levels including intrapsychic, intracouple, or to maintain family homeostasis" (p. 210). Drinking may be tied to fun and recreation and symbolize a time when people can set aside depressive behaviors and enjoy themselves. The notion may be, "If I'm drinking, I'm having fun, and I can only have fun if I'm drinking." Asking this person to give up alcohol would also be asking him or her to give up fun. Alcohol consumption may maintain physical distance to avoid sexual contact. Intoxication may be the only state that allows couples the intensity to make contact by fighting or that decreases inhibitions enough to allow for sexual behavior. Drinking may inadvertently allow for stabilization of the family or maintenance of social isolation.

Determining the adaptive consequences of alcohol consumption is important because the goals of treatment are to produce adaptive behaviors during sobriety and to develop effective ways to achieve positive consequences without alcohol consumption.

Steinglass, Davis, and Berenson (1977) further developed a model to demonstrate how drinking behavior is maintained (Figure 6-10). It is based on three concepts: "interactional behavior cycling between the sober state and the intoxicated state; patterning of behavior that has reached steady state; and the hypothesis that alcohol use in the alcoholic family has become incorporated into family problem-solving behavior" (Steinglass, 1979, p. 167). Figure 6-10 demonstrates the circular pattern of the alcoholic family, beginning with three ways a family can experience a problem. These parallel the patterns families present for family therapy. The first problem is pathology in an individual family member. The second difficulty is interactional conflict between family members, and the third area involves the family's inability to adjust to the social environment.

Figure 6-10 Circular Pattern of Maintenance of Drinking in the Family

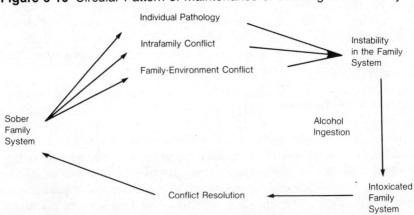

Source: Reprinted from "Observations of conjointly hospitalized 'alcohol couples' during sobriety and intoxication: Implications for theory and therapy," by P. Steinglass, D. Davis, and D. Berenson with permission from *Family Process*, 1977.

When any of these problem areas threaten to unstabilize the family, the family will seek an equilbrium that is associated with changing from sober to intoxicated behaviors. Steinglass believes that intoxication adds stability because of the rapid change in behavior due to the physiological effect of alcohol and the predictability of the intoxicated behavior.

REFERENCES

Anderson, C.M. & Malloy, E.S. Family photographs: In treatment and training. *Family Process,* 1976, *15,* 259-264.

Bailey, M.B. The family agency's role in treating the wife of an alcoholic, *Social Casework,* 1963, *44,* 273-279.

Bandler, R., Grinder, J., & Satir, V. *Changing with families.* Palo Alto, Calif.: Science and Behavior Books, Inc., 1976.

Bing, E. The conjoint family drawing. *Family Process,* 1970, *9,* 173-194.

Clarken, J.F., Frances, A.J., & Moodie, J.L. Selection criteria for family therapy. *Family Process,* 1979, *18,* 391-403.

Davis, D.J., Berenson, D., Steinglass, P., & Davis, S. The adaptive consequences of drinking. *Psychiatry,* 1974, *37,* 209-215.

Guerin, P. Evaluation of family system and genogram. In P. Guerin (Ed.), *Family therapy: Theory and practice.* New York: Gardner Press, 1976.

Hanson, K.J. & Estes, N. Dynamics of alcoholic families. In Estes & Heinemann (Eds.), *Alcoholism: Development consequences and interventions.* St. Louis: Mosby Co., 1977.

Irwin, E. & Malloy, E. Family puppet interview. *Family Process,* 1975, *14,* 179-191.

Kaufman, E. The application of the basic principles of family therapy to the treatment of drug and alcohol abusers. In E. Kaufman & P. Kaufman (Eds.), *Family therapy of drug and alcohol abuse.* New York: Gardner Press, 1979.

Kwiatkowska, N.Y. Family art therapy. *Family Process,* 1967, *6,* 37-55.

Landgarten, H.B. *Clinical art therapy.* New York: Brunner/Mazel, 1981.

Minuchin, S. *Families and family therapy.* Cambridge, Mass.: Harvard University Press, 1974.

Minuchin, S., Montalbo, B., Guerney, B., Rosman, B., & Schumer, F. *Families of the slums.* New York: Basic Books, 1967.

National Institute on Alcoholism and Drug Abuse. *An assessment of the needs of and resources for children of alcoholic parents.* P.B. 241. Rockville, MD: NIAAA, 1974.

Papp, P., Silverstein, O., & Center, E. Family sculpting in preventive work with well families. *Family Process,* 1973, *12,* 197-212.

Rubin, J. & Magnussen, M. A family art evaluation. *Family Process,* 1974, *13,* 185-200.

Satir, V. *Conjoint family therapy.* Palo Alto, Calif.: Science & Behavior Books, 1967.

Sherr, C. & Hicks, H. Family drawings as a diagnostic and therapeutic technique. *Family Process,* 1973, *12,* 439.

Simon, R. Sculpting the family. *Family Process,* 1972, *11,* 49-59.

Steinglass, P. Family therapy with alcoholics: A review. In E. Kaufman & P. Kaufman (Eds.). *Family therapy of drug and alcohol abuse.* New York: Gardner Press, 1979.

Steinglass, P., Davis, D., & Berenson, D. Observations of conjointly hospitalized "alcohol couples" during sobriety and intoxication: implications for theory and therapy. *Family Process,* 1977, *16,* 1-16.

Walsh, W.M. *A primer in family therapy.* Springfield, Ill.: Charles C. Thomas, 1980.

Watzlawick, P. A structural family interview. *Family Process,* 1966, *5,* 256-271.

Wegscheider, D. *If only my family understood me.* Minneapolis: Compare Publications, 1979.

Chapter 7

A Prescription for Family Treatment

This chapter introduces the process of family therapy. Volumes have been written on the theory and techniques of family therapy, and it is a popular subject for research and innovation in programming.

This chapter will discuss possible treatment strategies to use with the four types of alcoholic families discussed in Chapter 6. These include approaches for the family with chronic alcohol problems and techniques for families in which alcohol problems are secondary or not chronic. The chapter will be structured in the chronological order that the treatment methods are used in family therapy. That is, chronic emotional issues are covered initially, followed by a discussion of Haley's (1976) model of family therapy with the nuclear family. The chapter then follows the course of family therapy as it leads to marital therapy and marital couples groups. The final stage is family of origin work.

The last section of this chapter is a brief overview of treatment approaches used by four major theories of family therapy: the communication model, the systems model, the structural model, and the social learning model.

First, the therapist must decide which treatment mode is most appropriate for the client. Clarken, Frances, and Moodie (1979), in reviewing the literature, have listed some guidelines for discriminating between cases appropriate for family/ marital therapy and those that would be more successful in individual treatment. Family or marital treatment is recommended when individual treatment has not been successful or has involved family issues. Family and/or marital treatment is also recommended if improvement in the identified patient leads to symptoms in another family member.

Individual treatment is indicated when "the presenting problem of the individual does not have a significant etiology or an effect upon the family system" (Clarken, Frances, & Moodie, 1979, p. 395). This is unlikely in an alcoholic family. Individual treatment is also indicated in the following situations: (1) when family therapy is misused to deny personal responsibility for a major personality disorder; (2) when psychopathology of a family member would be prevented by individual work; (3) when there is massive unworkable pathology in a parent that would point to working with the child individually to teach him or her to cope with the parent; (4) when parents are deceitful in treatment; (5) when individuation would be enhanced (this is disputed by authors who believe family work is the best way to individuate); (6) at the end of family treatment, if individual pathology remains; or (7) if detoxification or medication is needed before family therapy.

Once a decision has been made to engage family members in treatment, an assessment should be conducted to determine the family's motivation for treatment and to decide which treatment method would be most appropriate.

Chapter 6 lists four types of alcoholic families that ask for therapy. First, a family may require therapy when there is hidden alcoholism in one or both parents and a child is the symptom bearer. These families may give clues to alcohol abuse through reports of alcoholism in the families of origin; overfunctioning in one parent and underinvolvement in the other; role reversals; attempts by children to protect their parents; children's fear of talking about the family; denial or isolation; reports of physical abuse or incest; scapegoating of a child; or irrational fear of teenage alcohol or drug abuse. The symptom in the child might be alcohol or drug abuse. Because the alcohol abuse is hidden, it is difficult to assess the chronicity of the problem. The therapist must initially focus on the presenting problem while looking for ways to incorporate the drinking problem into therapy. If the family leaves therapy before the parental alcoholism is discovered, the scapegoated child will be angry that his or her efforts failed and may progress to worse symptoms. The therapist should begin with Haley's (1976) approach (described later in the chapter) or a similar family therapy approach. If the alcoholism surfaces, a shift to Berenson's (1976b) chronic approach may be necessary.

In a second type of family, members may openly talk about drinking but are more concerned about other family problems. The history of alcoholism in these families is not very significant. The drinker usually does not have a marked behavior change when drinking. The spouses' relationship is symmetrical at first impression. Alcohol problems in these families seem to result from other problems and will recede if the contributing problems are solved. Since it is unlikely that alcohol is a chronic emotional factor in these families, the therapist should focus on the presenting problems and follow the Haley model.

The therapist should not ignore the issue of drinking and should connect the family difficulties to the excessive drinking at every opportunity.

In the third type of family, alcohol abuse is a major problem since the family is organized around the alcoholic's drinking. There is intense conflict, and the drinking makes other problems worse. The alcoholic may be physically addicted to alcohol and have definite behavior changes when drinking. If the spouses are in intense conflict and the emotionality of the family is high, an initial cooling off period may be required with the therapist taking control of the sessions. These families would probably respond to Berenson's chronic family model discussed later in this chapter.

The fourth type of alcoholic family may seek help when an alcoholic member has completed treatment and is sober. These families are often out of balance. Marital problems may revolve around issues of control of the family, or a new symptom bearer may be produced. If the child's behavior is the presenting problem, the family may have realigned in a negative way. The therapist should assess the family system and look for the adaptive consequences of past drinking. Families who are referred after the alcoholic member has received individual treatment may resist looking at their own limitations or the part they play in the problem. These families need to view drinking behavior as only one part of family interaction and allow the alcoholic to get rid of this label and reenter the family with new interaction patterns. The family members must also recognize that they played a role in the drinking behavior.

In all four of these family styles, the issue of drinking must be squarely faced, at some point, by the therapist. It must be understood that the drinking problem will be dealt with and not ignored. This does not mean that the therapist will allow the family to blame all of their problems on the drinking of one member, nor must every session include work on this area.

In a fifth kind of family, the alcohol problem occurs in an adolescent. These families may have hidden parental alcoholism, no parental problems, or parents that are recovering alcoholics. Treatment methods for working with these adolescents are covered later in the chapter.

FAMILY THERAPY AND AA

A further decision by the therapist should be made about the involvement of families in Alcoholics Anonymous or Al-Anon. This issue is similar to the decision on sobriety discussed in Chapter 6. Some therapists insist on attendance as a prerequisite for therapy. Others make distinctions in which clients are encouraged to attend AA. Since attendance at AA meetings may not be appropriate for all problem drinkers, a rigid position on AA attendance may rule out help for some families who might benefit from family therapy alone.

Family therapy and AA may seem to be working at cross-purposes, with AA and Al-Anon "focusing on the alcoholic person as the 'patient'—the antithesis of the family systems approach which identified alcoholism as a family dysfunction and directs treatment at the entire family" (Hindman, 1976, p. 7). Actually, these self-help groups and family therapy have several common factors. They agree that: (1) family members other than the alcoholic suffer; (2) change can occur when significant others are engaged in the process; (3) family members can resist change by the alcoholic; (4) if the alcoholic recovers emotionally and the other family members do not, a crisis may occur; and (5) the individual is responsible for personal change.

Davis (NIAAA, 1978) warns of a pitfall that can occur when both approaches are used simultaneously: "As family members begin working on a thorny problem in either the therapy or self-help group and there is a resulting rise in anxiety, they may attempt to avoid facing the problem by escaping to the other treatment approach" (p. 4). This problem can be avoided by coordination efforts between the therapist and the AA sponsor. If the family therapy shifts away from the drinking issue to reduce anxiety, AA may be avoided in favor of family sessions. While other problems are appropriate to address in family situations, the connection with alcohol should continue to be a main concern. A choice of family therapy as the sole treatment may be flattering to the therapist, but the decision to change treatment methods should be made on a therapeutic basis and as a joint decision between the family and the therapist.

Berenson (1976b) believes that "continuation in AA and Al-Anon is up to the client, with the therapist being careful that an early decrease in attendance may be a warning of an impending resumption of drinking, and that continued and frequent attendance for many years may become a stress in the marriage" (p. 292).

THE CHRONIC ALCOHOLIC FAMILY

If the therapist is working with a family that has a chronic, ongoing drinking problem (in one or both spouses) and a high degree of emotionality about drinking, treatment initially should focus on drinking management. Berenson (1976b) has developed a two-phase treatment approach for families who are organized around alcohol consumption. Such families may have: (1) a drinker who consumes a moderate amount of alcohol but whose spouse is angry and accusing; (2) a drinker who consumes alcohol intermittently but has severe arguments with family members; or (3) a situation in which both spouses drink excessively with much related conflict. This treatment approach is based on Bowen's (1974) family system theory, the concurrent use of Alcoholics Anonymous and Al-Anon, and Berenson's clinical experience (Berenson, 1976a).

The initial phase involves management of drinking and setting up conditions that will terminate drinking. The evaluation portion of this treatment should note changes in behavior of the drinker and the other family members when intoxication occurs. Adaptive consequences of this behavior should be noted, and a history of drinking patterns in the families of origin should be included. Care should be taken in this phase to avoid blame (which can lead to nonproductive arguments) and a continuation of the existing family system. Each family member must view his or her behavior as a part of the total problem. History taking is a neutral process that allows an overly emotional system a chance to cool off and begin emotional distancing. Berenson believes drinking may continue in these families but that work on family dynamics cannot occur until drinking stops. He achieves this by encouraging an emotional distance in the marriage. By working with the person who is most motivated (usually the nondrinking spouse), he tones down the emotional involvement and helps the family detach from the alcoholic. Al-Anon can be used in this phase as support, and the Al-Anon sponsor is suggested for the nonalcoholic to move toward emotionally while distancing from the alcoholic.

In this stage, "the focus is on the nonalcoholic becoming more responsible for self, rather than attempting to control the alcoholic" (Berenson, 1976b, p. 292). In Fogarty's (1976) terms, the spouse, who is the emotional pursuer, must learn to stop chasing the distancer, who is typically the alcoholic. This advice applies to the therapist as well. It is useless to pursue alcoholics in treatment if they are using their drinking behavior to distance themselves emotionally. In systems terms, it is better to focus on the family by facilitating changes in the motivated spouse.

To stop the nonalcoholic from pursuing, Fogarty (1976) suggests the pursuer must resolve the emptiness he or she is trying to fill through pursuit. He says, "The therapist should take the pursuer into his own inner emptiness by asking questions like, "What would it be like inside of you if you lost your spouse?" (p. 326). Nonalcoholics must learn to achieve for themselves what they are trying unsuccessfully to get from their spouses. Distancing may be a new behavior, but these techniques can be learned if the nondrinker observes the drinker. When the distancer is no longer pursued, loneliness may begin to occur. This can be very helpful to the alcoholic, who may become interested in self-examination and change. "The more a spouse takes a position for herself, the more likely the alcoholic is to stop drinking; the more the spouse takes a position in order to get the alcoholic sober, the more likely such a move is going to be a failure or transient success; or, if successful, the more likely there will be other family problems when the drinking stops" (Berenson, 1976b, p. 293).

If the therapist is able to work with both the alcoholic and the spouse, the therapist must maintain control of the sessions and reduce the affective content of treatment. In these emotionally charged families, defensiveness and blame can spark a conflict that is difficult to stop. Discussions should avoid the relationship between husband and wife, if it is volatile, and move toward problems that both people brought with them from their families of origin. This discussion takes the attention away from the spouses and cools the system. It also provides a view of how each member contributed to the drinking. This discussion can lead to an examination of marital expectations and periods of history that were happy times for the marital couple. Work and children are also safe subjects and can provide ways of discussing the family structure without direct conflict. If these techniques do not cool down the marital subsystem, the therapist may need to see the couple separately.

When the emotional distance has been achieved, Berenson (1976b) has found that a state occurs that he refers to as "walking on eggs" for fear the drinking will resume. At this point, the second phase of treatment attempts to decrease this emotional distance without the resumption of drinking. An attempt is made to reproduce in the sober state adaptive behaviors that were present during intoxicated states.

A good example of this form of treatment is presented by Carter (1977), and it involves a case study of a family who came for family therapy with a 14-year-old son with school problems. Carter (1977) approached this issue with what she calls a "Minuchin-Bowen sequence." She "begins work by focusing on the presenting problem and recommending tasks around that problem, as Minuchin does, and then will either glide into extended family work, or make an explicit second contract with the family to go on in that direction, i.e., coaching parents in work on their families of origin as taught by Bowen" (p. 50).

In this particular case, it became evident that a parental separation was contributing to the son's school problem. In working with the parents, she constructed a family genogram that included questions about drinking patterns. She discovered that both families of origin were from Ireland. All of their grandparents were born in Ireland, and the families lived within blocks of each other in the Bronx. The proliferance of alcoholism in both families was astounding. The father came from a family in which both parents were alcoholic, and they had come from alcoholic families as well. The maternal grandmother had six brothers who were all alcoholics and seven sisters who "drank a lot" except for one who became a nun. The mother's family of origin included an alcoholic father, a mother from an alcoholic family, and eight older brothers and sisters all of whom drank with some degree of difficulty.

Although this was clearly a family with a chronic, longstanding history of alcoholism, neither parent saw alcohol as a problem, and both vehemently refused to have anything to do with Alcoholics Anonymous. The father refused to stop drinking completely, and the mother defined alcoholics as "falling down drunks" or "skid row bums" that had nothing to do with any of her drinking behaviors.

Carter abandoned her usual approach of insisting on AA attendance and used Berenson as a consultant and support person while attempting a new approach to family therapy.

With this approach, the adaptive consequences of drinking were identified, and Carter found that alcohol allowed this family to have a good time. While drinking, they were able to express tenderness and affection (a rare occurrence while sober), have sex (with which they otherwise had difficulties), and/or express anger and bitterness that they otherwise avoided. This certainly did not get problem areas dealt with functionally, but it did get them expressed. Simply stamping out drinking, in this framework, would also be stamping out good times, affection, sex, and emotional release. Carter's goal was to modify the drunken behavior that was serving a functional purpose into the repertoire of the sober behaviors. This treatment lasted two and a half years and was successfully completed when new roles and behaviors eventually replaced old ones. Predictions were made that efforts to change would fail if the drinking continued. A videotape of the mother's drunken behavior was used to help produce the adaptive part of the drunken behavior when she was sober. Extensive family of origin work was done with the mother that restructured family relationships and allowed the mother to shed her victim role.

FAMILY THERAPY WITH NONCHRONIC ALCOHOLIC FAMILIES

In families of recovering alcoholics and in families where alcoholism or problem drinking is not the presenting problem, alcohol may not be the central issue of the early family sessions. If the therapist redefines the problem as alcohol abuse, the family may become anxious or may feel unheard and pull out of therapy. It is important to initially begin with what the family has identified as their problem. If the therapist can remain flexible and spontaneous, an initial solvable problem can be a good starting point.

This beginning period allows the family to experience the "familiness" of their problems. The entire family should attend the early session, and the network of support people who are involved with the family are useful for the initial interview.

Haley (1976) has developed a structure for the first family interview. He defines four stages: (1) social; (2) problem; (3) interaction; and (4) goal setting.

The social stage establishes a comfort level and provides a naturalizing of the social environment. Family members are allowed to sit where they wish. The therapist has a greeting exchange with family members to get their names, ages, and additional innocuous information. The idea is to demonstrate that each person is important and can contribute to the session. At this point, it can be determined who is missing from the family and if any members of the extended family would be important contributors.

The issue of blame may arise at this time with the alcoholic family. Either the family is uncomfortable with the unstated alcohol problem and blames a child for their presence in therapy, or the family continues to scapegoat the alcoholic and remains uninterested in his or her contributions to the family problems. The therapist should focus on the here and now and avoid discussion of specific problems initially. The family will present a dominant mood that the therapist should attempt to match.

With parents and children all in one room, parent-child interactions, discipline modalities, and sibling relationships may also be noted. This, however, only represents how family members act in front of others and may be different from behavior at home. Also, at this time the parents may be openly in disagreement, in agreement, or overly agreeable about the child's problems. One of the spouses may be reluctant to participate in the session.

Additionally, the therapist can observe the seating arrangement to see if the identified patient is isolated or sitting between the parents or if the parents have an allied child near them.

It is best at this time to keep all conclusions about the family interaction tentative, and therapists should not share their observations with the family. At some level the family is aware of these dynamics and would see this as an invasion. Haley (1976) says, ''To point out something like a seating arrangement is asking the family to concede something they might prefer not to concede, and thus that action could arouse defensiveness and cause unnecessary difficulties in the therapy'' (p. 19).

The second stage is the problem stage, and it begins with an inquiry about the family's view of the problem that has brought them in for therapy. It signals the end of the social atmosphere stage and indicates that it is time to get down to business. It may be very confusing to the alcoholic family to be in family therapy when it is obvious to them who has the problem. The therapist must clarify why the entire family has been asked to participate. The problem orientation can remain, but the therapist may state that it is important to get everyone's opinion of the problem. Usually the therapist has some prior knowledge of the family from a referral source or from the family member who called for the appointment. If the family seems secretive, it is beneficial for the therapist to share this information with the family.

During questioning about the problem area, the therapist needs to decide who to ask and in what way. If the family is simply asked what the problem is, the therapist may receive a long history of all of the negative behavior of the identified patient. The therapist can offer hope for change and ask questions like, ''What do you want changed in your family?'' To assess what caused the family to ask for help, the therapist may ask, ''How did the decision get made to call for this appointment?'' or ''What has happened recently that motivated you to call for the appointment?'' Haley (1976) suggests ''As a rule, the more general and ambiguous the inquiry of the therapist is, the more room there is for the family members to display their point of view'' (p. 21). The therapist should avoid being overly specific because the family may focus on one area such as problems of the child or the alcoholism. This focus will simply reinforce the notion that only one person has problems.

It is difficult to present these questions to the family as a whole, and usually there is a therapist bias in selecting who is addressed. If the therapists are alcohol counselors, their sympathies may be with the alcoholic, who seems victimized by a nagging spouse. If the therapists are child oriented, they may be angry at the parents, who have neglected and hurt the children. A decision about who to address can best be made by first examining the family hierarchy of power and influence. Usually one parent is more motivated to work than the other, and one parent has more power to get the family to return for further sessions. Haley (1976) believes the person who can get the family back to therapy should be treated with respect, but the underinvolved parent should be engaged first.

Sometimes the most detached family member is a child. In this instance, it is best to start talking with the person who is least involved and sits furthest away and work through the family to the most involved member. It is inadvisable to begin with the identified patient as it may look like the therapist is blaming him or her. Identified patients are used to getting attention when the family is anxious, and this pattern must be broken by the therapist. Haley says, "Every therapist must watch out for a tendency to turn to, or on, the problem person in a benevolent way when he or she (the therapist) is anxious and under stress" (p. 25).

In addition, the problem that brought the family to therapy must be clearly stated and not minimized. If there is a tendency to extend the social stage and not deal with issues, the family will be confused. If alcohol abuse is the presenting problem and a direct discussion of this issue is skirted, the problem will grow in magnitude and take on the aura of being unmentionable. Even if the therapist does not agree that the presenting problem is the main issue of the family, it can be used as a lever to create change. For instance, if the presenting problem is child-oriented but the therapist is certain of marital conflict, the marital relationship can be approached by addressing disagreement on parenting issues. Haley states, "Usually family members say that one person is the problem. The therapist's job is to think of the problem in terms of more than one person. By thinking that way he is most able to bring about change" (p. 33).

As the problem is being presented, the therapist should simply listen to the family and observe behaviors. The therapist should avoid making interpretations, giving advice, or encouraging emotional reactions with inquiries about feelings and not facts. One member of the family must not be allowed to monopolize the discussion. The therapist must have enough control of the session to allow everyone to speak. If the therapist is not in control, things will go on as they have in the past, and change will not occur.

If the family requested therapy because of a problem with a child, the chances are good that the parents may be talking metaphorically about marital problems. If the mother says her daughter is unaffectionate, it is possible that the mother is also saying her husband is not affectionate. These hypotheses should not be shared with the family. There is a reason that things are not talked about directly, and the child's behavior should not be outwardly connected with the marital situation. If the problem statement is left open and ambiguous, it will allow for these dynamics to be expressed to the therapist indirectly through safe subjects.

Alcoholic families have many areas that have become forbidden to discuss, and the children may be protecting the parents by withholding information or taking the blame for family troubles. The alcoholic couple may be unable to talk about certain subjects in a sober state but can let the therapist know they exist in indirect ways. The therapist can observe all the levels of communication and interaction and can begin to think about the family's problems in a systems context. The therapist does not have to convince the family of this approach; the family will experience it in the process of treatment.

The third stage Haley describes is the interaction stage. Here, the therapist begins to direct people to speak to one another, rather than having all comments directed to the therapist. At this stage, family members may be able to act out some of their problems. A role-play situation of family interaction around a problem can be set up, allowing the therapist to observe the structure of the family and interaction patterns.

The fourth stage is the goal setting stage, which requires a more detailed definition of the problem. The desired changes are defined, and a clear therapeutic contract is negotiated. In order for the family to begin change, it is necessary to put the problem into terms that are solvable, observable, and measurable. This is important for observing therapy outcomes and for giving the family a clear direction for working. At this stage, the therapist can ask specific questions about the symptoms, such as when they occur, if they are constant or periodic, if they come on quickly or gradually, or how intense they are. It is useful to find out what everyone does in reaction to a problem. If the problem is drinking, questions can be asked about shifts in everyone's behavior and how it is different from behavior around sober states. In families who present a problem in an area other than alcohol abuse, the goal of the family may not be to stop the drinking of one member. If the therapist insists on abstinence instead of the family's goal, they may leave treatment. But if abstinence is the goal, it is easily observable and can be defined in terms of family behavior. The alcoholic may also be in the victim or scapegoat role in the family, and it would be dangerous to try to convince the family otherwise at this stage. If the therapist has been involved with the individual treatment of the alcoholic, the temptation may arise to defend the alcoholic and fight the rest of the family. If the therapist works too hard to free the alcoholic from this negative position, the family may have to make the alcoholic worse to show the therapist they were correct. This is also true of a family who has a scapegoated child the therapist wants to save.

In this initial session, the therapist is working to join the family by making everyone feel at ease, allowing everyone to contribute, involving everyone with each other, and including everyone in the decision-making process. If done in a genuine manner, this joining allows the therapist to enter the family and to begin to bring about change from within.

If the family seems hesitant about committing to a course of therapy, it may relieve their anxiety to set a certain number of sessions after which an assessment of progress will occur and a decision to continue can be made.

Giving Directives

When the therapist has a good idea of the family structure and functioning he or she can begin to give directives or assignments for the family to do in the session and between sessions. These directives are designed to break a rule or pattern in the family interaction in order to bring about change in the system. Every interaction the therapist has with the family has some impact and can be seen as a directive. The behavior of the family around these assignments will give the therapist additional information.

Directives can be stated in two different ways. The therapist can tell the family what to do, or the therapist can tell them the opposite of what to do, assuming they will rebel against the directive and do the opposite.

In the first case, it is difficult to tell people to do something and have them obey without a great deal of therapist credibility. Haley (1976) says, "If someone drinks too much, sometimes it is a good idea to tell him not to drink. He might stop. But if the problem is severe, he is likely to drink more, and a therapist does not usually have the power to enforce the directive" (p. 52). If the directive comes in the form of good advice, it is not likely to be useful in making change. Directives that are used to change a sequence of behaviors are more helpful and will be carried out more often if the family members can see gains for themselves. The therapist and family need to agree on a task that will achieve movement toward the goal that was agreed upon. In this direct approach, the therapist must use what has been learned about the family as encouragement to complete the task.

Similarly, it is beneficial to find out what unsuccessful means the family attempted to use in the past to solve their problem. If the family can be made to see how desperate their situation is, they will be more motivated to change. Predictions of worse problems in the future can motivate the family to take action.

If the family is not desperate and they feel they are improving or if they are in aftercare and are looking for maintenance of sobriety, the therapist can promote continuation of this improvement and design a directive that will continue progress.

In stating the directive, the therapist must make precise task assignments and make sure everyone understands the tasks. If the purpose of the directive is to demonstrate unity, everyone must be included. If boundaries need clarification, the subsystems may need to be divided and directives given only to members of the subset. For instance, to increase marital involvement, an assignment can be given to the parents that would exclude participation of the children.

If the family seems resistant or excessively stuck in their patterns, it is helpful to predict that the family will think the assignment is silly and useless or that they will be unable to do the task. If the task is not done, the therapist should not excuse this disobedience but should help the family see they have failed themselves. If the family wishes to have a second chance, the same directive should not be used. The family should experience the loss of a chance for improvement by their reluctance to carry out the directive.

The second form of directive is referred to as a paradoxical directive and should be used carefully with families who are resistant to change, who gain from drinking, or who are practiced at causing the therapist to fail. When the family homeostasis is in a stable state, they will be comfortable and less motivated to try a different way to behave. Even if the alcoholic continues to drink, the family may feel more comfortable staying in a predictable pattern of behavior and will resist a direct approach from the therapist. Families in aftercare may be unstable due to the change in one person and easy to motivate, or they may be stable in their pattern of interaction with the alcoholic in the role of the victim or scapegoat. By using this rebellious, resistant stance, the therapist can assign a behavior opposite to the desired behavior and can predict failures or assign a directive that involves a request for an increase in the symptom.

When the therapist predicts difficulties, the outcome is usually positive. The idea is to gain the family's compliance whether or not they follow the directive. By predicting that therapy goals will not be achieved if drinking continues, the therapist will be correct if problems occur, and a connection will have been made between drinking and problem behavior. But if there are no problems, then the therapeutic goals have been achieved.

Similarly, if a task assigned in a paradoxical way (opposite of intended goal) is carried out, the therapist and client are working together even if the therapeutic goal is not achieved. If it is not done or the opposite of the directive is carried out, the goal will have been achieved. Whichever way the family chooses, positive change will occur. The family followed a directive or resisted and changed for the better.

In stating paradoxical directives, the therapist must show how these actions will benefit the family members or they will see the therapist as being sarcastic. For example, the therapist might say, "It would be too unsettling for this family for Dad to discipline; so he should continue in not correcting the children's misbehavior." Such a statement will confront the family's need to maintain homeostasis at all costs and will present the maladaptive behavior in positive terms.

The successful use of paradox requires much skill and practice and an ability to think of serious problems in a gamelike way.

Haley (1976) has listed eight stages of paradoxical intervention, as follows: (1) establish a relationship that can bring about change; (2) define the problem clearly; (3) set goals clearly; (4) offer a plan or a rationale to make the directive seem reasonable; (5) disqualify the person in the family who has become the authority on solving the problem; (6) give the paradoxical directive; (7) observe the response to the directive and continue to prescribe the symptom; and (8) as improvement occurs, avoid taking credit for the change because the family or person is doing the opposite of what is being requested. The therapist should act puzzled by the improvement.

When assigning direct or paradoxical tasks, the therapist should be certain that they are easy enough for the family to carry out in terms of the time involved and financial limitations, so that if they are not completed the therapist can assume resistance to direct attempts to change the system. In setting the tasks, the therapist should combine what the family feels is important (the presenting problem), with what the therapist feels is important (organizational change).

TRANSITION TO A MARITAL FOCUS

Once improvements have been made in the presenting problem (i.e., reduction in symptoms in a child or reduction in abusive drinking in a family member), the focus of therapy should shift to the underlying problems that were producing the symptoms. If the family leaves therapy without making a major shift in structure, it is likely that the identified patient will return to the original symptomatic behavior or gain new symptoms. Furthermore, another family member may become symptomatic.

If the family is in therapy due to a problem with a child, it is likely that the child is acting out the marital difficulties of the parents. When improvement in the child is created by separating the generational subgroups, the marital issues may surface. These issues may be very difficult for the couple to discuss. Haley (1976) says, "In most therapy with disturbed children, it can be assumed that if parents could easily concede their marital difficulties the child would not be the problem" (p. 155).

If the family has initiated therapy because of alcoholism in a parent and the symptoms have been reduced, the marital issues will most likely surface. Haley states, "Whenever a married person has a severe symptom it inevitably has a function in the marriage, and there will be consequences in the marriage when a symptom is cured" (p. 155).

If the marital issues can be acknowledged and openly talked about, a contract can be negotiated with the marital couple to work on these difficulties. If the family is unable to directly confront marital problems, these issues may be discussed indirectly by the use of analogies and metaphors.

As the parents begin talking about the presenting problem, the therapist will be able to detect subtle differences of opinion between the spouses. The marital couple may talk about their issues in global terms of the problems of all men or all women, or they may talk about another relationship that is similar to theirs. The therapist should respond to these analogies in the same context and not make the interpretation that the spouses are talking about themselves. As the family talks about their problems, the therapist can connect these problems to the relationship of the parents. When the couple is able to admit their difficulties in the marital relationship, a contract can be developed to work in this area.

Marital Work

When the marital couple identifies issues in the marital relationship that need intervention, the marital stage of family therapy begins. It is most productive to work with both spouses so that the therapist does not take sides or have a distorted view of the relationship. Haley states, "Often a marital therapist may feel like a labor negotiator, or a diplomat, involved in conflictual issues. If he joins one side against the other, he becomes part of the problem rather than part of the solution" (p. 161). Remaining impartial is very difficult and the therapist's bias cannot be entirely eliminated. Therapists should be aware of their sex role biases, their attitudes about marriage, and their own struggles with marital relationships.

If possible, the therapist's values in these areas should be kept to a minimum in the course of marital therapy, and the therapist should resist joining in a coalition with one spouse against the other. The focus of marital work should be on interpersonal issues and not on individual problems of the spouses. Fogarty (1976) states, "In dealing with these situations, it is important for the therapist to remember that there is no such thing as an emotional problem in one person, no matter how it looks" (p. 147).

To begin to bring about change in the system, the therapist must determine which spouse will be the easiest to change. Berenson (1979) feels that the spouse of the alcoholic is suffering more and therefore is more motivated to change. Bowen (1974) states, "Those family members who are most dependent on the drinking person are more overtly anxious than is the one who drinks" (p. 116). Spouses of alcoholics are often overfunctioning and will respond more quickly to attempts to tone down their overinvolvement than the underinvolved alcoholics will respond to efforts to increase their involvement. In terms of Fogarty's theory of the pursuer and distancer, the spouse becomes the pursuer in an attempt to change the alcoholic, and the alcoholic becomes the distancer, moving away from the spouse. Alcoholics often focus more on the behaviors of the pursuing spouses than their own behaviors.

The therapist can, if deemed appropriate, see the spouse alone as a way to stop the pursuing or overfunctioning. If both spouses are willing to attend, they can be treated as a unit. Bowen (1974) believes that families in which both spouses attend therapy have better outcomes. Berenson (1979) sees a further advantage in working with both spouses if the alcoholic attends a therapy session drunk.

Berenson says, "In the session, the therapist defines it as the spouse's problem rather than his own and may proceed to do a session while the alcoholic is drunk, pointing out either in the session, or by means of videotape after the session, how the drinking affects the interaction within the couple" (p. 235). The pursuing spouse gains the opportunity to establish a feeling of self-determination and responsibility for his or her own behavior, rather than blaming someone or something else. Bowen refers to this as taking an "I-position."

The next step in working with an alcoholic family is building an emotional support system. These supports can be connections with friends, extended family members, social agencies, vocational training, and the self-help groups of Al-Anon and AA. However, Berenson (1976b) says, "AA may be a problem if the alcoholic has an impression that he can only share his thoughts and feelings at AA meetings or with his sponsor, not with his spouse" (p. 294). Instead of alcohol, the alcoholic may use the AA meetings as a distancer against the spouse.

Marital Couples Groups

An alternative to working with an individual spouse or marital couple is a marital couples group. This approach combines marital therapy, based on a family treatment approach, with group theory, which has been found useful in working with alcoholics. The combination of these two approaches has been a popular family-level therapy approach to alcoholism, and several research studies of this method have been reported (Cadogan, 1973; Cadogan, 1979; Gallant, Rich, Bey, & Tevanova, 1970; Steinglass, 1979; Steinglass, Davis, & Berenson, 1977). Cadogan (1979) finds that, "The very existence of a group of people with similar life circumstances and similar problems coming together for the purpose of resolving their difficulties, and sanctioned by the authority of a professional therapist, lends hope to its members" (p. 189).

Cadogan uses group dynamics and problem-solving principles with groups composed of four to six alcoholic couples. These groups focus on interpersonal relations and link human relations problems with emotional difficulties. By making the group more homogeneous, Cadogan has found that marital, child-rearing, and in-law problems can be worked on that are relevant to all members. Also, the effect of alcoholism on the marital relationship lends itself to group cohesiveness.

Cadogan (1979) has also found these groups to be useful in reestablishing a homeostatic level based on factors other than problems in the family. The groups are additionally beneficial in restructuring interpersonal relationships both within marriages and with other group members. Social isolation, common to alcoholic families, is reduced by participation in the group, and there is pressure on the couples to extend their social contacts outside of the group members. A couple's communication skills are improved since repressed feelings are expressed.

Another important function of these groups is to identify and change pathological family interactions. Cadogan (1979) states:

Some marital unions are formed by immature individuals who are not ready for a meaningful and adult relationship. These marriages are based on a desire on the part of both members to parentify each other. As a result, the anxiety-producing features of the original parent-child relationship are often reproduced and reexperienced, and the self-defeating coping mechanisms used in childhood are again utilized (p. 194).

The group is particularly useful in helping people see these pathological relationships in other members and thus acknowledge responsibility for difficulties in their own relationships.

Family of Origin Work

If dysfunctional patterns originating from the couple's families of origin are not addressed, they will eventually be repeated. Framo (1976) uses a marital couples group to examine these intergenerational carry-overs. He has found that a spouse's irrational demands are often caused by voids he or she has never filled from his or her family of origin. Framo (1976) has found that when couples reach a point in therapy where marital issues have been fully explored and they are unable to reconcile further differences, they are in what he refers to as the "dirty middle" of therapy, where someone must change. Framo suggests the families of origin be included in a session with the couple. This is almost always met with resistance and refusal, but the marital couples group is used to encourage couples to involve their families. Although the resistance is very strong, Framo is so convinced of the strength of this method that he eventually persuaded 60% of his clientele to comply.

Sessions are composed of the husband or wife and his or her family. In order to avoid discussion about the marriage, the other spouse is not included. The goal of these sessions is to establish an adult-to-adult relationship between the husband or wife and his or her respective parents. These sessions center on the life cycle of the family, the key events, happy times, traumatic occurrences, and family structure. The process is similar to working with the nuclear family and often leads to the discovery of information about the family of origin that was previously unknown. Clarification of misunderstandings and misinterpretations of childhood perceptions can occur. Parents become real people, and patterns of the past are broken. Framo (1976) states, "The client, by having sessions with his or her family of origin, takes the problems back to where they began, thereby making available a direct route to etiological factors" (p. 197). Once these issues have been cleared up with the family of origin, the need to make irrational demands on the other spouse is gone, and the nuclear family can continue at a new level.

If clients' parents are dead, Framo suggests they bring in siblings—aunts, uncles, or any close friend of their parents. Work is done to bring back the memory of the parents, and similar changes can be made with interaction patterns. Satir uses group members in a technique she calls "family reconstruction" to act the parts of the family members in order to produce a simulation of the family of origin.

Similarly, Julius and Papp (1979) have developed a technique called family choreography with alcoholic families during work on a project funded by the National Institute on Alcohol Abuse and Alcoholism. The focus is prevention of alcoholism in children of families that have a history of drinking. The process is similar to psychodrama and requires several therapists to play the parts of the family. The client becomes the director, and family scenes are acted out. First, the family of origin is portrayed, and then a similar scene is created that depicts the nuclear family. Julius and Papp state:

> This is particularly useful in the alcoholic family system, since it enables the people taking part to perceive the drinking problem across multi-generational family lines, to observe and experience the similarities of behavior of those surrounding the alcoholic in times past and present, and to realize that while the actors may have changed from grandfather to father to husband to brother to son, the roles and situations have remained exactly the same. (p. 202)

When a scene has been repeated many times, participants begin to see their own part in the patterns and can begin to change their behavior instead of blaming others. Problems can be resolved instead of perpetuated.

In this final stage of family therapy (working on family of origin issues), changes can be made in the interaction patterns of both spouses. It is designed to halt the multigenerational process of alcohol abuse.

The Therapist's Family of Origin

When therapists are working with families it is easy for them to identify with those who have similar life experiences or values. Once a family therapist starts to side with one member or begins to treat a client like someone in his or her own family of origin (or nuclear family), he or she can no longer be an agent of change (NIAAA, 1979). When a therapist becomes the third side of a triangle by taking sides in an issue between two others, the family is likely to blame the therapist for their troubles and avoid dealing with the issues between themselves. This is much like the projection process with two parents and a child. Therapists need to examine their own relationships and the dynamics of their families of origin so that they can recognize when they are being pulled into a family, are playing out their own family role, or are failing to keep a therapeutic perspective on the family. For instance, therapists should examine how they feel about father figures because when they are working with a family that has a father like theirs, it will affect their therapeutic decisions.

In working with alcoholic families, therapists need to further examine their feelings and thoughts about alcoholism and alcoholics. Therapists' perceptions in this area come from their experiences with their own family systems. Therapists from families where there was no alcoholism or strict abstinence will look at these issues differently than those who are alcoholic or whose parents or spouses are alcoholic. Therapists who have not examined their perspectives are at risk of joining the family system of their clients and impeding family change.

Therapists should evaluate the possibility of overinvolvement with the family if they are taking sides or are rescuing a family member or are confused after a family session. Another warning sign is a feeling of pride in the family's accomplishments. Therapists should beware of telling someone in the family how to act, failing to record certain information in the case records, and viewing members of the family as either victims or villains.

To combat these tendencies, therapists must evaluate their feelings, beliefs, and biases about alcohol, alcoholics, and their roles in the dynamics of their families of origin and their nuclear families. Relationships with parents and siblings, their own birth order, and geographic location as well as local values should all be examined. Therapists should receive feedback and supervision from other professionals or work in pairs if they are being enmeshed in family dynamics. Videotaping of family sessions can be extremely valuable to the therapist and can be used for supervision and self-analysis.

ADOLESCENT ALCOHOLISM

Families with alcohol problems or those in therapy because of symptoms in a child may be concerned about the drinking habits of their teenagers. If the teen is brought to family treatment as the identified patient, a family history of the drinking patterns of all family members should be taken.

In terms of treatment, Berenson (1976b) divides adolescents with drinking problems into two categories: (1) teenagers from families in which there is no significant history of drinking problems; and (2) teenagers from families in which drinking problems exist in the parental and/or sibling subgroups.

In the first instance, Berenson uses contingency and behavioral or reciprocal social contracting, similar to that of Malout and Alexander (1974) and Stuart

(1971), whose work has been primarily with juvenile delinquents and their families. Often families are concerned with drug use, truancy and misbehavior as equally disturbing problems.

> It is important to note that the major "drinking problem" among youth today is not alcoholism, not problems associated with heavy drinking over a long period of time, but the negative consequences of intoxica- tion. These consequences include impaired driving performance, acci- dents, aggression, and violence, disturbed interpersonal relationships, property damage and impaired school and/or job performance. In youth, alcohol problems are more often associated with episodic and binge drinking than with either physical or psychological addiction to alcohol. (U.S. Department of Health and Human Services, 1981, p. 6)

In Berenson's treatment of this first category of teen drinkers, observable, acceptable behaviors are rewarded, and unacceptable behaviors are punished by withholding privileges. Parents are advised that controlling the teenager's drink- ing outside of the home is not possible but controlling behavior, whether it involves drinking or not, is within their reach. Berenson (1976b) states, "The goal is to diminish the overconcern about drinking, set effective limits, and allow the teenager an opportunity to grow up and become a social drinker, someone whose behavior is seen as coming from within himself, not from a bottle" (p. 295). If the parents are put in charge of the adolescent's behavior, they may feel more able to make changes than with an approach that tries to change the teen's thoughts and feelings.

Alcohol abuse, drug abuse, and adolescent delinquency should be viewed as a symptom of possible family maladjustment. The teen may be using these be- haviors to attract attention to a family with a severe alcohol problem in one or both parents.

When a history of the adolescent uncovers alcohol abuse in the parents or a history of problems in several family members, Berenson (1976b) focuses first on the alcohol problems in the parental subgroup. He begins by working with the most motivated spouse, and this often encourages the other spouse to enter therapy. If both spouses are alcoholic, the problem is compounded. The therapist can begin by working with the spouse who is sober at the time and switch to the other spouse as the drinking pattern shifts. By connecting the drinking behavior to presenting problems and predicting difficulty in change, the therapist can avoid jumping in to save the family and can simultaneously allow the family to take responsibility for changing.

It is valuable to stop the multigenerational transmission of alcoholism with the parents so that abusive drinking by the adolescent can be controlled (by the parents) and turned around before becoming chronic in adulthood.

AN OVERVIEW OF TREATMENT TECHNIQUES FOR FAMILY THERAPY

In Chapter 3, the etiological and philosophical bases of the communication model, systems model, structural model, and social learning model were presented. This section will cover specific family therapy techniques attributed to each of these models. This is only a brief overview of each theory, and further reading is recommended in each of these areas.

Communication Model

The communication model focuses on the development of new methods of communication. The therapists are active, directive, and involved in the process of treatment. And, depending on the chaos of the family, they may at times be nondirective and covertly influence the sessions.

This chapter has already addressed the techniques of Haley (1976), whose work in developing his strategic problem-solving theory has evolved from the communication model.

Satir (1967) is also considered to be a pioneer in the communication model area, and she clearly outlines a step-by-step process for family therapy in her book *Conjoint Family Therapy*. Her approach focuses on making families aware of their communication processes.

Initially, Satir helps to establish trust in each family member for the others. Confidentiality is explained, and she works to elicit confidence in her ability as a therapist. Next, the focus is on family awareness of behaviors and communications. She uses the "here and now" behavior of the family to help them face their problems. She employs techniques such as the life chronology (discussed in Chapter 6), a description of a typical day, acting out of an "at home" conflict situation, and an investigation of an individual's role in the family's delivery of messages.

These techniques create a new awareness in the family that can be used to change communication patterns. The new behaviors are applicable to daily life routine, and may be role-played in the family therapy session.

The length of time the family is involved in this treatment depends largely on the degree of disorganization of the family and their willingness to change. This form of treatment would be useful to families who are currently operating with old role behaviors (even though the alcoholic is sober) or those families who are chaotic due to isolation, miscommunication, or misunderstanding, and who teach these processes to their children. Conjoint family therapy is popular in the alcohol field. The role behaviors that Satir defined (see Chapter 3) have been adapted to the alcoholic family. This theory is covered in more detail in Chapter 3.

Systems Model

The techniques used by the systems model are based on Bowen's (1978) concepts of personality. The focus of therapy is on the central triadic relationship of the parents and a child. The projection process is investigated, and part of the triangle is changed so differentiation can move to a higher level. If one part of the triangle or one of the triangles in the family is changed, the whole system will change.

In a family that is emotionally charged, such as an alcoholic family, anxiety must be reduced before change can occur. If change is requested prematurely, it will create too much anxiety in the family, and they may terminate further treatment.

Initially, short-term goals are set that include all members. However, the central figures may be worked with individually or included with other family members later in the therapeutic process. The therapist helps clients see their problems in a family orientation, facilitates communication between all family members.

In addition, a detailed diagnosis of the family system is done that includes the observation of relationship triangles, an analysis of the projection by parents onto children, and a determination of the degree of individual and family differentiation. The person who is most likely to respond is determined and is usually the one who is most differentiated. This move toward individuality will increase family tension, and the family will resist this change. This resistance may have an effect on the person trying to differentiate, and he or she may become emotionally distressed and withdrawn. But true differentiation has not occurred with a physical separation, and the family may reestablish a lower level of differentiation.

The therapist encourages rationality to counter emotional responses and thus convinces the person who is attempting differentiation that he or she is doing the right thing and should resist the pull back into the ego mass of the family. The therapist must be careful not to appear to be siding with one family member against the rest, while continuing to encourage the differentiating person to respond in a less emotional way and break old patterns. This allows the family to realign in a new manner.

The therapist should also encourage the use of "I" statements to help the individual express responsibility for his or her own beliefs, feelings, and behaviors. If the differentiating person develops a new way of speaking, the family may respond in alternative ways. This is only the beginning of change, and the family may continue to resist. Until the tension is released by the family, there is potential to revert back to the old process.

After the successful differentiation of one person, there is usually a period of tranquility that may be followed by other family members also seeking a higher level of differentiation. Termination with the family occurs when widespread change has occurred. This method of treatment can be useful in short-term symptom reduction or can involve a family in years of treatment. It is useful for chronic alcoholic families to reduce emotionality and eventually attempt marital and family of origin work. Bowen (1978) has worked with spouses and children of alcoholics, when the alcoholics refused to attend therapy, and has been successful in changing the alcoholic family system enough to influence change in all of the members. However, he prefers working with the entire family.

Structural Model

The structural model was developed by Minuchin (1974) who saw individual symptoms as system-maintaining devices. He believes they are expressions of family dysfunction or are at least supported by the family system. Minuchin observed that symptoms are reinforced by family members and that a restructuring of the family must occur to reduce the symptoms.

Minuchin developed a highly structured process for family therapy with three parts: (1) the therapist joins the family in a position of leadership; (2) the therapist uncovers and evaluates the family structure; and (3) the therapist creates a situation to change the family structure.

In the initial joining, the therapist uses counseling techniques of empathy and support to adopt the family's style and blend into their world. This joining is tempered with professional objectivity, so that the therapist does not become a pawn that is moved by the family rules like other members.

Joining and accommodation techniques include: (1) maintenance, that is, support of individuals, subsystems, and alliances that exist in the family; (2) tracking of family communication patterns with clarification and reflection to let the family know they are understood; and (3) mimesis or a reflecting of the mannerisms of the family and its individual members.

An interactional diagnosis or structural diagnosis is done that focuses on family interactions. This process has six areas of evaluation:

1. family structure as a whole, including transaction patterns
2. family flexibility and capacity for change
3. sensitivity of individual members to each other in an enmeshed or a disengaged family
4. family life context with attention to areas of stress and means of support
5. family developmental stage and ability to perform stage-appropriate tasks
6. use of individual's symptoms to reinforce family structure

After the diagnosis of the family structure, the therapist creates a map or guideline for restructuring the family and establishing goals. Minuchin has developed symbols for boundaries, affiliation, overinvolvement, conflict, coalition, and detouring. He uses letters to denote family members and therapists in drawing out these maps.

When a plan has been made for change, a "restructuring" process begins. The techniques of accommodation are the beginnings of the restructuring process, which attempts to move the family toward goals established in the mapping process. Restructuring is a confrontation and challenge to the family to make a change. The therapist tries to unbalance the family and move them toward new problem-solving methods. The following are restructuring techniques:

1. Actualizing family transactional patterns. In this process the therapist engages the family in interactions so their patterns and structure can be observed, including nonverbal behaviors that may be incongruent with their verbal behavior.
2. Marking boundaries. The boundaries in a family between individuals or subsystems may be too weak (enmeshed) or too strong (rigid). By changing rules or establishing specific functions for subsystems, the therapist can strengthen enmeshed boundaries and decrease rigid boundaries.
3. Escalating stress. The therapist tries to promote a healthier resolution of stress in the sessions. Stress is created when the therapist encourages conflict, joins alliances, and emphasizes differences. The therapist then has an example of how the family responds to stress and can work toward change in the stress-reduction patterns that are maladaptive.
4. Assigning tasks. These are the homework assignments that can begin in the sessions and can be assigned for clients to work on during the week.
5. Utilizing symptoms. The therapist may rally the family around the task of removing the symptom, may exaggerate the symptom so that the family will get rid of it, may deemphasize the symptom, or may move on to a new symptom to remove the secondary gains involved with the symptom.
6. Manipulating the mood in the family. The therapist observes the family atmosphere and predominant mood and attempts to match it, as Haley recommends. Change can occur when the therapist exaggerates the mood and points out this pattern to the family by outdoing the family. If everyone is yelling, the therapist can yell louder.
7. Providing support, education, and guidance. The therapist becomes a teacher and instructs the family how to behave in a more appropriate way.

This structural method works to aid the family in building a new structure that can deal more positively with stress. Termination results when the family can resolve its present problems via the new structure.

Social Learning Model

The social learning model is based on the theories of behavior therapy. A short explanation of this theory is needed to understand the social learning model of family therapy.

There are four main steps in the process of behavior therapy. The first involves gathering data to obtain a clear picture of individuals and their environment. Depending on the presenting problem, this evaluation may include questionnaires, personal histories, standardized tests, or simply an informal interview. The second step is a determination of the areas that need remediation. This decision is shared between the client and the therapist. The third step is the intervention phase, composed of smaller units.

The fourth step is a follow-up check to determine the success of the program and decide if further procedures are needed.

In the intervention step, the behaviors that need remediation are evaluated for strength. How long have they occurred, and how often do they occur? Behaviors are often charted to establish a baseline of occurrence. This baseline is needed to determine progress. Next, reinforcers are applied to behaviors that are to be increased, and concurrent techniques are used to decrease behaviors. If behaviors are to be increased, the therapist must pick from four kinds of reinforcing procedures: (1) respondent conditioning or giving a reward every time a behavior occurs; (2) shaping, rewarding successive approximations of the behavior; (3) scheduling reinforcement based on time or number of behaviors; and (4) modeling, the imitation of behavior that is seen in others. Once the procedure is selected, a program is set up that is closely monitored by the therapist. Early in the program, the therapist should observe the client's reactions and then make periodic evaluations until the desired behavior occurs.

If a behavior is to be decreased, the therapist selects from five procedures that will reduce the occurrence of these behaviors: (1) extinction, the removal of all reinforcers; (2) saturation, the overloading of reinforcements to make the reinforcements noxious; (3) punishment, a negative response to behavior such as a slap; (4) time out, the removal of the person from the reinforcing situation; and (5) systematic desensitization (developed by Wolpe, 1973), working with phobic reactions through pairing an anxiety producing situation with a relaxed state.

The social learning model is described in more detail by Patterson (1971).

Therapists in this model begin with families by asking what they are teaching each other and how they reinforce behaviors. The therapists also establish what the family is willing to do.

The steps of working with the family parallel those of behavior therapy. First, the family is asked what behavior they want changed, and what behavior they would like substituted for it. In the second step, the family is asked to count and record the target behavior to establish a baseline. In step three, a program is established by selecting goals and techniques that use social reinforcers. Respondent conditioning is the first choice of procedures, but if that is not possible a schedule of reinforcement is established. If the behaviors to be changed are complex, shaping is used. Patterson uses contracting between family members and reports these contacts to the therapist as a social reinforcer.

Once new behaviors have been internalized, there is no further need for reinforcement. This treatment is usually short-term and nonanalytical. The therapist is interested in overt, observable behaviors. Alcoholic families who exhibit predictable patterns of role behaviors are good candidates for the social learning model. If the adaptive consequences of the drinking behavior could be learned during sober states, the need for the family to reinforce drinking will be reduced.

REFERENCES

Berenson, D. A family approach to alcoholism. *Psychiatric Opinion,* 1976, *13,* 33-38.(a)

Berenson, D. Alcohol and the family system. In P.J. Guerin (Ed.). *Family therapy: Theory and practice.* New York: Gardner Press, 1976.(b)

Berenson, D. The therapist relationship with couples with an alcoholic member. In E. Kaufman & P. Kaufman (Eds.), *Family therapy of drug and alcohol abuse.* New York: Gardner Press, 1979.

Bowen, M. Alcoholism as viewed through family systems theory and family psychotherapy. *Annals of the New York Academy of Science,* 1974, *233,* 115-122.

Bowen, M. *Family therapy in clinical practice.* New York: Jason Aronson, 1978.

Cadogan, D.A. Marital group therapy in the treatment of alcoholism. *Quarterly Journal of Studies on Alcohol,* 1973, *34,* 1187-1194.

Cadogan, D.A. Marital group therapy in alcoholism treatment. In E. Kaufman and P. Kaufman (Eds.). *Family therapy of drug and alcohol abuse.* New York: Gardner Press, 1979.

Carter, E.A. Generation after generation. In P. Papp (Ed.). *Family therapy: Full length case studies.* New York: Gardner Press, Inc., 1977.

Clarken, John F., Frances, Allen J., & Moodie, James L. Selection criteria for family therapy. *Family Process.* 1979, *18,* 391-403.

Fogarty, T.F. Marital crisis. In P. Guerin (Ed.), *Family Therapy Theory and Practice.* New York: Gardner Press, 1976.

Framo, J.L. Family of origin as a therapeutic resource for adults in marital and family therapy: You can and should go home again. *Family Process,* 1976, *15,* 193-209.

Gallant, D.M., Rich, A., Bey, E., & Tevanova. Group psychotherapy with married couples; A successful technique in New Orleans alcoholism clinic patients. *Journal of Louisiana State Medical Society,* 1970, *122,* 41-44.

Haley, J. *Problem solving therapy.* New York: Harper and Row, 1976.

Hindman, M. Family therapy and alcoholism. *Alcohol Health and Research World,* Fall, 1976, 3-9.

Julius, E.K. & Papp, P. Family choreography: A multigenerational view of an alcoholic family system. In E. Kaufman & P. Kaufman (Eds.). *Family therapy of drug and alcohol abuse.* New York: Gardner Press, Inc., 1979.

Malout, R.E., & Alexander, J.F. Family crisis intervention, a model and technique of training. In R.E. Handy & J.G. Cull (Eds.). *Therapeutic Needs of the Family.* Springfield, Ill.: Charles C Thomas, Pub. 1974.

Minuchin, S. *Families and family therapy.* Cambridge, Mass.: Harvard University Press, 1974.

NIAAA Information and Feature Service. No. 49, July 11, 1978.

NIAAA Information and Feature Service. *Counselors should study own family system.* No. 62, August 6, 1979.

Patterson, G. *Families*. Champaign, Ill.: Research Press, 1971.

Satir, V. *Conjoint family therapy* (2nd ed.). Palo Alto, Ca.: Science and Behavior Books, Inc., 1967.

Steinglass, R. An experimental treatment program for alcoholic couples. *Journal of Studies on Alcohol*, 1979, *40* (3), 159-182.

Steinglass, P., Davis, D.I. & Berenson, D. Observations of conjointly hospitalized alcoholic couples' during sobriety and intoxication: Implications for theory and therapy. *Family Process*, 1977, *16*, 1-16.

Stuart, R.B. Behavioral contracting within the families of delinquents. *Journal of Behavior Therapy and Experimental Psychiatry*, 1971, *2*, 1-11.

U.S. Department of Health and Human Services. *Guide to alcohol programs for youth*. DHHS Publication No. (ADM) 81-437. Washington, D.C.: U.S. Government Printing Office, 1977, Revised, 1981.

Wolpe, J. (Ed). *The practice of behavior therapy* (Vol. 2). New York: Pergamon Press, 1973.

Chapter 8

Related Problems: Abuse, Sexual Dysfunction, and Divorce

INTRODUCTION

The family model of treatment acknowledges that alcohol abuse is only one of the problems dysfunctional alcoholic families may bring to treatment. Family relationships, marital relationships, vocational growth, educational achievement, social relationships, and intergenerational boundaries may be suffering in these families. This chapter will cover further serious problems that often accompany alcoholism in a family: spouse abuse, child abuse and neglect, incest, sexual dysfunction, and divorce. These problems can occur in any combination and do not necessarily result because of alcoholism, nor does alcoholism result from family violence. In a review of research published in English, Orme and Remmer (1981) found no empirical data to support an association between alcoholism and child abuse. Although there does not seem to be a cause and effect relationship between these factors, there are many studies and articles that describe alcoholic families who experience violence, incest, and neglect (Browning & Boatman, 1977; Hanks & Rosenbaum, 1977; Hindman, 1977, 1979; Sanchez-Dirks, 1979; Spieker & Mouzakitis, 1976; Virkkunen, 1974). Kempe and Helfer (1972), who were first to describe the "battered child syndrome," state that alcohol is involved in one-third of child abuse cases. Virkkunen (1974), while investigating 45 incest cases, found 22 of the perpetrators were alcoholic. Often these studies are based on subjective opinions rather than hard data, and the findings are contradictory. Definitions of drinking problems vary; samples are small; and data on drug and alcohol problems are sometimes combined. Yet, the family therapist must be alert for signs of family violence and incest as possible issues in working with the alcoholic family.

FAMILY VIOLENCE: ABUSE AND NEGLECT

For years child abuse was ignored, but in the 1960s dramatic child abuse cases stirred public awareness and encouraged research in the detection and prevention of this problem. Researchers have found four factors common in families where child abuse occurred: (1) isolation; (2) a history of abuse in the family; (3) young, inexperienced parents; and (4) greater than average complications with pregnancy (Kent, 1975; Smith, Hanson & Noble, 1974). The connection between physical abuse and alcohol can be seen in the isolation of alcoholic families and abusive families. Many alcoholics were themselves abused as children and have physical abuse and incest as part of their family history. Alcoholics often could be described by some of the characteristics that Spinetta and Rigler (1972) have found in the child abuser: (1) low frustration tolerance; (2) low self-esteem; (3) impulsivity; (4) dependency; (5) immaturity; (6) severe depression; (7) problems with role-reversals; (8) difficulty in experiencing pleasure; and (9) lack of understanding of the needs and abilities of infants and children. Cork (1969), in a study of children from alcoholic families, found that role-reversals are common, with the child performing the role of the adult and the alcoholic acting childlike in a preoccupation with self. There are other similarities in children from alcoholic families and those who are abused. Caffey (1965) found that abused children have the following characteristics: retardation, deformity, illness, behavioral problems, disobedience, delinquency, and emotional problems. Chafetz, Blane, and Hill (1971) have found that children of alcoholics have emotional and behavior problems as well as being disobedient. Children from alcoholic families and abusive families often feel ashamed of their situation and feel guilty about their part in it. Since disabled children are at high risk for child abuse, there may be a connection between fetal alcohol syndrome and child abuse. Children who have deformities or growth difficulties because of alcohol abuse by the mothers during their pregnancies may be at risk for physical abuse (Mayer & Black, 1977). Spieker and Mouzakitis (1976) found that the maltreatment children receive from alcoholic parents is not so much physical abuse as neglect.

Family violence, however, is not isolated to child abuse. The "battering family" is often seen by professionals working with abuse in families. The husband who beats his wife may beat his children, and this wife and the children may retaliate with violence against the husband as well as each other (Scott, 1974). This connection is often not made because the child protective services (who investigate child abuse) are not involved with spouse abuse. Conversely, the court system that has jurisdiction over marital disputes is not involved with child abuse. It is typical that spouse abuse often goes undetected or unreported. Often the spouse who is beaten is the wife, due to physical size and societal norms. The man plays out the "macho" role, and the wife is the victim. In American society, in the past, it has been accepted that what goes on in the home is a private domestic matter, and it may even be justifiable for a husband to beat his wife. Wives in these situations feel helpless and incompetent. They are often ridden with guilt and shame and may feel unable to make a change because they believe they deserve the punishment and can do nothing to stop it. Often, the wives are financially dependent and have children to support. They feel penniless and powerless.

Alcohol abuse does not cause marital violence, but the two behaviors seem to occur in family systems that look similar. These families are closed systems, isolated from the community, and they have many family secrets.

Beating does not necessarily occur during intoxication, and often violence is part of sober behavior (Roy, 1977). In families where violence occurs during drinking episodes, beatings do not stop when drinking stops. However, men will often drink when they feel like beating their wives because they will be released of responsibility if they are drunk (Gelles, 1974). Coleman and Straus (1979) believe the abuser uses alcohol for a "time out" from expected behavior, and they state, "Following this argument, individuals do not become violent because they are drunk, but get drunk so they may become violent" (p. 5). Violence is affected by societal values. Linking spouse battering to alcohol abuse neglects the subservient role of women in society, the problems of marriage as an institution, and the use of alcohol as a means of asserting power and dominance (Sanchez-Dirks, 1979). American society accepts violence as a way to solve problems—the West was settled by those who were fastest on the draw. Physical punishment was (and is) used in schools, and the death penalty has been established as a deterrent to violent crimes. Television and movies cash in on Americans' love for violence. As stress levels increase in our society, violence seems to become the way to solve problems. Similarly, as stress increases in the alcoholic family with alcohol abuse or sobriety, the tendency to use violence to solve problems increases. Steinmetz and Straus (1974) have found that the more intimate the relationships of a group, the higher is the level of conflict. Since the family is the most intimate group in society, the level of conflict is very high. They also believe that conflict is an integral part of the family, but as long as society does not see family conflict as wrong, there will be reluctance in the family to learn nonviolent ways to solve problems.

The problem of abuse in the family is multicausal. Poverty, negative family circumstances, and occupational and emotional problems contribute to abuse along with drinking behavior. In looking at the alcoholic-abusive family, Flanzer (1981) identified three areas of abuse and neglect: (1) the drinker hits others; (2) the drinker is hit by others (being an easy target); and (3) children are neglected. Flanzer has defined violence in the family as a stabilizing factor much like the function of drinking behavior. He says, "Family violence works! It is initially a very effective form of conflict resolution. The abuser uses it to reinstate the 'steady state,' i.e., to ward off any attempt at change taking place within the family" (p. 30). This necessitates rigid role behavior or a reversal of roles to allow the family to survive. Role models often come from the family of origin, where abuse occurred. Parenting styles are learned from the family of origin, as well as role expectations. If the family of origin's values designed men to play a macho role or if women were seen as victims and children were beaten, the chances are great that these values and behaviors will be recreated in the nuclear family.

When parents use violence to discipline their children, they teach them to hit if they are angry or to hit if they want to control. These children learn how to hit from the people who teach them how to love. Flanzer (1981) says, "The message is clear: hitting and loving go together. If you don't hit, you don't love" (p. 31). In this situation, parenting equals hitting. Flanzer further describes the potential abuser as longing to be a "big adult" and to be able to control children. If these are children of alcoholics, they learn two destructive methods of problem solving: drinking and hitting. Abusers rarely take responsibility for their actions, projecting blame for the abuse onto others. They usually have high role expectations of their victims, who never seem to meet the goals. Abusers are usually jealous and possessive of their victims and keep them isolated from others.

Flanzer describes the victim as socially isolated and ashamed of the scars of the abuse. The blame projected by the abuser becomes internalized and further isolates him or her from others. The victim takes the abuse deservingly in his or her own mind and never waivers in family loyalty.

Flanzer describes a third role in the abuse triangle—the "rescuer." The rescuer is a person with good intentions who enjoys controlling and becomes enmeshed in the problem between the abuser and the victim. The therapist can become a rescuer and reduce tension in the relationship between the abuser and the victim. If the rescuer takes sides, he or she will get blamed for everything and will also assume the role of the victim.

This nuclear family triangle is often a mirroring of similar triangles and ways of relating that were found in one or both of the spouses' families of origin. Abuse is intergenerational much like alcoholism. Hanks and Rosenbaum (1977), in a study of 22 women who had lived with violent alcohol-abusing men, found three distinct types of families of origin in these women. These histories suggest that they carried the conditions that existed in their families of origin into their marriages. The three types of family of origin were: subtly controlling mother/figurehead father, submissive mother/dictatorial father, and disturbed mother/multiple fathers.

In the first category of subtly controlling mother/figurehead father, the father seemed to be dominant on the surface, while the mother appeared passive and supportive. With a closer look, the mother's subtle control was apparent in the way she treated the father (as being childish and unable to cope). The mother was the controller but allowed the father to appear as the authority. Outwardly, these appear to be stable families. They never argue, and the daughters described these marriages as ideal and perfect. These perfect couples, however, produced daughters who became involved with violent alcohol-abusing men and who often have serious emotional disorders themselves. These daughters married to escape their home and did not know their husbands drank before they married them. They described their spouses as perfect, except for their drinking, and rarely brought charges against them for the abuse. These women did not feel they were in danger despite personal injury and physical damage. These couples reported being closer after violent episodes and would project the blame for these episodes onto outside sources (i.e., the police or friends). These violent encounters would occur when the women encouraged the men to do better, but the men saw this as criticism, which recreated situations like those in their families of origin and led to violent behavior on the part of the men.

In the women's families of origin the mothers were overprotective. The fathers overcompensated by being strict and punished the daughters severely. This situation put the daughters between their parents.

The parallels between the women's families of origin and their nuclear families were striking. Both mothers and daughters married men who needed rescuing. The fathers inappropriately and severely punished the daughters, and they married husbands who continued this pattern. Their mothers drove a wedge between the daughters and their fathers, and the daughters drove a wedge between their husband and their children. The marriages in both families were stable in spite of chronic unhappiness. The parents wanted to present a good face to the community, and these women and their husbands blamed the community. Both of these positions created isolation for the family; there was a difference between behavior in public and in their homes.

The second category within the family of origin for these women was the submissive mother/dictatorial father. The fathers in the families of origin of these women often deserted their families, drank, and put in long hours at work. The marriages were a series of separations and reconciliations. When at home, these fathers were verbally and physically abusive to their wives, and the mothers were dependent and unassertive; many were daughters of abusive fathers.

The daughters in this group were critical of their parents. They had either been involved in family abuse or had received excessive, unsolicited affection from their fathers. When their fathers were sober, they were irritable, harsh, and intolerant of weakness or imperfection. They were critical of the mothers who tried unsuccessfully to "keep the peace." The mothers turned to their daughters for support and created a cross-generational alliance with them as their "pals." This disturbance of boundaries went further as the daughters took on adult duties to help out and became parentified. Some of the daughters became tomboys to try to gain approval from their fathers and avoid their fathers' anger. The mothers viewed their adolescent daughters as competitors for the fathers' attention and would encourage the "pal-daughters" to defy the fathers and encourage the fathers to punish the daughters for this defiance.

The daughters selected mates in an impersonal manner that was usually situational and unrelated to the men. They knew the men drank heavily. These men were hypermasculine and felt no remorse for violence. The women sheltered these men from prosecution for their crimes, and they would often brag about their husband's physical abuse and strength, which had the effect of reinforcing their husbands. The children in these nuclear families were abused, and their mothers were unable or unwilling to protect them. There were many separations and reconciliations in the nuclear family as well as in the women's families of origin. These women either had no contact with their parents or maintained a hostile dependent relationship. If there was contact, the parents became overly involved with their daughters' marriages and were active in the violent episodes of their daughters' marital disputes.

The families of origin of the women and their nuclear families were parallel in several ways. Both mothers and daughters married men they knew were violent and abused alcohol like their fathers. The lives of both families were structured around violent episodes and absences by the husbands. These women were indiscrete about sexual involvements, and these actions led to abuse from their husbands that was similar to their fathers' reactions to their adolescent sexuality. These daughters, like their mothers, were seemingly unable to terminate their unsatisfactory marital relationships.

The third group of women came from a family of origin marked by a pattern of disturbed mother/multiple fathers. In these families of origin, the fathers were abusive to the mothers and daughters as well. Their families were very mobile since the mothers would often leave their mates and return to their own mothers. The children were neglected and frequently left with relatives or friends. The mothers' relationships with their daughters were either affectionately smothering, intrusive, and overly close, or withdrawn, angry, and rejecting.

The daughters repressed their anger and became "good girls" who were indispensable to their mothers. They were parentified in their role behaviors and were used by their mothers as counselors and confidants. These daughters frequently had no peer relationships and dropped out of school. Although these children worked hard to be productive, parent-like girls, they were often scapegoated for family problems and abused. The daughters fantasized about their "good fathers" and were silently angry at the mothers' degradation of these absent men. The daughters frequently witnessed their mother's sexual promiscuity and were victims of incest by their fathers or stepfathers.

The relationships these mothers had with their families of origin were ones of rejection or distant hostile-dependence, but the families of origin in these cases did not become involved in the violence of the nuclear families. These women were usually resistant to treatment, less educated than other categories, married young, and were not motivated to change unsatisfactory relationships.

The women were mysteriously attracted to their mates, possibly in a search for the fantasized fathers. They developed quick, intense, dependent relationships and made themselves indispensable to the men (as they had done with their mothers) to keep from being abandoned. The women knew the men they married were violent alcohol abusers and were unable to list any good points about them. These couples would often separate after the violent episodes, and it was the men who would initiate reconciliation. The women would allow the men to return because they were lonely.

The indispensability that the women created made these relationships overly close in a conglomerate "we-ness," and violence was used to distance the individuals in an attempt to recover individual identity. Often the men in these relationships had a history of maternal rejection. The women could bring on violent attacks by recreating this pattern in their nuclear families by divulging infidelities.

These nuclear families paralleled the women's families of origin in several ways. First, both the mothers and daughters had difficulty maintaining consistent relationships. The daughters functioned as indispensable to both their mothers and their spouses and related to their own children much like they had been treated by their mothers, alternately smothering and neglectful. The mothers and daughters lived with a series of abusive men and because of their environments had come to expect violence and abuse.

The families of origin for these women influenced mate selection and the pattern of their nuclear families. The men that they chose were parallel to those in their own families of origin. Similarly, the nuclear families as a whole mirrored the families of origin. In these couples there appears to be no one person who is responsible for the violence. It appears to be an intergenerational pattern that perpetuates itself.

In working with these families, the person who has been abused is often the most motivated for change. Hanks and Rosenbaum (1977) found that the degree of stability in the families of origin predicted the probability of these women entering therapy. They also found a commonality in the severe degree of isolation of the women and the families. This isolation caused these women to become depressed and further dependent on their mates, making separation difficult. The goal of therapy often is to change these women's patterns of reaction to their spouses to avoid abuse and increase self-protection. If these women have left their spouses, the goal may be to provide an understanding of patterns of their families of origin and the intergenerational process of alcohol abuse and violence in order to prevent them from recreating a similar situation.

It is also useful to look at the role of the abuser in these families. Elbow (1977) found, in an attempt to maintain homeostasis, the usual coping mechanisms of the family may fail. When tension is not relieved, a person may find it difficult to maintain self-control, and violence may erupt. Elbow (1977) also conducted a study of abusers in violent marriages. She found that abusers tend to project the blame for their violence on others, may deny the need for counseling, and may deny their mates the freedom to seek counseling. The abusers insist that their mates conform to their definitions of role behavior, and the mates are often treated as possessions or ego extensions. The abusers see their mates as symbols of "significant others," often projecting attributes of their parents onto their spouses in a parentification of the mate. The abusers usually expected their marriages to be replications of their parents' marriages or antitheses of these relationships.

It is difficult to understand why battered spouses stay in these marriages unless intergenerational familial factors are examined. Several factors can contribute to the strength of this attachment: (1) frequency and severity of abuse; (2) a childhood background of abuse; (3) the degree of the victim's power and resources; (4) low self-esteem of the victim; (5) a sense of shame in the victim; and (6) love for the spouse that provides need fulfillment in the victim (Elbow, 1977).

Elbow has categorized abusers into four syndromes based on the emotional needs of each group. "Homeostasis is maintained if that basic need is met. Central, too, is the significance of the mate to the abuser" (Elbow, 1977, p. 518). These four syndromes are: (1) the controller; (2) the defender; (3) the approval seeker; and (4) the incorporator.

In the first category, the controller, the emotional need is autonomy. These abusers project blame for their behavior onto others and have no internal controls. They are controlled by external sources, and they resent these controls. Controllers are in charge of their mates' outside friendships and refuse to allow their spouses to enter therapy. The spouses are seen as possessions that cannot be lost. Violence occurs in these relationships when the abuser's authority is threatened. Abuse is then considered justifiable. Anxiety occurs for the controller when there is a loss of control or autonomy. The mate often symbolizes the parent who controlled the abuser as a child, leaving little room for autonomy. Mates are often attracted to controllers due to their ability to control events and make things happen.

The second category is the defender, whose emotional need is protection. These abusers have internal control, and their conflicts stem from a difference between desires and internal limits. Because the defender fears harm, violence is often a defense—hit before being hit. Defenders are self-righteous and are attracted to mates they perceive to be less powerful. They need their mates to cling to and depend on them so they will feel strong. They are rescuers and protectors with limits and moral prohibitions. Their mates are not allowed to leave them because defenders need to protect someone.

The third category is the approval seeker, whose emotional need is confirmation or approval of behavior. Although approval seekers have well-internalized control, they have very low feelings of self-worth. They set high expectations for themselves and are achievers but never gain satisfaction. They go out of their way to please others and become depressed when they do not succeed. Self-esteem is based on the acceptance and approval of others and must be constantly reinforced. Violence occurs when their self-worth is threatened. These abusers are usually children of overdemanding parents who withdrew approval if their high expectations were not met. The spouses of the approval seekers are often isolated because of the insatiable demands of the abusers for constant reassurance from their spouses. Withdrawal from the abusers to seek relationships with others is seen as abandonment or disapproval. Drinking may be part of the pattern of the approval seekers. They are frightened of their anger and must reduce their inhibitions with alcohol. These abusers cannot achieve intimacy, and sexual intimacy is often unattainable because of the projection of inadequacy onto the spouses. Unlike controllers, approval seekers reject therapy for themselves but will allow their spouses to go. On the other hand, abusers may come into therapy when their spouses have left the marriage or are threatening to leave. The loss of the spouse would be intolerable to the approval seeker because it indicates failure.

The fourth category is the incorporator, whose emotional need is affirmation. Incorporators need to validate their being and gain a sense of who they are. To do this they incorporate others into their personality. Thus, a good wife would make an incorporator a good husband. Incorporators need to incorporate the ego of another to experience themselves as whole people. In Bowen's terms, an incorporator has a highly undifferentiated sense of self (Bowen, 1978). These abusers may become desperate and cling to their mates. Often heavy alcohol and drug abuse occur. Incorporators came from families where children were dependent on their parents and were not allowed to develop their individuality.

Their mates are attracted to them by their strong desire for a close family. This closeness can become a prison for these mates as the incorporators control their every move out of a fear of losing their spouses.

In working with these couples, there are several things for the therapist to remember. First, never berate the abuser in front of the victim. There is a reason for the marriage, and the victim's needs are involved as well. The victims are usually ambivalent, and the therapist can work in this area of conflicting feelings. If the abuser is condemned by the therapist, the victim will feel the need to come to the spouse's defense. If the emphasis is placed on a family systems approach, the battered spouse can begin to see his or her part in the familial pattern without having to feel blamed. If the couple plans to remain together, the therapist can help the spouse find a way to avoid violence and thus instill in this person a sense of mastery. Mastery can be gained by helping the spouse make a choice and finding the best way to live with that choice. Elbow (1977) points out to these spouses that they have essentially three choices: (1) they can leave; (2) they can choose to stay and hope for change; or (3) they can stay and give up hope for change. Most often, battered spouses will choose one of the last two options. There are many reasons for maintaining these marriages, and therapists who push these victims of violence to prematurely leave their spouses may lose their clients. Therapists should be aware of three indicators that may signal a victim's readiness to leave an abusing spouse: (1) planning; (2) investment in self as a person; and (3) coming to grips with the reality of the situation (Elbow, 1977). Only after these victims search out shelter and community help, develop self-worth, find a job or decide on ways to gain financial support, and recognize that the pattern of abuse will continue are they ready to change in situations.

Intrafamilial Sexual Abuse—Incest

Another form of child abuse seen in conjunction with alcoholism is intrafamilial sexual abuse or incest. Justice and Justice (1979) state, "Incest is any sexual activity—intimate physical contact that is sexually arousing—between nonmarried members of a family" (p. 25). This can range from fondling of erogenous areas to mutual masturbation, oral-genital relations, or sexual intercourse. The most common form of incestuous relationship is father-daughter. However, incest occurs in mother-son, brother-sister, uncle-niece, grandfather-granddaughter, stepfather-stepdaughter, and any other combination of family relationships. Since this discussion is limited by the nature and scope of this book, the remainder of this discussion will focus on the most common form of incest, father-daughter.

Families that become involved in incest are not very different dynamically from abusive families. Justice and Justice state, "In both types of families, the parents are turning to the child to get their needs met. In the physically abusive family, the parent tries to beat the child into meeting his or her needs. In the incestuous family, the parent uses sex and seduction" (p. 256).

There is no one cause of incest in a family. However, there are some similarities in families where father-daughter sexual relationships occur. Usually there is an authoritarian, powerful father and a weak and helpless mother, who often suffers from depression. The daughter is in a role reversal with the mother and has assumed her sex-role position. This family is a closed system that is socially isolated from the community, and family members have a low level of differentiation. Family values are religiously conservative and moralistic. Family members see the world as black and white, and this view eases their uncertainty and low sense of self-worth by supplying definite answers to unsolvable problems.

The mother in these families is often the keeper of the secret. She refuses to choose between her husband or her daughter and allows the relationship to continue. This mother in many cases was abused herself. Summit and Kryso (1978) state, "Just as abused children are at risk of becoming abusing parents, sexually abused girls are at risk of selecting an abusive partner and failing to protect their children from intrusion" (p. 245).

In these families, the marital relationship may be in a fixed distance emotionally and sexually. Both spouses are unable to meet their needs in the marital relationship because of serious emotional cutoffs with their parents in terms of inadequate affection and nurturance (Brown, 1978). The mother will try to get the nurturance from her daughter that she did not receive from her mother, and the roles will reverse. The marital couple frequently will not be at home together during the time the children are there. The mothers may be doing shift work or working at night as a nurse or hospital aide to avoid the dysfunctional emotional and sexual relationship. If the father remains home with the daughter, a pseudomarital relationship is set up between the father and the daughter so that the father's nurturance needs can be met. Often these fathers feel such low self-worth that they are unable to go outside of the family to have their needs met due to fears of rejection.

Brown and Tyson (1978) have listed fourteen characteristics of incestuous families:

1. availability of victim—mother works at night
2. role confusion
3. sexual dysfunction in marriage
4. inability of father to meet unresolved sexual needs outside of the family
5. recent changes in the family pattern, stressors
6. extreme overprotection or overrestrictive involvement of the father in the daughter's social life
7. heightened fear of separation or abandonment by all family members
8. overprotection of younger siblings by the incest victim
9. acting out behavior by the victim
10. a child who is frequently victimized
11. male children who molest other male children; female children who molest other female children
12. unrealistic attitude of the child that the happiness and well-being of the family is her responsibility
13. parents sexually abused as children
14. a mother who spontaneously sacrifices the children's emotional or physical well-being to protect the marital relationship

If a family has some of the above characteristics and there is no incest occurring, it is probably due to: (1) a weak attachment between the father and the daughter; (2) the father has adequate inner defenses; (3) the father can meet his sexual needs outside of the family; or (4) there is a good sexual relationship between the father and the mother (Brown, 1978).

If a family comes to therapy with no previously reported incestuous relationships, yet there are some of the cues present in the family dynamics that signal incest as a possibility, a further check can be made of the individual members. Justice and Justice (1979) state, "One of the most obvious signs that incest is taking place can be seen in the mood and behavior of the daughter" (p. 155). The daughter is often depressed, withdrawn, and suspicious of others. In school, she may feel isolated and may fear that others will stare at her. As previously stated, the daughter may act as a parent, taking on adult roles and blurring generational boundaries. There is also a degree of secretiveness surrounding the daughter that may stem from the father threatening harm if their secret is not kept. This secretiveness can resemble withdrawal. These cues are common in preadolescents or adolescents while other more somatic cues are present in younger children. Justice and Justice state,

> The behavioral cues in a small child may include enuresis (bedwetting), soiling, hyperactivity, altered sleeping patterns (sleeping a lot or little at all), fears, phobias, overly compulsive behavior, learning problems, compulsive masturbation, precocious sex play, excessive curiosity about sexual matters and separation anxiety. (p. 158)

These symptoms in isolation are not sufficient to indicate sexual activity but should be coupled with family dynamics, observations, and factual data before any accusations are made. There are also cues in the father that can support assumptions. The most obvious cue is the crossing of generational boundaries by the father who behaves impulsively, irrationally, and immaturely. Another possible paternal behavior is romantic pursuit of the daughter. The father may appear to be acting more as his daughter's peer than her parent. In the same vein, the father may become jealous of his daughter's social contacts and become so authoritarian that he restricts all social contacts outside the house. The daughter may feel further trapped and hopeless and may run away from home. These families often seek therapy to get help in setting limits with their daughter. Running away is also a behavior that will alert youth service systems and police departments to potential family difficulties. However, this is not a guarantee that the incest will be uncovered unless someone working with the family can be skillful enough to recognize the potential for incest and can support the family enough to allow a member to report the occurrence of an incestuous relationship.

Other family members exhibit behaviors that can give these hypotheses support. For instance, the mother may become both a rival and a dependent childlike person to her daughter. The roles are reversed, yet there is still competition between the mother and the daughter for the father's affection. If the daughter (who is engaging in the incestuous relationship) is gaining special favors from her father over the other siblings, the mother may be angry at this daughter for occupying her special position.

Alcoholism is a possible indicator of incest if it is coupled with other cues. Browning and Boatman (1977) in a study of 14 incest cases found, "There was a strikingly high incidence of alcoholism among the fathers, and almost all were described by their wives as being prone to emotional outbursts and physical violence'' (p. 71). Virkkunen (1974) studied 43 cases of incest in which 22 cases involved alcoholism. His findings indicated that the alcoholics had been involved with criminal activities and violence prior to the incest more than the nonalcoholic group. Virkkunen states:

> In the study it was clearly discernible that alcoholized subjects experi-
> enced more often than others sexual rejection on the part of their spouse,
> and, thus, this could be regarded as a contributing factor in the evolution
> of the incest offense. . . . The cause of this appeared to be mainly
> disgust at the abuse of alcoholic drinks and its consequences, as well as
> the result of a large family and/or poor living conditions. (p. 127)

If this is the case, alcohol abuse may be a contributing factor in deteriorating marital and sexual relationships that set up a family pattern leading to incest between the father and daughter. Another possibility is that the poor marital relationships may have existed prior to the alcohol abuse. But from a systems perspective, it is not important which came first, but rather how one symptom perpetuates another in a circular pattern. The family therapist needs to evaluate the abusive family system and be aware of the possible existence of alcohol abuse, physical abuse, and sexual abuse within that system. To prevent sexual abuse or keep it from reoccurring once it has been reported, the therapist must break the cycle and remove a piece of the interaction that sets up the atmosphere for sexual abuse. To do this, the therapist can: (1) work for reduction of overinvolvement of the father and daughter; (2) improve the marital and sexual relationship of the parents; and (3) draw a boundary between the parent and child generations. This may be accomplished by reducing inappropriate role behaviors of the father and daughter or the role reversal of the mother and daughter, and encouraging the mother to assume a parental role. A further option is to work with the abusing father on family of origin issues. These are the roots of his inability to get nurturance and sexual satisfaction in an appropriate way and the source of his extreme insecurity and low sense of self-worth. In working with a sexual abuse family it is important to reduce the amount of dysfunctional role behaviors used by family members. Abusive fathers cover their insecurity and fear with hostility and play out their roles as they imagine the world sees them—as the monsters. It is most difficult for therapists to help people they view as monsters; they can only punish. The view of the parent as a monster denies that children are sexual beings and that the parents have sexual feelings for them (Justice & Justice, 1979). It also denies the strength of the circular, behavior-producing family system. Likewise, it is equally dangerous to treat the mother and daughter as victims. If the mother was a victim of incest, this may have precipitated her depressed role-behavior that contributed to the atmosphere that allowed incest to occur. This victimization of the daughter may be the beginning of a lifelong role that she continues to perpetuate by placing herself in similar positions, such as marrying an abusive man. There is a current movement to eliminate the word "victim" as a description of someone who has experienced incest and replace it with the word "survivor." There is some danger here. The connotation could be that they have survived the abuse and thus are not in need of help. Although theorists disagree on the severity of the problems of children who experience incest, there is potential for various consequences for both the child and the parents.

Justice and Justice state, "Incest does not affect every child to the same extent. Since people are unique, so are their responses to stressful and traumatic events" (p. 181). The consequences may be resolvable in a short time, or the incest may leave scars that never disappear. These consequences may occur at three different times: (1) during the incest; (2) at the discovery of the incest; and (3) when participants later have difficulties in their life-functioning and suffer long-term consequences for themselves and their children (Justice & Justice, 1979). Since incest occurs in families on an intergenerational basis, lack of attention to the children who experience incest may sentence the next generation to reexperience the family pattern.

Although sexual abuse affects the entire family at any time, possibly the most traumatic event is the discovery of the incest by someone outside the family system. Justice and Justice (1979) say, "Although in our experience the most lasting consequences usually come from the disturbed family relationships that give rise to the incest, we agree that the discovery can produce a traumatic effect" (p. 174). At the time of the discovery there is a gaping hole in the closed family structure; others have discovered the inner workings of the family. At this time, outside persons or agencies need to continue to call attention to these issues to stop the family from closing ranks and resisting change. At the time of the report of incest, the family mobile that was in a delicate balance is blown by a strong wind, causing a great disturbance in the system. The family is easier to change in this state of flux than when the wind dies down and the family regains a static balance.

Justice and Justice (1979) outline one form of working with the incestuous family in their book *The Broken Taboo*. They believe "The whole family is a 'victim' and steps must be taken to strengthen and support the family, not traumatize it further" (p. 241). To help the child, they stop the child's feelings of self-blame by: (1) giving the child support; (2) explaining that incest does happen; it is not supposed to happen; and it will stop; and (3) stating that the child is not responsible. The position they take with parents is one of understanding, without condoning or dismissing the incestuous behavior. They support the family and confront their problems. Three important points are made: (1) there are legal charges that must be dealt with; (2) incest is not acceptable and must stop; and (3) the role reversal in the family is harmful.

Justice and Justice (1979) have found that during the first therapy session the family may be angry, resentful, distrustful, and frightened. They begin with all of the family members and ask them what happened and what family problems exist. Next, they ask what has happened since the discovery of the incest. During the session the therapist observes how the family relates and begins to teach them new ways of interaction. The parents are encouraged to take responsibility verbally for the occurrence of the incest and to express their regrets for this exploitation to the child.

The next step in therapy is to place the parents in a couples group to work on marital issues. The children are added later. Justice and Justice (1979) state, "The typical problems we work on with each parent include symbiosis, marital relationship, stress reduction, sexual climate, isolation and alcoholism" (p. 246). They make three-month contracts with each couple to work on: (1) reducing symbiosis—a parent turning to the child to meet the needs of the parent; (2) strengthening the marital relationship by exchanging complaining and angry ways of communicating for active listening and the use of "I" messages that contain no blaming, defending, or judging; (3) improving the sexual climate by strengthening generational boundaries as the sexual relationship of the marital couple is improved; (4) reducing stress by eliminating stressors and using relaxation techniques; (5) reducing isolation through contacts with couples in the group; and (6) curbing alcoholism by making contracts with alcohol abusing members to stop drinking either with the help of Alcoholics Anonymous or by using the group in conjunction with family therapy.

The adults in these couples' groups work through their old feelings of depression, guilt, shame, and anger. They improve their self-images and receive information on how incest occurs in a family. Marital couples rejuvenate their sexual relationship and obtain help for sexual dysfunctions.

A second method of working with incestuous families was developed at the Child Sexual Abuse Treatment Program (CSATP) in California by Giaretto (1976). He has found in his program that family members must receive separate counseling before family therapy is useful. The Giaretto team first works individually with the child, mother, and father. They then see the mother and daughter together, then the husband and wife. After the marital counseling, the family is seen as a unit.

In 1972, some parents from this program created a self-help group for incestuous families called Parents United who employ a professional mental health worker and a paraprofessional as coleaders. The daughters of these families formed a teen group called Daughters United. These self-help groups are a useful adjunct to therapy for breaking down the isolated family. However, they can become an isolated refuge that allows the family to maintain isolation from the remainder of the community. Families need treatment even if the incestuous relationship is no longer in existence.

SEXUAL DYSFUNCTION

A brief discussion of sexual dysfunction is included in this chapter because of the occurrence of poor sexual relationships in alcoholic and abusive marriages, and the potential of sexual abuse of children in families where there is sexual dissatisfaction between the spouses. Although this is a problem that should not be overlooked, it is a subject that cannot be addressed in earnest while the issue of alcohol abuse is unresolved and there are family dynamics that maintain the dysfunction. One of the adaptive consequences of drinking may be to avoid sexual relations, or drinking may be psychologically connected to sexual intercourse. Thus, if the alcoholic gives up drinking that has been connected to sexual activity, sexual intimacy may be sacrificed when sobriety is achieved. Further, a spouse who has given up her power in the family when her husband sobers up and regains the authority position may withhold sexual favors as her last hold on power. This perpetuates sexual dysfunction in the marriage after the alcohol abuse stops. There are further connections between alcohol and specific sexual dysfunctions in both men and women. However, except for the unique interaction of alcohol and sex, sexual dysfunction in alcoholic marriages is no different from sexual dysfunction in the general population. While there are connections between alcohol abuse and sexual dysfunction, the most pervasive etiological factor of sexual difficulties in alcoholic marriages is the inability to form intimate relationships (Forrest, 1978; Howard & Howard, 1978).

Before working with couples on their sexual relationships, therapists should evaluate their own comfort level with sexual problems and their own values and feelings of sexual adequacy. Prior to making a decision to work with the couple on sexual problems or to refer to a sex therapist, an assessment should be made with the couple to evaluate their readiness to work on sexual difficulties. Clarken, Frances, and Moodie (1979) have established criteria for deciding on sex therapy or marital therapy. They found that sex therapy is indicated when: (1) the marital problem is clearly focused on sexual dysfunction; (2) there is a willingness and ability to carry out the sexual functioning tasks that would be assigned during treatment by the therapist; and (3) there is a strong attachment to the marital partner and both partners are interested in reversing the sexual dysfunction. If one of these factors is missing, the couple will probably sabotage efforts by the therapist to reverse the problematic behaviors, and task assignments will not be carried out due to a fear of being hurt (in both spouses) and a lack of trust in the relationship.

Marital therapy is indicated prior to sex therapy if: (1) sexuality is not an issue, or it is just one of many issues in marital dysfunction; (2) anger and resistance are too intense to carry out the extra session tasks around sexual functioning; and (3) the couple is not committed to each other or there are covert or overt behaviors to dissolve the marriage (Clarken, Frances, & Moodie, 1979).

If sex therapy is the choice, the therapist should work with the relationship between the couple and not allow one spouse to blame the other for sexual difficulties. In the alcoholic marriage, problems are perpetuated by blame and projection of inadequacies onto the spouse. Barnard (1981) gives an example of this relationship interaction in the maintenance of alcohol-sexual difficulty:

> The more alcohol is consumed the more difficult it becomes to perform adequately. As the male experiences erectile failure, more and more, he becomes more and more anxious, which lessens the likelihood of his developing and maintaining an erection. In order to protect his own fragile and threatened sense of masculinity he cuts his wife with hurtful remarks, and she becomes angry and likewise feeds into his anxiety and anger, which makes it unlikely either of them are going to be able to be sexually responsive. (p. 113)

Renshaw (LoPiccolo & LoPiccolo, 1978) has proposed a circular theory of the three A's, anger, anxiety, and alcohol, which are all connected in a circular fashion (see Figure 8-1). Anger and hurt interfere with the relaxation that is necessary to experience sexual pleasure. This results in fear of failure and anxiety. Alcoholics have often learned that anger and anxiety can be reduced by alcohol, and they turn to the old problem solver when they are worried about sexual performance. Alcohol consumption, however, interferes with sexual functioning, producing further frustration, anger, and anxiety over performing adequately.

Figure 8-1 Anxiety, Anger, Alcohol Cycle

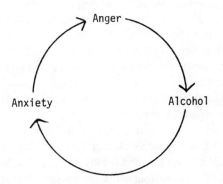

In treating the sexual relationship and attempting to break this self-destructive cycle, the therapist must not view the relationship as having an isolated sexual dysfunction that can be cured by a prescription of task assignments, but must view the relationship as made up of two people whose life experiences have brought them to the point of a self-perpetuating dilemma. The relationship is composed of two sexual beings who view their sexuality as more than just sexual intercourse. It also involves intimacy or the affective part of the relationship, the sharing, caring, and risk taking between two people. It involves reproduction and family planning, sexual identity, self-concept, role identity, and sexualization, the use of sexuality to gain a better position. All areas must be examined in the course of sex therapy.

A relationship is more than the sum of its two parts, and each member must be seen as having a unique contribution. Society and families of origin set up sex role and sex performance expectations for men and women, yet keep factual sexual information hidden, producing misconceptions and faulty ideas.

Men who abuse alcohol frequently are acting out the macho role by being aggressive, and they may appear to be without emotion or concern for the feelings of others. They are expected to be sex experts. If they fail sexually, their self-images are damaged, and they become anxious and fearful of further failure. This leads to avoidance of sexual contact or reduction of anxiety by the use of alcohol. When the condition achieves problematic proportions, men are silent and do not talk to others about an unacceptable weakness. Men from alcoholic families usually have had no model of intimacy and affection and do not know how to discuss the issue with their wives. This silent suffering can lead to loneliness, fear, despair, low self-esteem, and alcoholism (Barnard, 1981).

Women are confused about their sex role and societal expectations for their sexual functioning. They may not be certain if they are supposed to enjoy sex or participate only for purposes of reproduction and to please men. If these women are from alcoholic families, they can be playing out roles from their families of origin, or they may have negative opinions of sex if they were sexually abused by their alcoholic fathers. Because women tend to talk less about sex than men, they may have more misconceptions and believe that their self-worth is defined by the degree men value them. Self-worth, then, becomes dependent on another. Women also make a cognitive connection between alcohol and sexual functioning and may be unable to differentiate the two (Barnard, 1981).

When family, marital, individual, and family of origin dynamics have been explored and the therapist feels comfortable in working on sexual issues, there are several books available that contain specific techniques for working with sexual dysfunction (Fleit, 1979; LoPiccolo & LoPiccolo, 1978; Masters & Johnson, 1970; Sager, 1974). When working with motivated families, Masters and Johnson (1970) and Sager (1974) have found that many sexual dysfunctions have extremely high cure rates: vaginismus, 100%; premature ejaculation, 98%; ejaculatory incompetence, 82%; organismic dysfunction in the female, 83%; secondary impotence, 70-80%; and primary impotence, 55%. Sex therapy can be very rewarding for marital couples who had previously resolved issues that would preclude working on sexual dysfunctions. This area should not be overlooked by therapists working with alcoholic or problem drinking families. If the therapist is uncomfortable in working with a couple on their sexual dysfunction, a referral should be made to a sex therapist.

DIVORCE

A therapist who works with alcoholic abusive families will frequently have to address the issue of divorce. Families may see divorce as a solution to unresolvable difficulties; they may need help in making a decision to stay together or separate; or the family may already be in the process of divorce. Although marital issues are best worked out if the children are not involved, divorce is a family issue. The children are affected and should not be ignored by the therapist. This does not mean that the children should share in making the decision if the parents should divorce. Once this decision is made, however, it should not be kept a secret from the children.

Divorce is a major stress for the family. Even if it means an end to the violence, it is still a broken promise of ''till death do us part'' and may be seen as a failure to play out the husband and wife role. The parents can be so involved in their own adjustment and grieving that they overlook the reactions of their children. Children have different reactions to divorce according to their developmental levels and the amount of anger and fighting that continues between their parents after the divorce (Wallerstein & Kelly, 1980).

Divorce does not necessarily cause pathology in the parents or the children. In fact, divorce can improve the functioning of family members who have been living in a chaotic environment. Gardner has written two books to help families get through this stressful time with the least amount of problems, *The Parent's Book of Divorce* (Gardner, 1977) and *The Boys' and Girls' Book of Divorce* (Gardner, 1970). In these books, Gardner gives information, practical solutions to common problems, and dispels irrational ideas that children often develop during this stressful period. Children tend to blame themselves for their parents' divorce or think they can behave in certain ways to cause the parents to get back together. Children in alcoholic families can be especially vulnerable to these misconceptions because of the family's secretiveness. Children's own role behavior is also tied to their parents' behaviors.

Spouses of alcoholics may have a difficult time resolving the divorce and fully cutting the ties with the alcoholic person and the drinking behavior. The confusion can slow down the grieving process after the divorce. This process is the reverse of grieving over a death. In death, the survivor tends to view the deceased as perfect, initially, but as resolution proceeds, imperfections are remembered until the memory of the person becomes the reality of the person. In divorce, the spouse views the mate as all bad with no redeeming qualities, and as resolution proceeds positive attributes begin to surface until this mate is remembered as a real person with both good and bad traits. To help with this resolution process, the therapist can ask the spouse of the alcoholic to make two lists of characteristics of his or her mate. One column consists of the characteristics of the person, the other the features of the drinking behavior. The spouse can then recognize the positive qualities of the mate that he or she has disregarded due to the negative alcohol abuse. This step begins a healthier grieving process that will lead to resolution.

The children in an alcoholic family's divorce can have difficulties in their resolution as well. If the father is alcoholic, the mother may feel justified in restricting visitation of the children, so they will not be hurt as she was. This is a painful game that the wife can use to further punish her husband in the name of security for the children. However, this tactic deprives the children of a parent.

Children need to have a realistic picture of their parents as well. If the custodial parent denigrates the noncustodial parent or excuses his or her behavior, the children are robbed of their own opinions. In an alcoholic family, the children may be told their father or mother is sick or has a disease called alcoholism, and so the parents are getting a divorce. This can confuse the children who already have opinions about the parent and may now feel guilty about being angry at a parent who is sick or may feel deserted by a parent with whom they are aligned. Children can become angry and confused by the logic of the parents divorcing because a parent is sick.

Therapists working with alcoholic families in the process of divorce should educate the parents and the children about potential problems and misconceptions. They should help all of the family members express their ideas and feelings about the divorce. After the divorce, attention should be paid to communication processes so that the children are not used as messengers or spies between parents, and triangulation of children into unfinished parental issues is stopped.

REFERENCES

Barnard, C. *Families, alcoholism and therapy.* Springfield, Ill.: Charles C Thomas, Pub., 1981.

Bowen, M. *Family therapy in clinical practice.* New York: James Arnson, 1978.

Brown, A. A family systems approach to incest victims and their families. *The Family,* 1978, *6*(1), 9-11.

Brown, A. & Tyson, C. *Fourteen characteristics of incestuous families.* Workshop presentation to the Graduate School of Social Work, University of Utah, Salt Lake City, Utah, January, 1978.

Browning, D. & Boatman, B. Incest: Children at risk. *American Journal of Psychiatry,* 1977, *134* (1), 69-72.

Caffey, J. Significance of history in diagnosis of traumatic injury to children. *Journal of Pediatrics,* 1965, *67.*

Chafetz, M., Blane, H., & Hill, M. Children of alcoholics. *Quarterly Journal of Studies on Alcohol,* 1971, *32,* 687-698.

Clarken, J.F., Frances, A.J. & Moodie, J.L. Selection criteria for family therapy. *Family Process,* 1979, *18,* 397.

Coleman, D.H., & Straus, M.A. *Alcohol abuse and family violence.* Paper presented at the American Sociological Association Annual Meeting, 1979.

Cork, M. *The Forgotten Children.* Toronto: Paperjacks, in association with Addiction Research Foundation, 1969.

Elbow, M. Theoretical considerations of violent marriages. *Social Casework,* Nov. 1977, 515-526.

Flanzer, J. The vicious circle of alcoholism and family violence. *Alcoholism,* January-February, 1981, 30-32.

Fleit, L. *Alcohol and sexuality.* Arlington, Va.: H/P Publishing Co, 1979.

Forrest, G. *The diagnosis and treatment of alcoholism.* Springfield, Ill.: Charles C Thomas, Pub., 1978.

Gardner, R. *The boys' and girls' book about divorce.* New York: Bantam Books, 1970.

Gardner, R. *The parent's book about divorce.* New York: Bantam Books, 1977.

Gelles, R.S. *The violent home: A study of physical aggression between husbands and wives.* Beverly Hills: Sage, 1974.

Giaretto, H. The treatment of father-daughter incest: A psychosocial approach. *Children Today,* 1976, *5,* 2-5.

Hanks, S. & Rosenbaum, P. Battered women: A study of women who live with violent alcohol-abusing men. *American Journal of Orthopsychiatry,* 1977, *47*(2), 291-306.

Hindman, M. Child Abuse and Neglect: The alcoholic connection. *Alcohol Health and Research World,* 1977, *1,* 2-7.

Hindman, M. Family violence. *Alcohol Health and Research World.* Fall 1979, (1), 1-11.

Howard, D., & Howard, N. Treatment of the significant other. In S. Zimberg, J. Wallace, & S. Blume (Eds.), *Practical approaches to alcoholism psychotherapy.* New York: Plenum Press, 1978.

Justice, B., & Justice, R. *The broken taboo: sex in the family.* New York: Human Sciences Press, 1979.

Kempe, H.C., Helfer, R.E. *Helping the battered child and his family.* New York: J.B. Lippincott Co., 1972.

Kent, J.T. What is known about child abusers? In S.B. Harris (Ed.), *Child abuse present and future.* Chicago: National Committee for Prevention of Child Abuse, 1975.

LoPiccolo, J., & LoPiccolo, L. *Handbook of sex therapy.* New York: Plenum Press, 1978.

Masters, W.H., & Johnson, V.E. *Human sexual inadequacy.* Boston: Little, Brown & Co., 1970.

Mayer, J. & Black, R. The relationship between alcoholism and child abuse/neglect. In Seixas (Ed.), *Currents in epidemiological studies.* New York: Grune & Stratton, 1977.

Morgan, D. *Alcohol, disinhibition, and domination: A conceptual analysis.* Presented at a conference on Alcohol and Disinhibition sponsored by the Social Research Group, Berkeley, Calif., 1981.

Orme, T. & Remmer, J. Alcoholism and child abuse. *Journal of Studies on Alcohol,* 1981, *42*(3), 273-287.

Roy, M. Current survey of 150 Cases. In M. Roy (Ed.), *Battered women.* New York: Van Nostrand Reinhold Co., 1977.

Sager, C.J. Sexual dysfunctions and marital discord. In H.S. Kaplan (Ed.), *The new sex therapy.* New York: Brunner/Mazel, 1974.

Sanchez-Dirks, R. Reflections on family violence. *Alcohol Health and Research World*, Fall 1979, (1), 12-16.

Scott, P.D. Battered wives. *British Journal of Psychiatry*, 1974, *125*, 433-441.

Smith, S.M., Hanson, R., & Noble, S. Social aspects of the battered baby syndrome. *British Journal of Psychiatry*, 1974, *125*, 568-582.

Spieker, G. & Mouzakitis, C. *Alcohol abuse and child abuse and neglect: An inquiry into alcohol abusers' behavior toward children.* Paper presented at Alcohol and Drug Problems Association of North America, 27th Annual Meeting, New Orleans, Louisiana, September 12-16, 1976.

Spinetta, J.J., & Rigler, D. The child abusing parent: A psychological review. *Psychological Bulletin*, 1972, *77*, 296-304.

Steinmetz, S.K., & Straus, M.A. *Violence in the family.* New York: Harper and Row, 1974.

Summit, R., & Kryso, J. Sexual abuse of children: A clinical spectrum. *American Journal of Orthopsychiatry*, 1978, *48* (2) 237-251.

Virkkunen, M. Incest offences in alcoholism. *Medicine, Science and Law*, 1974, *14*, 124-128.

Wallerstein, J. & Kelly, J. *Surviving the breakup: How children and parents cope with divorce.* New York: Basic Books, 1980.

Chapter 9

Children of Alcoholics

INTRODUCTION

Chapter 8 addressed the impact of violence, sexual abuse, and divorce on children living in an alcoholic family. These are extreme circumstances and should not be ignored in the treatment of alcoholic families. However, exposure to a parent who is alcoholic or life in a family where alcohol abuse is a central dynamic that affects all of the family members can be equally damaging to the children. Children of alcoholics have been ignored by alcohol treatment agencies in favor of working with the alcoholic individually or working with the alcoholic and his or her spouse. Agencies who treat children are often unaware of the alcohol abuse in the family, or they believe that only people with special information can treat alcohol problems. It is typical to refer such families to alcohol treatment agencies as soon as alcohol becomes an issue in treatment. This would seem logical if treating the alcoholic would produce positive change in the children. However, in a study of alcoholic families in Pennsylvania, Booz-Allen and Hamilton (1974) found "the treatment and recovery of the alcoholic parent does not appear to reduce the problems experienced by the children" (p. 63).

The family system often was out of balance and unable to adjust, and the children did not give up their coping roles. Cork (1969) did a study of 115 children, between the ages of 10-16, who lived in alcoholic homes. She found that the home situations of the abstainers were not much different from those who continued to drink. These children did not report that family life became significantly better when drinking stopped in the absence of family therapy. One child described the impact of his father's sobriety in this way:

Dad's changed now that he's not drinking. He's friendlier, and he talks more. Sometimes he even tries to act like a father and makes some rules, but he never sticks to what he says. I think he's afraid we won't love him

173

if he does. My parents don't fight quite as much now but they're not really happy. Mom never lets Dad forget about his drinking days. She's still the one who runs things. Dad seems more like one of us kids. (Cork, 1969, p. 53)

This family continued to operate with a poor marital subsystem and a parent who crossed generational boundaries. The child who spoke these words is still affected by the marital fighting and a lack of consistent parenting. Children living in homes where alcohol abuse is occurring or has occurred in the past total 28-34 million (Booz-Allen & Hamilton, 1974). These children are at high risk for developing social and emotional problems, and they are twice as likely to develop alcohol-related problems as children of nonalcoholics (Bosma, 1975; Goodwin, Schulsinger, Hermansen, Gruze, & Winokur, 1973). The alcoholic parents who are raising these children, in 52% of the cases, came from homes where one or both of their parents had a drinking problem (Fox, 1968). In light of this information, it does not seem appropriate to exclude children from the treatment process. Children need to develop new channels of communication within the family, and they should have an opportunity to explain their perspective of the family process.

PROBLEMS OF THE CHILDREN

Many studies and reports have found various problems in children who live with alcoholics. Sloboda (1974) found that parents often do not live by society's rules; discipline is inconsistent and the children become confused and unable to predict parental behavior. Chafetz, Blane, & Hill (1977) did a study comparing 100 alcoholic families with 100 nonalcoholic families that were seen at a child guidance center. They found that marital instability, poor marital relationships, prolonged separations, and divorce were considerably more prevalent in the alcoholic families (41% vs. 11%). Family theory views marital disruption as a major contributor to children's symptoms. Additionally, these researchers discovered more serious illnesses and accidents (possibly as a result of neglect), as well as more school problems in alcoholic families versus nonalcoholic families. Children from alcoholic homes externalized conflict and were more often involved with police or the courts. According to Chafetz, Blane, and Hill, "this suggests that children of alcoholics have a difficult time becoming socially mature and responsible adults" (p. 696).

Hindman (1975) writes that alcoholic families are chaotic, confusing, and unpredictable to the children. Children often experience neglect, abuse, and inconsistent discipline, and they rarely experience structure. As a result, they become isolated, develop adjustment problems, and have difficulty with peer relationships.

Booz-Allen and Hamilton (1974) reported, "Having an alcoholic parent is an emotionally disturbing experience for children. If children do not resolve the problems created by parental alcoholism, they will carry them the rest of their lives" (p. 73). The most frequent disturbances they found (60%) were emotional neglect of the children and family conflict, defined as violence, aggression, fighting, arguments within the home, and spouse abuse. Emotional neglect occurred when the alcoholic withdrew from the child, building a wall that did not provide the child with communication, affection, or parenting. These families also experienced the full range of other family problems, including nonfulfillment of parental responsibilities, instability, divorce, separation, death, physical abuse, and inappropriate physical behavior to meet the needs of the parent.

The children in this study expressed strong feelings about living with an alcoholic parent. Most frequently they resented their situation, particularly the parental duties they had to perform and not having "normal" parents. Often they expressed embarrassment about their parents' inadequacies and lack of responsiveness. They did not bring their friends home because they did not want them to witness the chaos of their home. They also expressed a full range of feelings, including love, admiration, respect, fear, anger, hate, guilt, and loneliness. The children had a need to love their parents, but they had ambivalent feelings that caused them confusion.

As the children grew up in these families they experienced various problems. Young children developed school problems, delinquency, and fighting. A high percentage of the children had difficulties in developing relationships with peers of the opposite and same sex. Less common problems included alcohol and drug abuse, depression and suicidal tendencies, repressed emotions, and a lack of self-confidence and direction.

Children were at a higher risk of developing problems when they: (1) belonged to a lower socioeconomic group; (2) witnessed or experienced physical abuse; (3) were six years old or younger at the onset of the parental alcohol abuse; (4) were an only or oldest child; and (5) lived in a nonsupportive family situation. These are the children who gain the least from parental treatment and need to be included in a family treatment process. Although children's personalities, attributes, and personal internal resources determine the degree of difficulties they will have, the researchers felt, "the nuclear and extended family had the greatest potential for positively affecting the child" (Booz-Allen & Hamilton, 1974, p. 76).

Hecht (1973) focused on the alcoholic family and concluded that communication was often incongruent, unclear, and led to the isolation of family members. Children observed their parents say one thing and do another and would not know which message to respond to. If these messages became "double binds," the children could not win with either choice. Spouses of alcoholics would often protect the child with halftruths about the alcoholic, but unfortunately the children came to believe that parents could not be trusted. To survive in this environment, the children learned to ignore verbal messages and watch for actions and deeds. Similarly, the children imitated the parental communication style of fighting and hostile sarcasm, often acting out their impulses. Children living in these systems felt alone and had difficulty trusting others.

These families had further difficulties with role behavior. The parents did not perform parental duties, and sex role models were distorted or nonexistent. Children had also crossed generational boundaries and were functioning as parents in many areas. Also, family members took on survival role behaviors when the alcoholic was drinking.

Inconsistencies in discipline made it difficult for children to see a clear cause and effect structure of the world. Family rules were not clear cut and frequently changed. It is generally axiomatic that, when the parental unit is overly involved with alcohol, it is difficult for them to understand their children's dilemma.

Hecht (1973) reported that children, on the other hand, had a great need to love their parents, but when their parents were abusing alcohol or neglecting them, they become angry. This anger was not directed at their parents but turned inward. The children also were afraid that matters would worsen, and their home would disappear. If the children lived in a single parent family, this fear often became reality if the parent entered inpatient treatment or was incapable of providing a home for the children. The children could be placed in a foster home or institution until the parent was capable of parenting again. This need to love a parent and have that love returned caused the children distress when the parent was drinking. They then became ashamed of the parent. Their anger and resentment were translated into rebellious behavior. Ironically, this rebellious behavior may have been the very thing that led the children to be placed away from their parents. The child often became the "bad" person, and the alcoholic was hidden and protected by other family members.

Clinebell (1968) has reported four factors that produce damage in the lives of children of alcoholics. The first factor is role reversal. Children may undertake parental duties because the parent is unable or because responsibilities are forced on the children. Also, the alcoholic may be treated as a child and, in return, act helpless. In incestuous families, the daughter and mother switch roles. Second, an inconsistent and unpredictable relationship with the alcoholic is emotionally depriving to the child. Third, the nonalcoholic inadequate parent is struggling with major problems, and because his or her own needs are unmet, he or she is unable to attend to the needs of the children. The fourth damaging factor is social isolation of the family as protection from further pain and suffering. Due to embarrassment, the family builds a wall of defenses around itself that leaves no room for social relationships or adequate peer relationships for the children. Although these conditions do not occur in all alcoholic families, they are damaging when they do exist.

Cork (1969) interviewed 115 children who lived in alcoholic families to gain an understanding of the child's perspective. She found that children became so absorbed in family problems that they were unable to develop a sense of responsibility or an ability to solve problems. These children were dealing with adult problems and had not expressed their feelings about this with others. As Cork interviewed them, they enthusiastically talked about a subject that was ordinarily taboo.

The following is a list of some of the children's concerns:

1. They would not go to a friend's house because they would not dare reciprocate and invite friends to their homes due to the unpredictable and embarrassing behaviors of their parents.
2. They were angry at everybody.
3. They were preoccupied at school with worry about what would happen when they returned home.
4. They envied their friends who seemed to have fun with their families.
5. When they were only children, they felt alone.
6. When both parents were drinking, the children felt neglected.
7. The children felt they had to be parent-like, especially if the mother was drinking.
8. If the parents were separated, the children worried about each parent's loneliness. They wished for their parents to reunite even if the home was calmer during the separation. The children seemed to feel an even deeper loss of the alcoholic parent if this person moved out of the home.
9. Adolescents were unable to separate and individuate from their parents. They did not experience a sense of responsibility or control over their lives. It was difficult to break away from somebody with whom they had no ties. One child said poignantly, "I want to be somebody, but I feel like a nobody."
10. The children often excused the alcoholic for his or her behavior and condemned the nonalcoholics for being hostile and angry. Children could deduce from this that love and caring would cure alcoholism. Research unfortunately indicates that many do marry alcoholics to try out their hypothesis.
11. These children experienced multiple separations and reunions of their parents and learned not to depend on any consistent state.
12. Even when the alcoholics stopped drinking, the children continued to have problems.

Additionally, the study surveyed: (1) children's focus of concern in their family life; (2) how they felt they were affected by having an alcoholic parent; (3) their views about drinking; (4) problems caused by drinking; and (5) their attitudes about their own future use of alcohol. Interestingly, the children's primary concern about their family was not alcohol consumption. The main concerns were parental fighting and quarreling and a lack of interest in them by both parents (see Table 9-1). Children felt affected in many ways by parental alcoholism, and the largest group made a choice not to drink because they were afraid of being like their alcoholic parents. Approximately two-thirds said they would never drink for various reasons, and one-third said they would drink in moderation. Five children were already drinking. Ironically, if previous research is correct, 50%-60% of these children who have decided not to drink or drink moderately will become alcoholic. If this is the case, making a decision about drinking alone, without further therapy to eliminate the child and family problems, is not enough to prevent alcoholism in these children. Cork was distressed by the fact that the children she had rated as most disturbed were the children who planned to drink moderately or were already drinking.

Cork also looked at the grandparents of these children and found that two-thirds of the fathers of alcoholic parents were alcoholic and 10% of their mothers were alcoholic. One-half of the fathers and 7% of the mothers of the nonalcoholic parents were alcoholic. This seems to substantiate theories of an intergenerational process and makes these third-generation children truly at high risk, even though they have cognitively decided not to drink like their alcoholic parents.

Although this could point to a genetically inherited problem, there are many other characteristics of interpersonal relationships and interpersonal problems that may be contributors as well. Cork deduced from her work that, "the key to alcoholism lies in the interpersonal relationships within the family" (p. 79). She felt the major environmental stresses of the parents and grandparents in this study were difficulties in marriage and family life.

Table 9-1 Children's Focus of Concern in Their Family Life

Concern	No. of Children
Parental fighting and quarreling	98
Lack of interest of alcoholic parent	96
Lack of interest of nonalcoholic parent	73
Unhappiness of parent	35
Drunkenness	6
Drinking	1

*Some children responded with more than one answer.

Source: Reprinted with permission from the Alcoholism & Drug Addiction Foundation, Toronto, Ontario, Canada. December, 1981.

Studies of the children of alcoholics have revealed a wide range of child and family problems that occurs in alcoholic families, depending on the nature of the study and the questions asked. There appear to be two focuses, an individual focus on the problems of children and a second focus on family relationship problems. Table 9-2 is a grouping of the reported problems of the child who lives in an alcoholic family. The areas of difficulties are: (1) physical and emotional neglect; (2) acting out behaviors; (3) emotional reactions to alcoholism and chaotic family life; and (4) social and interpersonal difficulties. It is possible that all of these individual problems are a result of living in a system that is not functioning in the best interests of its members.

When the mother is alcoholic, children experience more of these problems than when they live with an alcoholic father. When both parents are alcoholic, the child

---

Table 9-2 Problems of Children Who Live in Alcoholic Families

Physical Neglect or Abuse

serious illness
accidents

Acting Out Behaviors

involvement with police and courts
aggression
alcohol and drug abuse

Emotional Reactions to Alcoholism and Chaotic Family Life

suicidal tendencies
depression
repressed emotions
lack of self-confidence
lack of life direction
fear of abandonment
afraid of future

Social and Interpersonal Difficulties

family relationship problems
peer problems
adjustment problems
feeling different from norm
embarrassment
overresponsible
feel unloved and unable to trust

is without a parental resource (Cork, 1969; Fox, 1968). Table 9-3 is a list of family problems divided among the dyadic marital relationship, the parental relationship, and triadic parent-child relationships. Family therapy treats dysfunctional family relationships, separates overinvolved coalitions and joins underinvolved members, reduces family tension, and creates a new family balance at a higher level of functioning. This allows for each member to feel more fully centered and self-determined. As a result, the adaptive consequences of alcoholism are reduced or eliminated, and problem symptomatology in the children and parents often disappears. Family conflicts produce persons with a high degree of inner tension who may reduce anxiety with alcohol consumption (McCord, McCord, & Gudeman, 1960). If this family conflict is reduced, the inner tension of the alcoholic and the drinking may also be reduced or eliminated. With a reduction of family tension, individual members are able to survive in the family without role behavior and can pursue self-determination that is not dependent on another family member.

Table 9-3 Problems of the Alcoholic Family that Affect More Than One Person

Marital

marital instability and fighting
prolonged marital separation
divorce
death of a spouse
physical abuse of a spouse

Parental

inadequate parenting
lack of structure
inconsistencies
emotional neglect of children
inability or unwillingness to perform parental duties

Cross Boundaries — Parent and Child Relationships

physical and sexual abuse of children
parentification of a child
role reversal
family conflict
isolation of family from society
isolation of individual family members within the family
incongruent communications
lack of trust between family members
family secrets

Role Behavior in Children of Alcoholics

Satir (Bandler, Grender, & Satir, 1976), a pioneer in family therapy, identified role behaviors that family members play when they are under stress. Family members work hard at these roles to save the family system at the expense of their own emotional and physical health. Satir identifies these roles as:

1. the placater who agrees with everyone, appears helpless, and feels worthless.
2. the blamer who disagrees and blames but feels lonely and unsuccessful.
3. the superreasonable or computer who is logical and computes in a calm way but feels vulnerable.
4. the distractor or irrelevant who makes no sense, is obtuse and off the subject, and feels nobody cares.

These roles hide the true feelings of these people and interfere with clear, congruent communication. When these role behaviors fail and the stress continues, family members change roles in a desperate attempt to cope.

Wegscheider (1981), a student of Satir's, has identified role behaviors specific to an alcoholic family. These are seen as defenses that cover the true feelings of the person and make communication difficult. These role behaviors are:

1. the dependent who is angry, rigid, perfectionist, charming, righteous and grandiose but feels guilt, hurt, shame, fear, and pain.
2. the chief enabler—a spouse, parent, or coworker who provides responsibility but feels hurt, angry, guilty, and afraid.
3. the family hero, usually the oldest child, who provides self-worth for the family with hard work, achievement, and success, but feels lonely, hurt, and inadequate. The achievement is for others and the family; the hero is not rewarded with self-worth.
4. the scapegoat, the child who acts out, abuses alcohol and drugs, and takes the focus off the seemingly unsolvable family problem of alcoholism. The scapegoat volunteers for this position but feels lonely, rejected, hurt, and angry.
5. the lost child, the child who offers relief by not being a problem. These children withdraw and are quiet and independent, but they feel lonely, hurt, and inadequate.
6. the mascot, often the youngest child, who provides fun and humor and distracts family members. They are protected from what is really happening but sense the family tension and feel insecure, frightened, and lonely.

Wegscheider has seen people play out these roles to survive in their families in her years of work with alcoholics. She uses a family approach to help all of the family members recover and reestablish a functional family system.

Black (1979, 1981) has defined the role behavior of children of alcoholics in two categories: (1) the misbehaving, obviously troubled children; and (2) the mature, stable, overachieving, behaving children that Black believes are the majority. These behaving children develop survival roles to provide their own stability. They learn the family rule—don't talk about what is happening. They detach from others, repress feelings, and organize to take care of others. In the alcoholic family, the children learn to trust only themselves, and in school they are self-reliant and set short-term goals that will lead to accomplishment. Consequently, these children develop a good self-image through their successes outside of the home. This process works well until long-term life decisions have to be made, and children of alcoholics find themselves in their midtwenties unable to cope with adulthood. Alcohol provides a reduction of loneliness and pain that these children have learned to be sensitive to. They repeat the stress reduction process that worked in their family of origin. Another option for these children is to find an alcoholic spouse to perpetuate their role behavior and take care of someone again.

In her research, Brown (1979) has found that adult children of alcoholics are unable to trust their own feelings and are afraid of not being in control. They have problems with intimacy, responsibility, identification, and expression of feelings. As children, these people learned to avoid upsetting their parents by holding in their feelings at all costs. Their parents were unpredictable, and the children never could be certain how they would react to their outward expression of feelings.

As long as these children are getting some secondary gains for their role behaviors, they maintain a positive self-image. However, when the easily achievable, short-term goals disappear and become long-term adulthood goals, there is no foundation of self-worth to fill the gap. Lack of self-worth, in the cases of these achieving children, often leads to alcohol abuse as a pain reliever.

Black (1979) divided these children into three types of role behavior:

1. "Responsible" ones are usually the oldest children who feel responsible for everyone. They provide structure for the family and become angry at themselves if they cannot control. These children are adult-like, serious, rigid, and inflexible. They have little time for play or fun. Their self-reliance leads to loneliness, and they often marry alcoholics. This role is very similar to Wegscheider's family hero.
2. "Adjusters" follow directions and must be flexible to adjust to the fighting, separation and multiple life changes of the alcoholic family. They feel they have no power over their own lives.
3. "Placaters" are emotionally sensitive children. They take care of others first to reduce their own pain and make life easier. They believe they do not

deserve to have their own needs met. They smooth over conflicts and are rewarded for their help. They work too hard at taking care of others and neglect their own feelings and needs. Placaters can become "empty-nest" alcoholics when their own children grow up and no longer need care.

An example of one of these rules is shown in the following case study. An 11-year-old girl, an adjuster, lived with an alcoholic father who was divorced when his daughter was less than a year old. His transient life style took the two of them throughout the country, and his daughter had never gone to the same school for a whole year until she was placed in a foster home (after it was discovered that she had been sexually abused by her father for five years). This child explained to a child protective services worker that she did not mind the life style except for the sexual abuse. When her father was not making progress in treatment, she explained this by saying, "You can't expect a lot from him, or you'll be disappointed." Her acceptance and adjustment was a desperate attempt to hold on to the only family member she had ever known.

Adjusters work hard at taking care of others and deny any feelings of their own. They are adaptable and adjust to many situations, but they are manipulated by others and can lose their self-esteem.

Although there are rewards for these role behaviors (responsible ones are successful; adjusters are adaptable; and placaters are appreciated), there are negative consequences for playing these roles. These children have difficulty expressing feelings, especially feelings with a negative connotation. Anger and sadness go unnoticed or were punished in their family.

These roles do not change when they leave the alcoholic family or when the alcoholic achieves sobriety without a positive change in the family system. The children relate to the behavior and attitudes of their parents and not their drinking (Cork, 1969). The children learn to deny their feelings because they are unable to tolerate their strong reactions to the family situations. They protect themselves with denial and will continue to do so even when the drinking stops.

In their report, Booz-Allen and Hamilton (1974) identified four coping mechanisms that parallel the role behaviors of children:

1. Flight—these children avoid the alcoholic by not being at home, hiding in their rooms, running away, becoming involved in activities outside of the home, going to college, getting married, getting a job, emotionally withdrawing, blocking memory, or turning to religion.
2. Fight—these are the aggressive, rebellious, acting out children that are seen as behavior problems. They sometimes end up in court or are placed out of the home.
3. Perfect child—these children never do anything wrong. They mind their parents and excel in school. Parents bring them out of the shadows to show them off as examples to the others.

4. Supercoper—these children usually are the oldest children and can become confidants of nonalcoholic spouses. They are parentified children who feel responsible for the other family members.

These role behaviors of children of alcoholics are not separate categories. Children have blends of several of these behaviors and use different ones at different times or switch to different roles. A family hero who goes off to college and is influenced by his peer group to drink abusively (and fails at school) can quickly become the scapegoat. If a scapegoat leaves home and the family is still in need of one, the next youngest may fill the scapegoat position.

Table 9-4 is a chart that combines the child behavior roles of Black, Wegscheider, and Booz-Allen and Hamilton, Inc. in an attempt to see the similarities of these role behaviors. The Satir role behaviors that pertain to all of the family members parallel the role behaviors of alcoholic children.

Table 9-4 Coping Roles

Black	Booz-Allen and Hamilton	Wegscheider	Characteristics	Satir
Adjuster	Flight	Lost Children	loneliness, isolation, escapes, never complains, "I will not cause you further problems"	Irrelevant (no place for me)
(no role)	Fight	Scapegoat	hurt, anger, rejection, feelings are close to the surface, takes the focus off of the alcoholic	Blamer (lonely and unsuccessful)
Placater	Perfect Child	Mascot	provides relief, emotionally isolated, makes others feel good	Placater (worthless)
Responsible One	Super Coper	Family Hero	loneliness, over-achiever, parentified	Super Responsible (vulnerable, no feeling)

TREATMENT TO HELP THE CHILDREN

Children who live in alcoholic families may be identified as "the problem" or may seem like perfect children. Both of these roles take the focus off the central problems of the family dynamics, the marital stress, and the tension around the abuse of alcohol. The best way to help children who live in alcoholic families is to improve the functioning of the nuclear family. Improvement in family communication patterns, rebuilding of marital and parental relationships, reestablishment of trust and respect, and facilitation of emotional contact will change the environment that is damaging to children.

If the alcoholic is still drinking, work with the nonalcoholic spouse could lead to establishing one parent that could protect and care for the children. The spouse must stop taking responsibility for the alcoholic's drinking or sobriety. It is difficult for anyone to solve a problem when someone else has taken responsibility for it. The spouse could then begin to take care of himself or herself and begin to structure the home environment, as well as consistently parent the children. Hecht (1973) states, "The spouse, as much as possible, must avoid assigning tasks to the children that they are not ready to undertake, and avoid directing toward them the anger the nonalcoholic parent feels toward the alcoholic" (p. 1767).

In addition to the family work, children can benefit from group work with other children. The group provides them with a place where they can express feelings without fear of reprisal and where role behavior is not necessary. Children also experience that they are not alone and that they can establish relationships with peers. Ackerman (1978) says, "Helping children of alcoholics to work through their feelings and establish effective relationships with others will be very helpful in overcoming the impact of an alcoholic parent" (p. 109). When the children can develop self-confidence, they feel they can control themselves and have an influence on the outcome of their lives. These feelings are preventative medicine for the children who are high risk for turning to alcohol as a problem solver.

Black (1981) uses group work with children to let them know they are not alone, that their parents' alcoholism is not their fault, that addiction is hard to stop but the parent can get help, and that the children need to take care of themselves. Black uses art therapy in her children's groups to help them talk about difficult subjects. Black (Patterson, 1980) says, "Asking youngsters to draw pictures of their family life and their views on alcoholism helps reverse a tendency in the children to deny the existence of a problem."

TREATMENT PROGRAMS

In looking at treatment programs for children from alcoholic families, it is impossible to avoid the idea of prevention. Treating the behavioral or emotional problems of children who have lived with an alcoholic parent is surely a major step in preventing these high-risk children from becoming alcoholics themselves.

Although the children have been overlooked in alcohol treatment in favor of working individually with the alcoholic or the marital couple, they are becoming a target population for prevention efforts in some areas. Treatment centers are pioneering special programs for children of their clients. Some centers provide groups for children of their clients. These are support groups with structured activities. Black (1979, 1981) has been using art therapy with groups of children in a California treatment center.

School systems are becoming aware of this high-risk group and are developing educational programming and support groups. Children Are People from Minneapolis, Minnesota train school personnel and interested communities in the techniques of beginning these programs.

Some treatment centers are beginning to include children in their treatment programming. The Johnson Institute of Minneapolis, Minnesota has a family therapy program designed to impact on the system that makes these children "at risk."

State and federal alcohol agencies are funding more prevention programming and targeting high-risk populations.

The Cambridge and Somerville Program for Alcoholism Rehabilitation (CASPAR) program in Somerville, Massachusetts has been funded by the National Institute on Alcohol Abuse and Alcoholism (NIAAA). It provides alcohol education and support groups for children from alcoholic families (Deutsch, 1982). The Nebraska Division on Alcoholism and Drug Abuse recently funded an innovative prevention-treatment program for children with alcoholic parents called Children from Alcoholic Families. This program is based on the theory of prevention through reduction of risk in the physiological, sociological, and psychological areas. There is little that can be done to move children from high risk to low risk in the physiological area. Genetically, these children may be unable to drink without problems. However, children can be educated about this high-risk factor and can be taught warning signals if they should choose to drink. Changes can be made, though, in the sociological and psychological factors that make these children high risk.

Sociologically, these children have lived in an environment where alcohol has been used abusively. People have modeled drinking to get drunk and to avoid reality. Often the other parent drank abusively, as well, or abstained and was morally critical of the spouse. Neither of these positions models a responsible approach to alcohol. In this program, parents become more aware of the model they are setting for their children, and they talk about appropriate and inappropriate drinking with their children. They can educate their children about alcohol and begin to open up communication processes in the family so that the children can come to the parents when they need answers to difficult questions. Parents are also taught new parenting strategies. Improvement in parenting skills can lower the risk factors of the children. Children who learn to make good choices, who feel responsible for their behavior, and who can control their environment are children who will grow up with more self-assurance and tolerance for stress.

Ethnic factors are examined, and the family history of alcoholism for three generations is charted in a genogram. Generally, an effort is made through education and family therapy to improve the family system, including communication patterns, parenting skills, and drinking-related values, all of which affect the child.

Psychologically, prevention of alcoholism in these children of alcoholic families involves improving self-esteem and allowing the children to feel they can make good decisions and be capable people. Chemically dependent persons are low in self-esteem, unable to cope, unable to relate to others, and lacking in decision-making ability. They also have unhealthy dependencies and a low tolerance for tension (Glenn, 1981).

To decrease these children's risk factors, work is done to promote positive self-images and to give them enough life skills to create successful life experiences. Group work is used to improve their ability to relate to peers, enhance their ability to make decisions, increase their independence, and develop positive techniques to help them deal with stress.

Another way of looking at this prevention-treatment strategy is Albee's model for prevention problems that are multicausal (Albee, 1981).

Figure 9-1 is an equation that can be viewed as a fraction. Prevention occurs when the numerator is reduced or the denominator is increased. Children of alcoholics can do little about the organic factors of inherited genetic predispositions to alcoholism, and it is impossible to eliminate stress from the environment. It seems more possible to increase the denominator by teaching coping skills to the children and their families, increasing the competence and self-esteem of all of the individuals involved in the program, and connecting these people with support networks in the aftercare portion of the program.

The Children from Alcoholic Families program works in three areas to increase the denominator of the prevention fraction. The children's groups increase the coping skills of the children, give them competence, and improve self-esteem. The family therapy improves the communication skills, enhances family relationships, and increases problem-solving abilities. The aftercare component provides support groups and connects families and individuals with community agencies and resources that build support networks for these children and their families.

Figure 9-1 Prevention Fraction

$$\frac{\text{Organic Factors} + \text{Stress}}{\text{Coping Skills Competence} + \text{Self-Esteem} + \text{Support Networks}}$$

The Children from Alcoholic Families program is housed in a child guidance center and is not affiliated with any alcohol treatment program, nor does it support any one treatment philosophy for alcoholism. It was created to prevent alcoholism by interrupting the intergenerational processes of alcoholism. The focus is on the children.

The program has five components:

1. Intake component. The goal of the intake component is to screen and evaluate children and families to determine family goals, degree of risk, and areas in need of ramification. Families are eligible if at least one parent has had a drinking problem or currently is drinking abusively. These families may include a parent with long-term sobriety, a parent having recently entered or completed chemical dependency treatment, or a chemically dependent parent without sobriety.

   At the intake, children are referred to an age-appropriate group; parents are placed in the parents' group; and a case manager/family therapist is assigned to the family. The groups are closed and time limited (six weeks). Family therapy occurs once a week in addition to the groups.

2. Parents' component. The parents are offered a two-pronged approach, a psychoeducational group and individual treatment for stress management. The parents' group is a forum for discussion of prevention strategies, role behaviors, family systems, and parenting education. Individual treatment includes biofeedback for increased control of automatic functions that mediate and impact upon levels of bodily tension and progressive relaxation. The client is taught how to obtain more complete relaxation in the bodily musculature most vulnerable to tension buildup.

   At least one parent is required to attend the parents' group. If the alcoholic will not attend, work is done with the spouse to improve the family environment and possibly change the family system.

3. Children's component. The children experience alcohol education, socialization, and treatment for emotional and behavioral problems through a peer group modality. Therapists attempt to induce a level of comfort conducive to the spontaneous expression of feeling. The intent of the group is that reasonable freedom of expression should exist without fear of reprisal, and rigidified role behavior should be unnecessary.

   The goals of these groups are: 1) to let the children know they are not alone; 2) to inform them that it is not their fault that their parents are alcoholics; 3) to teach the children about the nature of addictions and the difficulty their parents have in achieving and maintaining sobriety; 4) to reassure them that alcoholism is treatable; 5) to help them learn about themselves and take care of themselves; 6) to allow for expression of positive and negative feelings; 7) to foster improved peer relationship skills;

8) to teach problem-solving techniques; 9) to evaluate the level of coping skills, social skills, and overall function in conjunction with the family. This diagnostic information is needed to determine a reasonable plan for aftercare or continued treatment involvement.

4. Family component. Each family has a family therapy session once a week for six weeks. Family therapy goals are established that are unique for each family. The goal of this component is to allow the family to view the effects of alcoholism on each member and the system as a whole. The family can then view the problem existing within the family system and begin to move from an unhealthy system to a healthy system. That is, they can move from a family with secrets and limited intimacy, a family with hidden rules in which only performance has value, to a healthier family system. The healthy state allows open communication and can accept differences, negotiates rules openly, and values the feelings of its members.

Because each family is unique, the type and degree of change needed varies. However, the overall goal is movement toward a healthy system that produces children who are emotionally strong.

5. Aftercare component. When the family members have completed the six-week group and family sessions, an aftercare assessment is accomplished by gathering information from each counselor who is familiar with a family member, results of formal evaluations, and contacts with other sources in the community capable of providing a measure of social and emotional coping. The results of this assessment determine if the family member would benefit from further family therapy, inclusion in a long-term aftercare group, referral to self-help groups (i.e., Al-Anon, AA, Alateen, or Alakid), referral to the Child Guidance Center's Children of Divorce Project, or a networking of family members to outside supports and recreation facilities.

The long-term support groups are an extension of the children's groups with less intensity. Therapeutic camping experiences for these groups are being developed in conjunction with the YWCA.

The families in the program are remaining in the program beyond the six-week period and are establishing an Adult Children from Alcoholic Families Group to impact on the intergenerational issues of alcoholism.

Due to the varying range of problems and coping skills, each family is assessed individually, and risk for the children is estimated. The aftercare plan reflects the needs of the family. Booz-Allen and Hamilton (1974) determined that:

Parental alcoholism is not equally disruptive in all families. In some cases, alcoholism is a relatively minor characteristic in the total fiber of family life; the family functions well with a basically positive atmosphere, whether in spite of or because of the alcoholism of a parent. If the situation is not seriously uncomfortable, the child need not take extreme measures to defend himself against it; he simply accommodates the alcoholism as a limited problem. (p. 41)

The program focuses on the strengths of these families and gives them concrete methods for reducing the risk of their children. Families and children are not kept in the program indefinitely. They are given realistic projections for the success of their family and are encouraged to develop their own support networks and leave the program without further need for intervention.

SUMMARY

[Children of alcoholics are at high risk for developing behavioral and emotional problems, as well as alcoholism. These problems can be seen in aggressive, acting out behavior or hidden behind achieving, mature, perfect behavior. These seemingly perfect children can have difficulties in relationships as they grow older and are at risk for abusing alcohol. Even children who make a decision to avoid alcohol may turn to alcohol when they can no longer cope.]

Treatment methods for alcoholism must include the children if these problems are to be eliminated and if the intergenerational transmission of alcoholism is to be halted.

REFERENCES

Ackerman, R.J. *Children of alcoholics: A guidebook for educators, therapists and parents.* Holmes Beach, Fla.: Learning Publications, 1978.

Albee, G. Primary Prevention, a workshop presented at Kellogg Center, Lincoln, Nebraska, October 2, 1981.

Bandler, R., Grender, G., & Satir, V. *Changing with families.* Palo Alto, Calif.: Science and Behavior Books, 1976.

Black, C. Children of alcoholics. *Alcohol Health and Research World,* Fall 1979, 23-27.

Black, C. Innocent bystanders at risk: The children of alcoholics. *Alcoholism.* 1981, 22-25.

Booz-Allen & Hamilton, Inc. *An assessment of the needs of and resources for children of alcoholic parents.* Prepared for National Institute on Alcohol Abuse and Alcoholism, 1974.

Bosma, W. Alcoholism and teenagers. *Maryland State Medical Journal,* 1975, *24* (6), 62-68.

Brown, S. Kids of alcoholics. Newsweek, May 28, 1979, 82.

Chafetz, M., Blane, H., & Hill, M. Children of alcoholics: Observations in a child guidance clinic. *Quarterly Journal of Studies of Alcoholism,* 1977, *32,* 687-698.

Clinebell, N.J. Pastoral counseling of the alcoholic and his family. In R. Catanzaro (Ed.) *Alcoholism: The total treatment approach.* Springfield, Ill.: Charles C Thomas, Pub., 1968.

Cork, M. *The forgotten children.* Toronto: Alcoholism and Drug Addiction Research Foundation, 1969.

Deutsch, C. *Broken bottles, broken dreams: understanding and helping the children of alcoholics.* New York: Teachers College Press, 1982.

Evaluation Technologies, Inc. Issues and strategies in the provision of services to children of alcoholics. Rockville, Md.: National Institute of Mental Health, 1982.

Glenn, S. *Steve Glenn on Prevention.* A summary of Glenn's comments. A seminar on drug and alcohol abuse prevention, CETA Building, Omaha, Nebraska, April, 1981.

Goodwin, D.W., Schulsinger, F., Hermansen, L., Gruze, & Winokur, G. Alcohol problems in adoptees raised apart from biological parents. *Archives of General Psychiatry,* 1973, *28,* 238-243.

Fox, R. Treating the alcoholic's family. In R.J. Catanzaro (Ed.), *Alcoholism: The total treatment approach.* Springfield, Ill.: Charles C Thomas, Pub., 1968.

Hecht, M. Children of alcoholics. *American Journal of Nursing,* 1973, *73* (10), 1764-1767.

Hindman, M. Children of alcoholic parents. *Alcohol Health and Research World,* Winter 1975-76, 2-6.

McCord, W., McCord, J., & Gudeman, J. *Origins of alcoholism.* Palo Alto, Calif.: Stanford University Press, 1960.

National Institute on Alcohol Abuse and Alcoholism. *Guide to alcohol programs for youth.* Rockville, Md.: National Clearinghouse for Alcohol Information, 1980.

Patterson, R. Children of alcoholics: Focus for social worker. *The Oregonian,* March 31, 1980.

Sloboda, S. The children of alcoholics: A neglected problem. *Hospital and Community Psychiatry,* 1974, *25* (9), 605-606.

Wegscheider, S. *The family trap.* Crystal Minn.: Nurturing Networks.

Wegscheider, S. From the family trap to family freedom. *Alcoholism,* Jan/Feb. 1981, pp. 36-39.

Chapter 10

When Words Fail: Art Therapy

Much of this section on treatment has dealt with verbal techniques used in family therapy, with the exceptions of art and movement techniques covered in Chapter 6 on evaluation and diagnosis. This perspective can be limiting since people think in images as well as words. Adding the dimension of artistic expression to therapy is useful for those who are not masterful with words and for those who are skilled at verbal manipulation. Clients often make statements, such as, "I can't put it into words," or "Do you see what I mean?" Some clients have difficulty finding words or allowing themselves to talk about abstract subjects, emotions, or dilemmas. Their clarity of communication can be improved by giving them an additional mode of communication. Other people are so skilled at manipulating words that they can con their way out of receiving help in a therapeutic situation with rationalization and intellectualization. Alcoholics who have spent many years covering up their drinking and finding excuses for their behavior and absenteeism at work and in family life are often very skilled at excusing themselves from making change or clearly viewing themselves as needing to change. Art therapy has been used in alcohol treatment centers with positive outcomes (Albert-Puleo & Osha, 1976; Foulke & Keller, 1976; Schleicher, 1978). Albert-Puleo and Osha (1976), in their experience in using art therapy with alcohol and drug dependent people, found that:

Few addicts had previously participated in artistic activity. For them it is a novel form of expression offering opportunities for new kinds of mastery and it is not felt to be threatening. Because it is outside the scope of their customary manipulations, art does not readily lend itself to the intellectualization and rationalization on which addicts rely to justify their feelings and behaviors. (p. 29)

Art as a communication method can be beneficial for the other family members who have learned the family rule that if they talk about alcohol abuse, things will get worse. Art therapy is useful in breaking the silence and exposing family secrets. There may be no family rules to prevent family members from drawing the family as they view it. Sometimes it is easier for family members to talk about what they have drawn than what is happening within themselves.

Kwiatkowska (1978) describes working with a family whose presenting problem was an 18-year-old adolescent, diagnosed as schizophrenic. After working with the family in art therapy for several sessions, she used an evaluative technique to determine the family members' views of one another. Each family member was asked to use a symbol for family members to create an abstract family portrait. Kwiatkowska states, ''It introduced the problem of the father's drinking'' (pp. 145-146). The teenager, Donnie, had used a bottle of beer to represent his father in his picture. Kwiatkowska reports, ''Donnie was bitter, contemptuous and accusing; he spoke with disgust of his father's falling when drunk and his sleeping on the floor'' (p. 146). This, incidentally, was the first time a family member was able to talk about the family secret of the father's drinking.

Children have found art therapy to be helpful to them in expressing the powerful emotions they have about the parents' alcohol abuse and their own emotional and physical abuse (Black, 1979). Children can represent their feelings in their drawings and talk about how figures in the pictures are angry, without having to identify themselves as those children. Ginott (1961) states, ''Clay and paint allow fearful, fragile children to state feelings one moment and erase or negate them the next. They can commit acts that are reversible, acts than can be taken back, refined, and redefined to make it safe to explore their inner and outer world'' (p. 70).

Children often lack the verbal skills to express themselves and problem solve with words. From birth, much of the way they learn about the world is visual. Children are expert observers and store mental pictures of their world and their observations of those in it. But these children are not skilled in logical thinking and they may draw incorrect conclusions. They may carry these misperceptions into adulthood if their family environment does not allow for open discussion of all subjects. Drawing is a process that allows these images to be reexamined, clarified, and confronted, and helps the family and therapist to correct mistaken ideas such as self-blame for a parent's drinking.

Art therapy is a valuable treatment technique to use with families, children, and individuals. Denny (1969) states that it is a ''professional encounter between counselor and client where art materials and expression are introduced into the relationship in order to facilitate the release of feelings, to promote understanding of the self, to strengthen personal resources, and, most importantly to help the client take constructive action'' (p. 119). In other words, it is a form of psychotherapy that uses artistic creation as a means of communication rather than relying primarily upon verbalization.

Thus, the artwork of the clients must be treated with as much unconditional positive regard as their verbal statements. The art must be viewed as a true expression because the persons involved created the work as an extension of themselves. The artwork should not be evaluated in terms of artistic merit but be genuinely accepted for its value as a form of communication between people. The therapist is not an art teacher. Therapy is not a place for critical remarks about the quality or correctness of the artwork. Thus, if a child paints the sky with red and white stripes, the therapist will damage the therapeutic relationship by declaring that the sky should be blue. Often, writing becomes part of the artwork. If children misspell words, they do not need to be corrected.

The therapist does not need special skills in art to be able to use art expression in therapy. The therapist must, however, be open to any and all forms of artistic expression and have a desire to facilitate this expression in others. Artwork should be taken seriously, and drawings should be filed away for future reference. The clients should be discouraged from destroying their creations.

MATERIALS

Art therapy can be done with a minimum of supplies. However, it is helpful to have a variety of materials to fit various situations and to have a selection for clients to choose from. It is important to have a variety of sizes of paper. A good selection might include typing paper, 8½ by 11 inches; manilla paper, 24 by 36 inches; white school drawing paper, 18 by 24 and 24 by 36 inches; an assortment of colored construction paper; and paper rolls. Paper rolls can be purchased at school supply stores, or newsprint end rolls can be purchased very cheaply from newspaper printing plants. These are used for large wall murals. A small expenditure will cover a wide variety of media. Felt pens or markers are ideal because they are ready for use immediately and create brightly colored pictures. Cray-pas and oil pastels also give rich color and can be blended to achieve soft tones. Poster paints and brushes can be added as well. In addition to the art therapy supplies, magazines should be provided so that images and words can be cut and used for collages. These can be supplemented with wallpaper books, catalogs, comic books, scraps of cloth, yarn, and assorted items that can be glued to the collage. Clay is a refreshing departure from two-dimensional art. Plasticene is useful for including color in three-dimensional work, but red earth clay or gray clay puts people more in touch with the earth and can be kept indefinitely if stored in airtight containers and if water is added when it begins to dry.

If a large variety of materials is offered, clients may identify intuitively with a material that can express something they would otherwise not have considered.

However, visual material can be introduced into therapy with any kind and size of paper and any drawing medium. It is helpful to use adult materials (oil pastels, inks and pens) with adolescents and adults instead of media, such as crayons, that are reminiscent of childhood.

TECHNIQUES

There are many art therapy techniques and assignments that have been reported (Denny, 1969; Kwiatkowska, 1978; Landgarten, 1981; Schleicher, 1978). However, the techniques selected must incorporate the needs of the client, must be compatible with the therapist's theoretical orientation, and must be relevant to the situation.

Techniques chosen for the early sessions should be exploratory and nonthreatening since resistance may have to be overcome. In early sessions, techniques should be used to develop the relationship. Following sessions can be used to define problems, express feelings, set goals, and make behavioral changes.

Techniques can be used to promote exploration, the building of rapport, the expression of inner feelings, self-perception, and improved interpersonal relations.

Exploration

For the purposes of exploration, techniques such as automatic drawing, free drawing, or color exploration could be used. In automatic drawing or scribble drawing, the clients are encouraged to relax and make free-flowing scribble lines on paper. They may be asked to close their eyes. They make a series of drawings and then look for a pattern or design and finish by making a completed picture.

In free drawing, the choice of subject matter, material, and manner of expression are left up to the clients. They are told to express themselves freely. Clients may be asked to select a free drawing that they like least, best, or is most puzzling and then tell about it. When the clients are allowed to make choices, information can be gained by observing the process. For instance, if clients choose the same medium each time, they may fear loss of control.

In color exploration, the clients may be asked to choose the colors they like least and best and make a composition with them. They are then asked to discuss how these colors relate to each other and why they chose them. Clients may also paint or draw with colors that they feel express their moods, or they may be asked to explore one color. Figure 10-1 is a drawing done by an 11-year-old incest victim who used the color black to express her anger and the phrase "leave me alone" to refer to her anger at being sexually abused.

Figure 10-1 Black Used to Represent Anger

Rapport Building

Rapport building involves techniques such as conversational drawing and pairs projects. In conversational drawing, group members pair off and share a piece of paper between them. On this paper, they conduct a conversation with visual images. When they are finished, they discuss the process.

The technique of pairs projects requires partners to create an art object together. When they have finished, they examine the final product and talk about the interactions between them during the creation.

Expression of Inner Feelings

Inner feelings can be expressed through such techniques as: affective words; feelings x-rays; drawings of problems and feelings or dreams and fantasies; the road of life; life on a line; and paper bag masks.

Affective words are used as stimuli for painting. They can be chosen by the client or the therapist and may consist of one feeling or a combination of opposite feelings such as love and hate.

Feelings x-rays are used with children to help them identify how feelings can affect parts of their bodies and assess their impressions of where these feelings occur. The children are laid on a large piece of paper from a paper roll a little longer than their body. The therapist traces around them, hangs the paper on the wall, and says, "If I had an x-ray machine that could see inside of you that would see your feelings and not your bones, what would I see?" The children usually identify heart feelings, head feelings, and stomach feelings and can give clues to psychosomatic tendencies (see Figure 10-2).

Clients may be asked to draw problems and feelings. They may draw a recent or recurring feeling or mood. This technique requires people to become aware of their feelings and to put them into a concrete form. Figure 10-3 shows a drawing done by an incest victim who was describing her anger and sadness when she was taken from her family and placed in a foster home because incest was discovered.

Dreams and fantasies techniques can be used with children and adults. Dreams can be drawn in a sequence like a story or a cartoon. Dialogue can be added, and the interpretation should be elicited from the client. Figure 10-4 is the drawing of a 10-year-old daughter of an alcoholic. She had dreamed that a skeleton with raw meat for eyes had kidnapped her and had tricked her by being able to change into her father. In discussing the drawing, she was able to talk about her ambivalent feelings about her father and the monster he could become.

In the road of life technique, clients are asked to paint the road or path they have been following for the past several years or the road they see in the future. This allows the client to look at the directions of their lives in perspective.

In the life on a line technique, each person is given a piece of paper and is asked to draw a line representing his or her life from birth to the present. The highs and lows should be shown and identified with a word or age. On the same page, the client is asked to draw another line showing his or her drinking history. This can be helpful in connecting the increase in drinking with a decrease in life functioning (Schleicher, 1978).

Paper bag masks or paper plate masks can be used to help clients express how they feel inside or would like to feel (see Figure 10-5). Clients are simply told to draw a face on the bag or plate. These masks can also represent the various "faces" people wear at different times with different people. Clients can become more aware of the facades they use to protect or cover their real selves.

Figure 10-2 Feelings X-Ray

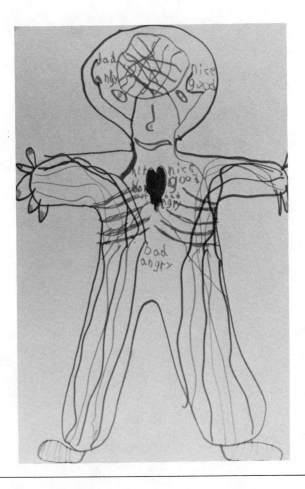

Self-Perceptions

Clients' perceptions of themselves can be shown in exercises such as, self-portraits, "my bag," and "two animals." Self-portraits can be done in a number of ways. Clients can be asked to simply draw themselves or their ideal, or the image they believe they present to others. Other versions are one-minute full-length self-portraits that force quick decisions. Clients may also represent the self-image as an animal they identify with. These self-portraits can be used throughout the therapeutic process to assess self-image or to set goals. It is

Figure 10-3 Sadness and Anger

Figure 10-4 Dream

Figure 10-5 Paper Plate Mask

interesting that incest victims often draw themselves with no bodies as if to reject their sexuality.

The "my bag" exercise is used in a group setting after the introductory stage when group members have some information about each other. Each person is instructed to bring a bag to the following session. On the outside will be a collage of pictures and words that the person assumes everyone knows about them. On the inside are the secrets that no one in the group knows. The bags are then discussed in the group, and feedback is given by the other group members.

In the "two animals" exercise, before the session, a string covered in black tempera paint or ink is dropped onto a white paper. The string can be lifted off or dragged on the paper to create a pattern. Clients are allowed to select a paper and are instructed to find two animals in the string pattern. These animals can be real or fantasy. The clients are then asked to write four statements about each animal. This experience draws on the polarities of the personality. Figure 10-6 shows a drawing of an 11-year-old girl whose alcoholic father sexually abused her for several years. Her first animal was a kangaroo who was learning how to hop. She described it as being different colors, cute, nice, and generous. The second animal was a crab arm that she described as pinchy, hard, sassy, and likely to pinch people's toes. A major difficulty for her was social relationships and her dilemma between accepting others and lashing out at others.

Figure 10-6 Two Animals

Interpersonal Relationships

Interpersonal relationships can be determined from family portraits. Each member of a family is given a piece of paper and is asked to draw the family. An alternate method is to give the family one piece of paper and ask them to make decisions about how the family will be drawn and who will be included. This can also be done with clay so that the figures can be arranged in different settings and in different proximities to one another.

Abstract family portraits where symbols can be used for the family members can be revealing (Kwiatkowska, 1978).

These drawings can give a wealth of information about the relationships of family members, coalitions, and boundaries. They are extremely useful with blended families who may be having difficulties integrating all of the members.

The family drawings of the Brown family (Figures 10-7 through 10-10) pointed out an extreme division between the parental subsystem and the sibling subsystem. This was evident in the separation of the two groups in each drawing. In two of the drawings, the parents were sitting at their bar drinking while the children watched television. This excessive drinking behavior was contributing to the inaccessibility of the parents for the children. In the stepfather's drawing (Figure 10-7), a tree was between the parents, and the children were working as a unit to "make waves." Mr. Brown explained that the children often stirred things up, and there were problems (the dead tree) between the parents. Goals for marital and family therapy were derived from this exercise.

Figure 10-7 Stepfather's Family Drawing

Figure 10-8 Mother's Family Drawing: Parents Drinking at Their Bar; Children Watching Television Upstairs

Figure 10-9 Teenage Daughter's Family Drawing: Parents at the Bar; Children Watching Television. Very Similar to Mother's Drawing

Figure 10-10 Oldest Daughter's Drawing: Similar to Stepfather's Drawing

ART THERAPY SESSIONS

In the art therapy sessions, clients are made to feel at ease, and the therapist explains that the art productions are not judged on their artistic value, but are used to enhance the therapy process. Landgarten (1981) states, ''Clients are introduced to clinical art therapy by being informed that this method is used to help them better understand themselves and how they function as individuals and/or part of a family or a group system'' (p. 4). Directives given to the clients can be in the nature of evaluation exercises, expressions of emotions, wishes, dreams and fantasies, future plans, self-images, or family constellations.

It is best to start with simple directives that require little artistic ability to reduce resistance and give the clients a positive experience. All directives should have some relevance to short- or long-term goals so that the clients are encouraged to make progress toward changing in a positive direction.

Clients are encouraged to discuss their artwork while they are creating it and after its completion. This reduces the chance the symbols will be misinterpreted by the therapist. People tend to have their own individual symbolism. Red may symbolize anger for one person while black is more descriptive of anger for another. It seems logical that clients are in the best position to make interpretations about their own work. The therapist may have opinions about interpretations, and these can be expressed as questions to the client about the work. When therapists make direct interpretations of other's work, the perspective and values of the therapist become projected onto the drawing and contaminate the interpretation. It is not necessary to convince clients of the correctness of an interpretation. It is more productive to use the artwork to stimulate communication, build rapport, encourage emoting and self-evaluation, and work toward change in a positive direction.

Drawings can be kept in files and brought to sessions to review progress and set future goals. This allows clients to review their work and take responsibility for their own change. This record of therapy is helpful for therapists. They can review the drawings for common themes and patterns that may be repeated, and the drawings can be used to confront the clients if incongruities exist.

Art therapy is especially useful for group work. The art products provide stimulation for group interaction. Quiet members can be brought into the group process when they have made a statement with a drawing or sculpture that other group members can respond to. Cooperative art tasks can be assigned to promote socialization and reproduce a situation that parallels social situations outside of the group. Clients can then try out new behaviors in a structured environment. Group murals or conjoint sculptures demand cooperative efforts, leadership and coordination among the group members. Art therapy has been used successfully in multifamily therapy groups where families take turns in focusing on their problems and receiving feedback from the other families in the group.

Family Art Therapy

Art therapy can be used in family therapy sessions for more than evaluation purposes. Art tasks can be used in the sessions in a "here and now" interchange approach. This can encourage a family to work together in new ways and develop more adaptive patterns of communication and interaction. Assignments are designed to impact on the areas that need change. If alcohol abuse is the subject of the artwork, its effect on family functioning can be examined. If alcohol abuse is absent from the work but present in the family, this contradiction can be brought out to allow the family secret to be openly confronted and discussed.

Landgarten (1981) says, "As one or more family members begin to change, the established family system is weakened" (p. 23). When the family is in this state of movement, the therapist can have an impact on the family to push this movement and help the family achieve a higher state of functioning. Often when one member changes, the family system will renew efforts to resist this change. The therapist can support the member who is changing to continue even against the pressure of the entire family.

Family art therapy is different from family therapy only in the addition of another mode of communication into the process. Instead of talking about goals, family members draw them or create them from clay. This forces a fresh examination of the family and its interactions by all members of the family and allows family members to experience each other in a unique way. When families begin to talk about experiences that occurred outside of the sessions, these can be translated into the present by assigning the family the task of recreating the scene with movable clay figures. The scene can be acted out by moving the clay figures, and alternative problem-solving and interaction techniques can be attempted by the clay family.

Family functioning can be quickly scrutinized by observing the interactions of the family. Family coalitions, boundaries, and rules can be observed, and tasks can be designed to impact on areas that need change. To increase empathy and understanding between generations and to identify projection of the parents onto the children, a drawing assignment can be made. Family members are asked to draw themselves at a time when they were younger. The parents must portray themselves as they were when they were the age of one of their children (Landgarten, 1981). This exercise will give information about alliances between parents and children. Often the father's drawing of himself as a child may be very similar to the perception of his son. This assignment brings this projection to the family's awareness.

Drawings are harder to deny or ignore than verbal expressions. When a family has to draw its problems, they must begin to face them. Landgarten says, "Laying out the family problems gives the children a sense of relief and the parents a greater awareness of the messages which they convey to the children" (p. 27). When the problems have been clearly stated the children do not have to hide them and protect the family. Often symbols reoccur in drawings, and the family does not acknowledge their presence. The therapist can bring these symbols to the awareness of the family, and family secrets can be uncovered.

In alcoholic families, members are unpracticed at expressing emotions directly, especially negative feelings. Direct expression of anger may be difficult for all of the members of the family. They may fear that direct expression of feelings will prompt a return to drinking by the alcoholic or result in an unpredictable negative response. Family members can be asked to draw their anger and give it to the family member it belongs to. This promotes direct channels of communication and eliminates triangulation of a third person. If Mother is angry with Dad for coming home late and not calling, she can direct it at him instead of yelling at her son who has forgotten to wash his hands before dinner.

Children who have withheld anger while their parents were drinking may have difficulty risking communications in a direct manner. Special task assignments can be given to the children to work on between sessions. This method was used with the Peterson family. Both parents had been through alcohol treatment and were attending several therapy groups. However, their 12-year-old daughter, Susan, was not achieving in school, was socially isolated, refused to bathe, and spent a lot of time at home in withdrawal. Shortly after the family entered therapy, Mrs. Peterson asked her husband for a divorce. Susan became more withdrawn and would rarely remember to do her household chores, and this infuriated her mother. Susan would not talk directly about her anger toward her mother for the physical abuse Susan received from her while she was drinking or her anger about the divorce. The Petersons had each aligned with one of their children and used them to intensify their own conflict. Susan had a close alliance with her father and had been compared in a negative context with her father for years. When her father moved out of the house, he left Susan alone to fight with her mother and sister. Task assignments were used to help Susan work on repressed feelings between sessions. Figure 10-11 is an exploding volcano that Susan doodled during the initial family session while her parents were talking. Figure 10-12 is the visualization of Susan's discussion, during a family session, of her struggle to communicate openly. She described herself as coming from the left side of the picture, a dark scary place where she had to hide her real self. She envisioned herself digging a hole in a wall, bit by bit, in an attempt to reach the other side, which she portrayed as a fairy tale world with a castle. The wall, she said, was the wall she had built around herself to keep from getting hurt. It was frightening to think about digging a hole in this wall because it allowed access to her from the outside world.

In later sessions, she began to identify her anger. Figures 10-13 and 10-14 show her anger as a black blob with a cutoff valve. Susan had chosen to keep this valve closed and knew that the hand in the picture that was turning the valve was hers. When the anger came out of the faucet it changed colors and looked different from

Figure 10-11 Volcano Doodle

Figure 10-12 Digging Through the Wall

the stored anger. Figure 10-14 includes her list of behaviors that would allow the anger to be released, "hit, yell, tell them I'm mad, questioning, argue, disagreement, tell friends, draw, beat pillow."

Susan was encouraged to practice these behaviors, and her mother was aware that her reaction to these expressions would be important for encouraging or discouraging Susan's efforts. Susan had difficulty in talking about her parents' drinking and her feelings about it. She was asked to write these feelings and bring them to the next session.

Figure 10-13 Anger

Figure 10-14 Dealing with Anger

Susan wrote:

I felt pretty scared when my parents were drinking. Everyday I would get snapped at for the tiniest little things, even things I didn't do. I was scared of my mom especially because she was home when I got home and she would get mad and hit me for what I thought was nothing, like leaving the cap off the toothpaste. When Dad came home things didn't change much. I would probably be at a friend's house. When I came home, usually at 5:00, dinner would be ready to eat, so we would eat dinner. After dinner we would go into the family room and watch T.V. or whatever. When I went to bed I could lay awake and listen to them fight. I would wonder about what was going to happen and when. I would wonder if they would ever quit drinking.

A lot of nights I would stay out late and come in secretly or I would spend the night at a friends (with permission, but they were just to drunk to remember). But I would come home. There was one time that I was told that if I was not home by 8:00, I should not come home for the rest of the night. So, I did just as I was told. I was out at Michelle's house past 8:00 and I wouldn't go home. I left her house about 8:30 and stayed outside in our yard for a while. I finally came in at about 8:45.

I guess things have changed since then. I only get hit when I need it (at least that's what Mom says. I think she does it just to make me mad). I don't get hit for just anything, but my Mom says that I still have a lot of my Dad's and Mom's bad qualities. The only thing I think is still bad is that I'm twelve years old and still can't stay out past dark, even in our own neighborhood.

Susan's writing allowed her to express some feelings she had held for a long time and pointed to further work to be done in the family. Both parents were projecting their own negative attributes onto Susan, and Susan was willing to assume them to maintain her place in the family structure.

Homework tasks were useful for another preadolescent girl, Nancy, whose mother divorced her alcoholic husband and moved her children thousands of miles away. The children had not had a chance to express their feelings about Dad's drinking and had a negative experience the previous summer when Dad came to visit and took the daughters shopping. He was intoxicated and passed out in a store. Nancy was asked to draw some of her memories of what it was like living with her father. The following is Nancy's description of her drawings, shown in Figures 10-15 to 10-21.

For the drawing in Figure 10-15, she said, "When the drinking of someone affects a person that cares, that person reacts back and tries to stop him from drinking." She explained Figure 10-16 as, "When someone is concerned about

Figure 10-16 Stop Drinking

Figure 10-15 "Let's go daddy!"

someone else's drinking problem they try to stop them from drinking.'' Figure 10-17 she explained as, "When someone is drunk they naturally scold or beat on someone else (not knowing what they're doing), sometimes causing that person to cry.''

For Figure 10-18, she said, "When children are hurt by words or actions they often scream or cry.''

She explained Figure 10-19 as, "The reactions of someone who is too young to understand what's going on and how it's affecting the other members (or friends) of the family.''

About Figure 10-20, she said, "When children see or hear things that they do not like it builds up in them and when they go to sleep and it forms a nightmare. Sometimes they dream what they saw—or heard but often their mind makes up scary figures to frighten them.''

About Figure 10-21, she said, "Children that have parents that drink don't like for them to drink, and all thoughts of their friends, family and how happy they appear to be, causes that child to dream of a happy family it'd like to be part of. Children with drinking parents tell themselves that when they're older they're not going to even go near a drink.''

Nancy was able to express anger, fear, and confusion and to wish for the happy family that she believed her friends had. Nancy could not claim the child in the picture as herself and needed to use general terms in her descriptions. These were her first contributions to the family sessions after many weeks of refusing to participate.

Individual Art Therapy

When it is not possible to work with families, children can benefit from individual art therapy. Changes in the family can occur through the way one family member responds to another. The following case studies are similar in that both girls were 11 years old and had been sexually abused by their fathers for several years. Only one father was alcoholic, but the family dynamics of both cases were similar. Both girls had taken on a parental role and were worried about their parents but were unable to admit or communicate negative feelings.

Cheryl

When Cheryl entered therapy, she had been living in a foster home for two weeks. A police officer had questioned her at school about her sexual abuse by her father and taken her to child protective services. She was placed in a foster home away from everything she knew. She had a new school, different friends, and only saw her family once a week for supervised visits. During her initial art therapy session, she stated that she was happy on the left side of the paper and that she was sad on the other. (See Figure 10-22.)

Figure 10-18 Crying

Figure 10-17 Scold-Cry

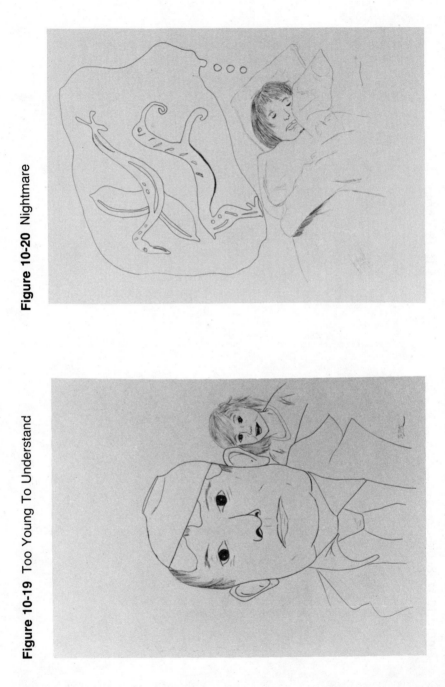

Figure 10-20 Nightmare

Figure 10-19 Too Young To Understand

Figure 10-21 Wish Dream

The girl who was sad had no body. After several sessions Cheryl drew her feelings as shown in Figure 10-23. The gray background represented her loneliness, and her expression was the emptiness and homesickness she was finally admitting to. Cheryl worked for a year making drawings about her feelings and reactions to life situations. This transferred to communication outside of the sessions, and she was able to express powerful emotions to her foster parents, friends, and caseworker. The last hurdle came in expressing these feelings to her family. Figures 10-24 and 10-25 depict the two ways she saw herself relating to her parents.

Figure 10-24 is the face she used most—one that expressed love. Figure 10-25 represents a face she hardly ever used, a face that expressed anger and blame. At this time, Cheryl was participating in family sessions in addition to her individual work. She was encouraged to take all of her drawings to her next family session to help her express these feelings to her parents. This attempt was successful and was

Figure 10-22 Happy—Sad

Figure 10-23 Loneliness

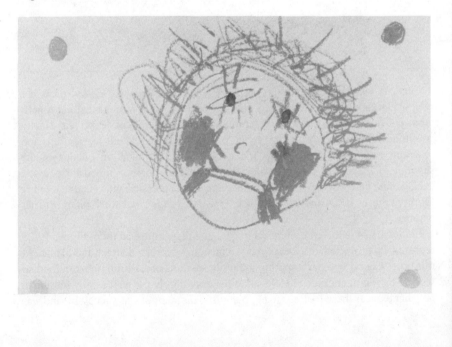

Figure 10-24 Used Most

Figure 10-25 Seldom Used

a beginning of a more direct communication pattern between Cheryl and her parents.

Figure 10-26 is the illustration of a story that Cheryl told about a princess and a wicked queen.

Cheryl was angry at her mother because she felt her mother was emotionally isolating herself from Cheryl. Cheryl wished to teach her mother to share her feelings as well. The princess in the story left the queen who was cold and did not care about the feelings of her subjects. The princess traveled through the forest of problems to the land where they needed a queen (the foster home had two boys and saw Cheryl as the daughter they never had). The people of the kingdom loved the princess and made her queen and gave her a large crown because she loved them and could express her feelings. One day the young queen invited the old queen to visit her in her new kingdom so she could learn how to be happy. The old queen came but only learned a little and then returned to her kingdom relatively unchanged. The young queen was sad but realized she might not be able to teach the old queen what she had learned. This story helped Cheryl realize she could only be responsible for her own feelings and not those of her mother.

In one of the last art therapy sessions, Cheryl took a piece of paper and spontaneously drew Figure 10-27.

She said, "Now that I don't have to hide my feelings, I feel as free as a bird who has flown out of the clouds."

Figure 10-26 Fairytale

Figure 10-27 Free as a Bird

Lee

Lee was living in a foster home when she entered therapy. Most of her life she had moved around the country with her alcoholic father. The father had taken her away from her mother when she was a baby because the mother was beating her and was unable to care for her. Lee had never attended the same school for an entire year, and her only long-term relationship had been with her father. He was often drunk, left her alone, beat her, and sexually abused her, but she would not express any displeasure for fear of losing the only family she knew. She took on parental duties and worried constantly about her father. Once she took a sixpack of beer outside and spilled it on the driveway. This ploy, she found, was unsuccessful because he just bought more. Figure 10-28 was drawn as she talked about her frustration in being unable to convince him to stop drinking beer.

In Figure 10-29 she says, "I was scared when my Dad was drinking. It made me think he was going to get in a car accident."

Much of Lee's therapy was geared toward allowing her father to solve his own problems and helping her to take care of herself. Many of her artworks contained themes of wishing to be older or living on her own. Figure 10-30 is a collage of pictures from magazines. On the left is a mother-daughter picture on which she has written, "I miss my Mom." In the center is a child descending into a hole in the

Figure 10-28 "Daddy, would you stop drinking beer!"

Figure 10-29 "I was scared when my dad was drinking. It made me think he was going to get in a car accident."

Figure 10-30 Collage

ground. This was a fantasy she had that if she could dig a hole in the ground, she and her Dad could live there and they would not need money. She was still taking on adult responsibilities by worrying about rent and paying bills. On the right side of the picture are the jaws of a shark and a picture of a makeup kit. She wrote, "I've always wanted makeup because it makes me feel older." Lee was worried that she would be left alone before she grew up.

After she had lived with her foster family for some time, her wish that these people could be her real family faded as she realized she could never occupy the same spot as the natural children in the family. Figure 10-31 is Lee's drawing of the jealousy she felt (left) while witnessing the foster mother give her natural daughter a present from her grandmother while telling Lee there was no present for her.

Figure 10-32 shows the foster family with their children and Lee (far left) feeling left out. Lee was encouraged to share these feelings with her foster family. She took the risk and achieved a new closeness that she had not experienced before.

Because Lee had moved so many times she was unskilled socially with her peers. She drew herself in Figure 10-33 as isolated in the world with everyone laughing at her.

In Figure 10-34 she drew herself popping off the page yelling, "help," while others were laughing at her. Work was done in the area of social skills, and Lee was put into a group of peers to work on these issues.

Figure 10-31 Jealousy

Figure 10-32 Foster Family and Lee

Figure 10-33 Isolated

Figure 10-34 "Help!"

SUMMARY

The addition of art activities to the therapy process can encourage emoting in families with frozen feeling, can encourage adaptive communication and healthy problem-solving techniques, and can reach those family members who are unskilled with words or who manipulate others. Art techniques have been used successfully with alcoholic clients, in group treatment, with families, and in helping children who have experienced life problems.

REFERENCES

Albert-Puleo, N. & Osha, V. Art therapy as an alcoholism treatment tool. *Alcohol Health and Research World*, Winter 1976/77, pp. 28-31.

Black, C. Children of alcoholics. *Alcohol Health and Research World*, 1979, *4*(1).

Denny, B. Art counseling in educational settings. *Personnel and Guidance Journal*, October 1969, pp. 119-124.

Foulke, W.E. & Keller, T.W. The art experience in rehabilitation. *American Journal of Art Therapy*, 1976, *15*, 75-80.

Ginott, H.G. *Group psychotherapy with children*. New York: McGraw-Hill Book Co., 1961.

Kwiatkowska, H.Y. *Family therapy and evaluation through art*. Springfield, Ill.: Charles C Thomas, Pub., 1978.

Landgarten, H.B. *Clinical art therapy*. New York: Brunner/Mazel, Pubs., 1981.

Schleicher, W.R. Art therapy with recovering alcoholics. In Goby & Keiler (Eds.). *Perspectives on the treatment of alcoholism*. Park Ridge, Ill.: Lutheran General Hospital, Inc., 1978.

SUGGESTED READINGS

American Journal of Art Therapy, 1976 to present.

Anderson, W. (Ed.), *Therapy and the arts*. New York: Harper and Row Publishers, 1977.

Art Psychotherapy, 1976 to present.

Bing, E. The conjoint family drawing. *Family Process*, 1970, *9*, 173-194.

Devine, D.K. A preliminary investigation of paintings by alcoholic men. *American Journal of Art Therapy*, 1970, *9*(3), 115-128.

Dilley, J. Adding a visual dimension to counseling. *Personnel and Guidance Journal*, Sept. 1971, 39-43.

Feder, B., & Feder, E. *The expressive art therapies*. Englewood Cliffs, N.J.: Prentice-Hall, Inc., 1981.

Forrest, G. The problems of dependency and the value of art therapy as a means of treating alcoholism. *Art Psychotherapy*, 1975, *2*, 15-43.

Gantt, L., & Schmal, M.S. *Art therapy—a bibliography*. 1940-1973, DHEW Publication No. (ADM) 74-51. Washington, D.C.: U.S. Government Printing Office, 1974.

Gardner, H. *Artful scribbles, the significance of children's drawings*. New York: Basic Books, 1980.

Harms, E. Art therapy for the drug addict. *Art Psychotherapy,* 1973, *1*(1), 55-59.

Isaacs, L.D. Art therapy group for latency age children. *Social Work,* January 1977, 57-59.

Jung, C.G. *Man and his symbols.* New York: Dell Publishing Co., 1964.

Jung, C.G. *Mandala symbolism, Bollingen series.* Princeton: University Press, 1959.

Kellogg, R. *The psychology of children's art,* 1967, New York: CRM-Random House, Inc., 1967.

Kwiatkowska, H.Y. Family art therapy. *Family Process,* 1967 *6,* 37-55.

Rhyne, J. The gestalt approach to experience art; art therapy. *Journal of Art Therapy,* July 1973, 237-248.

Rhyne, J. *The gestalt art experience.* Monterey, Calif.: Brooks/Cole, 1973.

Rubin, J. & Magnussen, M. A family art evaluation. *Family Process,* 1974, *13,* 185-200.

Sherr, C., & Hicks, H. Family drawings on a diagnostic and therapeutic technique. *Family Process,* 1975, *12,* 439.

There is a rainbow behind every dark cloud. Millbrae, Calif.: The Center for Attitudinal Healing, Celestial Arts, 1978.

Ulman, E. Art therapy at an outpatient clinic. *Psychiatry,* 1953, *16,* 55-64.

Ulman, E., & Dachinger, P. *Art therapy in theory and practice.* New York: Schocken Books, 1975.

Ulman, E., Kramer, E., & Kwiatkowska, H. *Art therapy in the United States.* Craftsburg Common, Vt.: Art Therapy Publications, 1977.

Virshup, E. *Right brain people in a left brain world.* Los Angeles: The Guild of Tutors Press, 1978.

Wadeson, H. *Art psychotherapy.* Somerset, N.J.: John Wiley & Sons, Inc., 1980.

Worthings, R. Children's art: The highroad to health. *Parent's Magazine,* 1974, *42,* 59-60.

Chapter 11

Treatment with the Alcoholic's Spouse

The purpose of this chapter is to examine the role of the alcoholic's spouse in the recovery process. The dynamics of the spouse's relationship to the drinker and the rest of the family will be discussed, as well as the implications for treatment of the spouse.

BACKGROUND OF THE PROBLEM

The Spouse as Emotionally Disturbed

For many in the field of counseling and psychotherapy, the spouse (usually the wife) of the alcoholic is seen not as a helpless victim of circumstances but a full contributor to a dysfunctional family unit. This is not surprising, given the large quantity of research establishing the alcoholic's spouse as stressed and in need. Whalen (1953) described four general personality types of wives of alcoholics. This work was based on interviews conducted at the Family Service Agency in Dallas, Texas. Whalen notes that husbands of alcoholic wives rarely accompany them to therapy, and she therefore has focused her comments on the wife of the alcoholic male. To begin with, Whalen feels that the wife of an alcoholic, in general, has as poorly integrated a personality as her husband, even though she may appear more functional in the eyes of society. The implication here is that the wife is an equal contributor to the overall destructiveness of the alcoholic family. Whalen goes on to assert that the alcoholic's wife is usually drawn to the alcoholic as a marriage partner due to underlying personality characteristics that are essentially negative and destructive.

Specifically, Whalen has identified four personality types that she feels recur frequently. The first she has labeled the "sufferer." This individual often chooses an alcoholic husband due to her need to be punished. She is not disappointed when the alcoholic becomes abusive, irresponsible, and incompetent. The sufferer is typically meek, apologetic, and a good homemaker. She probably comes from a family where she was abused, and her central problem is low self-esteem. Abuse becomes a self-fulfilling prophecy. Whalen points out that this personality type does not always marry an alcoholic but does seek a mate who is domineering, rejecting, and cold. Her role in the alcoholic family reinforces and tolerates the behavior of her husband; she is one-half of a dysfunctional symbiotic relationship.

The second personality type Whalen describes as the "controller." This woman seeks a mate who needs her, an alcoholic, a handicapped person, or someone from an inferior socioeconomic or educational background. Her basic personality structure involves distrust and resentment of men in general. She wants someone weaker than herself that she can dominate and manipulate. Often her initial reason for contact with a counselor is to find an ally who will help her stop her husband's drinking. It seldom occurs to her that she has a problem—it's all his fault. The controller is often the major breadwinner and a career woman. She seldom has an active interest in the family and is hostile and critical of her husband. In addition, she is unforgiving and distant from her husband, denying him support or love, reinforcing his feelings of inadequacy by conveying a scolding, maternal attitude. It is pretty obvious that this woman could undermine any attempts at rehabilitation by the alcoholic alone. She does not want a competent equal partner, even though she complains about his drinking.

The third personality type is called the "waverer." This woman also is attracted to someone she perceives as needing her, but for different reasons than the controller. The controller wants a husband who is weak in order to control him, but the waverer seeks this kind of person due to her fear of being abandoned. If he needs her, she reasons, he is unlikely to leave her. The waverer has a great need to be loved, coupled with great insecurity. She can only feel secure in relationships with dependent people. As a mother she appears devoted, but in reality, she attempts to keep her children small and needy. She is overly protective and smothering. As a wife, she may eventually become fed up with her husband's behavior and separate from him for a while. However, she can always be coaxed to return with sincere promises (which never last). She knows she is being mistreated, but she cannot resist the tender words she wants so much to hear.

The fourth personality style is the "punisher." The punisher's relationships with people, especially men, are characterized by rivalry and aggressiveness. She is often successful professionally and has little interest in a home life. Unlike the controller, she does not demand that her husband take care of her emotionally or financially; she takes care of him. She describes her husband as cute or sweet and basically protects him. She provides her husband with almost anything and castrates him emotionally in the process. On the other hand, when he drinks and is "bad" (making a boisterous nuisance or sleeping around) he is severely punished. According to Whalen, this is also a symbiotic relationship. In this marriage, the punisher finds an outlet for her aggressive impulses in partnership with a man who is dependent on her and who is constantly maneuvering himself into situations that justify punishment. The husband gets what he unconsciously desires—the punishment he feels he deserves due to his low self-concept and self-hatred as a "loser."

Whalen does not claim that these four personality types are exhaustive. Other types exist and are yet to be described. In reviewing this conception of the alcoholic's wife, several points need to be stressed. First, it is clear that the spouse must receive treatment concurrently with the alcoholic in order for him to have a realistic chance of recovery. Second, the effects on the children of these marriages are devastating. Both maternal and paternal roles are negative and destructive. Moreover, the stress inherent in these marriages creates confusion and anxiety in the children. Third, the children must also receive concurrent therapeutic support. And finally, Whalen emphasizes that the four personality types cited are not characteristic only in alcoholic marriages. These women often marry other types of problematic men who will be counterparts to their neuroses.

MacDonald (1956) also feels the wife of the alcoholic male needs psychotherapy. He reports research in which wives actually developed psychiatric symptoms as their husbands' drinking decreased. Furthermore, in many cases MacDonald found that severe emotional illness occurred in the wife just at the time the husband stopped drinking. He refers to this process as "decompensation," or the loss of ability to act as a counterbalance. What this implies, MacDonald believes, is that alcoholics and their spouses have a negative symbiotic relationship, and the cessation of drinking by the alcoholic may precipitate psychiatric symptoms in the spouse. He also believes that the wife may have longstanding emotional problems that can be disguised only while her husband is engaged in alcoholic behavior.

Another perspective on the decompensation hypothesis has been forwarded by Hansen and Hill (1964). They suggest that the family has only limited "emotional room" at any one time, and following a disaster the family must take turns displaying emotional disturbance. In this context, the wife of the alcoholic would "take her turn" by manifesting symptoms once the alcoholic appeared stable and she could abandon her role as "the strong one."

The Spouse as Not Disturbed

Up to this point, studies have been cited that describe the spouse (usually the wife) of the alcoholic as being emotionally disturbed. However, the question is whether this condition predates the alcoholic marriage or is a consequence of it (or exists at all). Many believe the alcoholic's spouse is not disturbed. For example, Corder, Hendricks, and Corder (1964) used the Minnesota Multiphasic Personality Inventory (MMPI) to compare wives of alcoholics to wives of nonalcoholics. Results described alcoholics' wives as having demonstrated more psychiatric symptoms, but they nonetheless fell in the "normal" range on the test and therefore were not viewed as "sick."

Other researchers have used the MMPI and found similar results. Rae and Forbes (1966) suggest that alcoholic wives are essentially normal people who are simply reacting to stress. Furthermore, James and Goldman (1971) have concluded that the stress an alcoholic spouse experiences is in direct relationship to the intensity and frequency of alcoholic episodes. Hill (1949) presents another argument against the "spouse as sick" hypothesis. He suggests that the reunion of families, especially spouses, after the alcoholic's recovery is a traumatic process and does not imply the spouse has been disturbed in the past. He points out that many nonalcoholic families also have readjustment problems in circumstances such as war separation. Adjustment to separation seems generally easier than adjustment to reunion for all families.

Other researchers in the area also reject the theory that the alcoholic's spouse is disturbed. Paolina, McCrady, Diamond, & Longabough (1976) argue that most empirical evidence fails to differentiate alcoholic and nonalcoholic spouses on personality variables. In this study, husbands and wives of alcoholics were compared with a norm group on the Psychological Screening Inventory (PSI) and were found not to differ significantly, with the exception of a single scale (defensiveness). However, the authors point out that even here alcoholics' wives' scores fell within the normal range.

In summary, it is the opinion of the authors that the degree of pathology of the alcoholic's spouse must be determined individually. It is just as difficult to draw generalizations about alcoholics' spouses as the rest of humanity. The important point here is that the spouse be assessed and not excluded from treatment. Whether the spouse contributes to alcoholism or is overstressed in reaction to it, the need for therapeutic assistance remains. It is also the authors' opinion that the spouse of an alcoholic is very unlikely to be emotionally intact. Human beings cannot be submitted to stress and discord for long periods of time without negative psychological consequences.

TREATMENT IMPLICATIONS

The disturbed spouse theory has several implications for treatment. First, the spouse may suffer from long-term conflicts that are independent of the alcoholic and that require therapy. Second, alcoholism may be, as Whalen (1953) refers to it, a "red herring," and not the central problem to consider in treatment. Indeed, Whalen feels alcoholism is incidental to the four personality types discussed earlier. Therapy for these individuals involves helping them understand their core conflicts and adopt new behaviors. The third implication for treatment is that the marital unit needs assistance. Since the marriage in this situation involves the symbiosis of two essentially destructive personality types, both partners need simultaneous treatment. Consider an instance in which only one-half of the relationship changes. The customary expectations and responses become modified, leaving both partners confused and anxious. Finally, Whalen calls for relatively long-term treatment, one year or more. She advocates a modification in the client's personality structure, accompanied by the accrual of a new behavioral set by the marital unit and the family.

In order to accomplish this task, several steps should be followed. The first is to establish trust and rapport with the spouse, who is initially seen individually. This step is important due to the inadequacy and distrustfulness that these clients exhibit. Also, Whalen specifies that women who essentially dislike or are competitive with men should be seen by a female counselor. During the initial stages, the spouse is given supportive counseling. The therapist should model a noncompetitive, accepting relationship. Eventually, the core personality issues are confronted. At this stage, the spouse comes to grips with her problems and drops the idea that everything is the alcoholic's fault. Behaviors are also examined, and it should be pointed out to the client how her behavior is destructive to herself and everyone close to her. Once this insight has been gained, new, healthier behaviors are suggested and attempted. In the final stage of treatment, the client understands her root personality disturbances and possible resolutions. Group therapy is recommended after the client is firmly rooted in the therapeutic process. Eventually, conjoint marital or family counseling is suggested.

Contrary to the disturbed spouse school of thought, the second theory proposes that the spouse is responding to the stress of the alcoholic marriage. The issue of whether or not the spouse's problems outdated the marriage has definite treatment implications. In the latter case, long-term psychotherapy is probably not necessary. Rather, efforts should be directed toward modifying or removing the stress situation or aiding the spouse in adapting to it with less anxiety. One advocate of the "wife in reaction to stress" concept is Jackson (1954) who also advocates Al-Anon for alcoholic spouses. She describes seven steps in family adjustment to alcoholism.

1. Incidents of excessive drinking begin and, although they are sporadic, place strains on the husband-wife interaction. In attempts to minimize drinking, problems in marital adjustment not related to the drinking are avoided.
2. Social isolation of the family begins as incidents of excessive drinking multiply. The increasing isolation magnifies the importance of family interactions and events. Behavior and thought become centered on drinking. Husband-wife adjustment deteriorates, and tension rises. The wife begins to feel self-pity and loses her self-confidence as her behavior fails to stabilize her husband's drinking. There is an attempt to still maintain the original family structure that is disrupted anew with each episode of drinking. As a result, the children begin to show emotional disturbance.

3. The family gives up attempts to control the drinking and begins to behave in a manner geared to relieve tension rather than achieve long-term ends. The disturbance of the children becomes more marked. There is no longer an attempt to support the alcoholic in his roles as husband and father. The wife begins to worry about her own sanity and about her inability to make decisions or act to change the situation.

4. The wife takes over control of the family, and the husband is seen as a recalcitrant child. Pity and strong protective feelings largely replace the earlier resentment and hostility. The family becomes more stable and organized in a manner to minimize the disruptive behavior of the husband. The self-confidence of the wife begins to be rebuilt.

5. The wife separates from her husband if she can resolve the problems and conflicts surrounding this action.

6. The wife and children reorganize as a family without the husband.

7. The husband achieves sobriety and the family, which had become organized around an alcoholic husband, reorganizes to include a sober father and experiences problems in reinstating him in his former roles.

The wife in this case is responding to the stress of an alcoholic husband and is not seen as psychopathological herself. Instead of therapy, the spouse is first offered information about alcoholism to better understand the aberrant behaviors of the alcoholic. This is felt to be important by stress theorists. For example, up until the time of intervention, the spouse may have disbelieved the husband's memory lapses involving drinking episodes. She may discover that blackouts are a symptom of alcoholism, and the alcoholic really does forget his or her behaviors. The spouse may also believe that the alcoholic has control of his or her consumption and drinks for spite. These and other misconceptions can be cleared up, and unnecessary anxiety can be alleviated. In addition to informing the spouse about the nature of alcoholism, stress theorists advocate emotional support and encourage the spouse to abandon futile attempts to make the alcoholic stop drinking, known as the "home remedy." Spouses are also given information about their enabling process (the inadvertent reinforcement) of their partner's drinking. They are instructed not to cover up for the alcoholic, such as calling work and saying he or she is ill. In this way the spouse can identify his or her role in maintaining the problem and is offered new behaviors and attitudes that are healthier. Stress theorists also underline the importance of marital and family counseling during the reunion process. They point out that this is perhaps the most difficult part of recovery, and the spouse will have to give up some control of the family's affairs, among other things. Finally, Jackson (1954), Bailey (1964), and others ascribing to this theory advocate Al-Anon as an important adjunct to counseling for the alcoholic's spouse.

Al-Anon

Research by Bailey (1964) and Wright and Scott (1978) has suggested that the best treatment predictors of an alcoholic's sobriety are his or her involvement in Alcoholics Anonymous (AA), coupled with the spouse's concurrent involvement in Al-Anon. In addition, Wright and Scott researched which treatment(s), if any, were important for a spouse in order to facilitate the alcoholic's recovery. Their conclusions indicated that the more types of treatment a spouse participates in, the better. They went on to specify Al-Anon and inpatient treatment as the most beneficial.

Many would agree with the effectiveness of Al-Anon. But what is it, and how does it work? In many ways, its functions are parallel to AA, such as the use of the AA traditions and 12 steps as a conceptual framework for alcoholism. But Al-Anon serves the spouses and friends of the alcoholic and does not deal directly with problem drinkers. Al-Anon, like AA, is anonymous and has no governing authority. It is a self-help group that gives support, information, and encouragement to its members. Participants are helped to help themselves and give up efforts to control the alcoholic. But perhaps the most effective aspect of Al-Anon is its practical, how-to approach, offered by people with similar experiences. Al-Anon can serve as an important adjunct to traditional psychotherapy. Many similar goals exist between counseling and Al-Anon (which are described in Chapter 6), and the two processes often work comfortably together.

A third perspective on the treatment of the alcoholic's spouse comes from the family dynamics school of thought. Many of these theorists, including Bowen (1978) and Papp (1979), believe that effective resolutions of alcohol-related problems in the family unit first require the resolution of the spouse's conflicts with his or her family of origin. Although the concept, family of origin work, has been addressed previously in this book, this approach is important in dealing with a spouse. This is true, the authors believe, because the spouse will continue to recreate and relive conflicts either in his or her current marriage or future relationships unless family of origin issues are addressed.

Bowen believes a key issue is the person's ability to differentiate from the family of origin. By this he means moving toward emotional independence and objectivity relative to past family conflicts. Without this differentiating process, the spouse (in this case) will be "stuck to" old roles that are often irrational and self-defeating. The person who is undifferentiated will continue to play the same pathological games with new players (an alcoholic spouse, for example) in spite of efforts to change.

In order to resolve this issue, Bowen believes renewed contact between the client and the family of origin must take place if possible. In situations where this is not feasible, surrogate relatives from the parent's generation are recommended (aunts, uncles, etc.). The client is coached by the therapist to undertake new behaviors in the presence of the family of origin. First, clients are directed to develop person-to-person relationships in their families. This means relating to one individual, rather than Mom and Dad as a dyadic unit, and relating personally to them, as opposed to talking about impersonal things or other people. This has the effect of removing time-honored stereotypes or roles. Second, the client is told to become an objective observer of his or her family of origin and the family's dynamics around some emotional issue. The client is instructed to remain a neutral party, without taking sides or blaming, and objectively observe the goings on. Also, the client is told to assess but control his or her own emotional reactivity. This homework assignment should not be revealed to the rest of the family, nor should an emotional confrontation be attempted. This new role, Bowen believes, not only leads to an awareness of emotional attachments and proclivities, but also helps to open up the communication process between the client and his or her family of origin. Once the client has become differentiated (unhooked) from old family issues, progress can be made in current or future relationships without contamination.

Papp (1979) approaches the same problem (family of origin issues) with a different technique. She prescribes a family choreograph process in which the client directs therapists to act out significant family events from the past. In this format, the clients can also cast themselves in the role-play. The therapist helps by asking the client what feelings or thoughts occur while these scenes are played, and the therapist clarifies insights that typically result. The advantage of this technique is that it allows clients to reexperience old conflicts and then reprogram the scene so new behaviors can be experienced. Also, Papp feels the choreography helps the client to graphically understand the dynamics of the family of origin and the current influence these have.

Although there are, of course, many other techniques for addressing family of origin work, these two examples underline the premise that present symptoms are rooted in the extended family.

SUMMARY

Two conceptions of the alcoholic's spouse were presented: (1) the spouse as emotionally disturbed; and (2) the spouse in reaction to stress. The treatment implications for each were outlined. In the first instance, long-term therapy specifically focusing on the spouse's pathology was recommended. In the latter case, education about alcoholism and supportive counseling along with Al-Anon were advocated. In both situations, marital and family counseling were viewed as important during the recovery process, especially during the family's reunion period. A third perspective outlined the family dynamic belief that family of origin issues are at the base of most marital conflicts, and spouses of alcoholics should be encouraged to explore these root problems before current ones can be adequately addressed.

REFERENCES

Bailey, M.B. The family agency's role in treating the wife of an alcoholic. *Social Casework,* 1964, *44,* 273-279.

Bowen, M. *Family therapy in clinical practice.* New York: Jason Arnson, 1978.

Corder, B.F., Hendricks, A., & Corder, R.F. An MMPI study of a group of wives of alcoholics. *Quarterly Journal of Studies on Alcohol,* 1964, *25,* 551-554.

Hansen, D.A., & Hill, R. Families under stress. In H.T. Christensen (Ed.), *Handbook of Marriage and the Family.* Chicago: Rand McNally, 1964.

Hill, R. *Families under stress: Adjustment to the crisis of war separation and reunion.* New York: Harper, 1949.

Jackson, J.K. The adjustment of the family to the crisis of alcoholism. *Quarterly Journal of Studies on Alcohol,* 1954, *15,* 562-586.

James, J.E., & Goldman, M. Behavioral trends of wives of alcoholics. *Quarterly Journal of Studies on Alcohol,* 1971, *32,* 373-381.

MacDonald, D. Mental disorders in wives of alcoholics. *Quarterly Journal of Studies on Alcohol,* 1956, *17* (2), 282-287.

Paolina, T.J., McCrady, B., Diamond, S., and Longabough, R. Psychological disturbances in the spouses of alcoholics. *Journal of Studies on Alcohol,* 1976, *37* (11), 1600-1608.

Papp, P. Family choreograph: A multigenerational view of an alcoholic family system. In E. Kaufman & P. Kaufman (Eds.), *Family therapy of drug and alcohol abuse.* New York: Gardner Press, 1979.

Rae, J.B., & Forbes, A.R. Clinical and psychonectic characteristics of the wives of alcoholics. *British Journal of Psychiatry,* 1966, *112,* 197-200.

Whalen, T. Wives of alcoholics. *Quarterly Journal of Studies on Alcohol,* 1953, *14* (4), 632-641.

Wright, K.D., & Scott, J.B. The relationship of wives' treatment to the drinking status of alcoholics. *Journal of Studies on Alcohol,* 1978, *39,* 1577-1581.

Chapter 12

Evaluation of Treatment

EVALUATION OF FAMILY TREATMENT

Throughout this text the authors have advocated a family systems approach for the amelioration of alcoholism. Many of the chapters have specifically addressed a variety of family approaches, with the hope that these techniques will be adopted and used by the reader. However, another pertinent issue surrounding family counseling has yet to be discussed—the evaluation of family therapy.

This chapter will first review several different approaches for evaluating family counseling that have been reported in the research literature. Following this, the results of these studies will be discussed.

It is an understatement to say that attempts to evaluate family treatment have met with a multitude of problems, both from a conceptual and methodological point of view. As DeWitt (1978) points out, "in all, previous reviewers have all noted that the research evidence as to the efficacy of family therapy is disappointing in terms of both quantity and quality" (p. 550). The difficulties in measuring the success (or lack of it) for this treatment model are based in the following areas. First, there is no generally accepted criteria for successful completion. For example, many studies rely solely on the clinical impressions of the practitioners who provided the treatment. Others rely on the subjective evaluations of the client(s) following termination (usually in survey form), and still others use statistical data, such as length of employment, arrests, or recidivism following treatment to verify success. Another problem in evaluation is the inability to use a control group—a similar population of families who do not receive treatment compared to those who do. The problem here is that it is unethical to withhold treatment from distressed families for the sake of research. A final example of methodological problems is the difficulty in standardizing the type and quality of treatment offered. Indeed, even within most agencies, there is a discrepancy between the styles and levels of expertise of the treatment staff. In general, the evaluation of family counseling presents many problems that, to date, have not been overcome.

Conceptually, the definition of family counseling (or therapy) remains nebulous. For example, many combinations of family members and therapists are possible under this heading. Family counseling may include the entire family with one therapist or two. In other situations, it may include members of the family of origin, as outlined in Chapter 3. Family counseling may involve the concurrent treatment of spouses and children, but in separate sessions. The term *family counseling* designates no consistent composition of therapist(s) and client(s).

Yet, given these (and other) obstacles, much attention and work have been focused on the evaluation of the family counseling process. Coleman and Stanton (1978) have approached this problem by developing an instrument to measure the extent of family therapy involvement for different agencies, called the Progress Index for Family Therapy Programs (PIFTP) as shown in Exhibit 12-1. This instrument does not measure the effectiveness of family treatment per se but evaluates the agency's overall performance. The PIFTP consists of items deemed important by a professional task force. Each item is weighed on its relative importance and reflects what the agency considers are cogent indicators of family therapy involvement.

Coleman and Stanton surveyed 500 agencies, including a preponderance of drug abuse centers. Many programs did, however, treat other problems (76 were community mental health centers). The results of this study were remarkable. The maximum score possible on the PIFTP was 58 (see Exhibit 12-1), but the overall mean for the total group was only 18.5. The mean for the community mental health centers was also 18.5. They additionally found that only 27% of the agencies had budgets for family therapy and only 4% conducted research to measure effectiveness. Another finding was that a mandatory requirement of family therapy for clients did not ensure as high a score on the PIFTP as was previously expected (42.5% of these programs scored less than 30 points). Finally, results showed that neither the characteristics (size) nor the client demography of the 40 most successful programs served as predictors of a family therapy requirement.

The use of this instrument can help agencies determine their level of maturity in terms of family counseling and can allow a comparison between themselves and other programs. But again, the PIFTP does not provide direct evidence of treatment effectiveness.

More to the point of evaluating the actual effectiveness of family counseling, Tittler, Fiedler, and Klopper (1977) have developed a system to determine change in families. To do this, they have tailored four established measures to fit the characteristics of individual families. The instruments used are: (1) the family life questionnaire; (2) the outside activities checklist; (3) the felt figures task; and (4) a two-part, family interaction task.

Exhibit 12-1 Progress Index for Family Therapy Programs

Family therapy in this index refers to therapy or counseling of family members in which a therapist or counselor helps a family solve its problems and achieve more positive and constructive ways of relating to one another. The family members who attend may vary from session to session, and it is very likely that all members do not meet together all the time.

Item	Response	Weighted Score
1. Is family therapy often or always introduced when the identified client enters treatment?	Yes ___ No ___	1
2. Do families often or always remain in family therapy until primary goals are attained?	Yes ___ No ___	1
3. Does family therapy take place in the home at least occasionally?	Yes ___ No ___	1
4. Is family therapy mandatory for all clients?	Yes ___ No ___	5*
5. Is family therapy the primary or only form of treatment at your agency?	Yes ___ No ___	5
6. Is the family therapist also the primary therapist for the identified client?	Yes ___ No ___	1
7. Does the family therapist have primary responsibility for therapeutic decisions which will affect the identified client and the family?	Yes ___ No ___	1
8. Does the family therapist have major influence on decisions regarding control of medication?	Yes ___ No ___	1
9. Do family therapists have only a minimal role in establishing family therapy policies such as client selection, timing of treatment, etc.?	Yes ___ No ___	−1
10. Is there supervision of family therapy within your agency?	Yes ___ No ___	3
11. Does training include group or individual supervision with live family sessions as a focus?	Yes ___ No ___	5
12. Does training include group or individual supervision without live families?	Yes ___ No ___	2
13. Does training include the use of audiotapes?	Yes ___ No ___	2
14. Does training include the use of videotapes?	Yes ___ No ___	5
15. Does training include the use of notes?	Yes ___ No ___	1
16. Does training include the use of seminars/lectures?	Yes ___ No ___	1
17. Does the agency have a budget allocation for family therapists' training?	Yes ___ No ___	3

Exhibit 12-1 continued

18. Do family therapists attend professional
    family therapy conferences or workshops?   Yes ____ No ____   3
19. Does the agency provide funding for attending
    conferences or workshops?   Yes ____ No ____   1
20. Is at least 25% of the total time allotted for
    training devoted to family therapy training?   Yes ____ No ____   1
21. Is your agency doing any family therapy
    research?   Yes ____ No ____   3
22. Which of the following best describes the
    specific family therapy training of the average
    family therapist at your agency?
    (Check one only)
    a) No training   a ____   0
    b) Conferences and/or workshops or course
       work in an academic program   b ____   2
    c) Intensive inservice training or training with
       a family therapy institute   c ____   3
23. The average family therapist at your agency
    has the following amount of experience as a
    family therapist: (Check one only)
    a) one year or less   a ____   1
    b) 2-3 years   b ____   2
    c) 4-5 years   c ____   3
    d) 6 or more years   d ____   4

*Originally received a score of 10 on this item.

Source: Reprinted with permission from "An Index for Measuring Agency Involvement in family therapy," by Sandra B. Coleman and M. Duncan Stanton in *Family Process*, vol. 17, p. 481, © 1978.

The procedure used to tailor these measures for specific families consists of, first, determining areas of family imbalance and discordance, followed by the development of specific expectations as to how the family needs to change (based on the data obtained from the four measures). Expectations are then formulated by the treatment staff and are expressed in terms of the directions in which selected problems should change. These authors stress that expectations should be within the capabilities of the family. Change is evaluated on the measures by selecting 10 expectations for each family and assigning a score of $+2$ or -2 for each, depending on whether the change occurred in a positive or negative direction. This procedure can be employed both during and following treatment and can provide information about areas that need more attention. This method can also serve as an evaluation of family treatment after completion.

A similar approach has been developed by Sigal, Barrs, and Doubilet (1976) who examined the "interaction" of the family and the "emotional involvement" of its members to see if these two variables could predict the outcome of family therapy. To do this, a questionnaire entitled "The Family Category Schema" was given to each of the 20 families in this study before and after treatment. Three judges then rated the various areas of family change based on this data to determine if improvement occurred. Families fell into three categories according to the judge's rating: "great improvement," "moderate improvement," and "no change." Following this, the families' levels of interaction and emotional involvement (rated by the therapist) were compared to the three outcome categories. It was assumed that families who initially had higher levels of interaction and more emotional involvement would change more positively, but this result was not found in this study. However, approach demonstrates an improved way to use clinical evaluation to determine success by the employment of independent judges.

Minuchin, Montalvo, Gurney, Rosman, and Shermer (1967) have also reported on the evaluation of family therapy. These researchers used the Family Interaction Apperception Test, a standardized instrument, in combination with the Wiltwyck Family Task (developed for their study) and a clinical evaluation of treatment. These measures were administered before and after treatment to determine if change occurred in the tested families. One drawback, however, is that both tests are projective in nature and require a considerable amount of interpretation. Nonetheless, this procedure represents the use of standardized instruments to evaluate therapy.

Another method for evaluating family therapy has been reported by Martin (1967). His approach is unique because family communications have been divided into the specific categories of "blaming" versus "nonblaming" statements. Martin compared families who received family counseling to a matched control group who did not. All the families were given pre and post therapy evaluation sessions that were recorded and transcribed. Trained, independent judges made blind ratings from the transcripts, and assigned all statements into blaming or nonblaming categories. The results of Martin's study indicated that families who had received family treatment showed a greater proportionate decrease in blaming scores following treatment than the control group. Although the results are not necessarily relevant to this section of the chapter, Martin has illustrated the use of a defined aspect of communicational behavior, judged by independent raters, as a criterion of change in family functioning.

Similarly, Langsley, Flomenhaft, and Machotka (1969) reported a large-scale study that focused on the evolution of family treatment. A total of 300 families with one identified patient (IP) were tested; 150 were randomly given family therapy, and 150 were referred for conventional hospital treatment. The two groups were then compared on several criteria before and after treatment and upon a six-month followup. The criteria consisted of: (1) rehospitalization rates following treatment; (2) the Social Adjustment Inventory, which taps four areas of social and environmental functioning; (3) the Personal Functioning Scale, which measures personal and emotional adjustment; and (4) the number of days of lost functioning following treatment.

Although the differences found between the family treatment group and the control group were small in this study, it represents sound research methodology that could be applied in other settings. To review this study briefly, these researchers used a large population (300); pre, post, and followup assessment; random assignment of subjects into the experimental and control groups; and multiple outcome criteria that were measurable.

A retrospective design was used to evaluate family counseling in research conducted by Sigal, Barrs, and Doubilet (1976). This study involved the assessment of 93 families who requested help with a child at the Jewish General Hospital's Department of Psychiatry between the years of 1962 and 1972 in Montreal, Canada. Families who participated in three or more family counseling sessions (63) were compared to those who participated in one or fewer sessions (following a diagnostic interview) and terminated contact against their therapists' advice. Since all families answered survey questionnaires four to five years following the termination of services, this study was retrospective in nature. The therapy provided was described by the authors as ". . . psycho-dynamically oriented, interactional family therapy, typified by an emphasis on explanation or interpretation and reference to non-verbal expression in the family" (p. 228). Three criteria for effectiveness were used: (1) the status of presenting symptoms as reported by a parent at least one year after termination of contact with the treating facility; (2) the appearance of new symptoms; and (3) the parent's report of the degree of satisfaction with the family's current functioning. Information was also gathered concerning the informants' satisfaction with the contact, whether they thought their problems had been understood, and whether they had subsequently sought help elsewhere for the presenting problems. Although the criteria for this evaluation model were subjective, the authors' rationale was that parents' reports of their children's behavior correlate well with reports obtained from outside observers (Glidewell, Domke, & Kantor, 1963). Furthermore, since consumers define the problems, it seems reasonable to ask them if they got what they needed (Mayer & Timms, 1970).

The results of this study, which will be addressed in the following section of this chapter, were not encouraging. However, as discussed earlier, the actual results of these research attempts are not germane at present. The authors have simply attempted to describe several different methods of family therapy evaluation that may be used by the reader.

Finally, two recent studies by Woodward, Santa-Barbara, Levin, and Epstein (1978) and Bond, Bloch, and Yalom (1979), respectively, will be cited. These studies represent further attempts to refine outcome evaluations of family therapy.

The first study used a scaling system for therapy goals. The goals for each family were individualized and constructed by the therapist. Each goal consisted of a five-point range, so that a level of attainment could be analyzed. It was stressed that once relevant goals were identified, they must be stated in the most concrete terms possible and also be behavioral and measurable. Next, the goal setter specified what expectations were less likely to occur and which were more or less desirable. The goals were assessed after a six-month followup period. Client deterioration or improvement could be determined from the distribution of goal attainment scores. Also, any number of scaled goals could be constructed for each individual. Table 12-1 presents an example of goal attainment scaling (Kiresuk & Sherman, 1968).

Notice that five goals for this client are outlined, each with a relative weight that is determined by the therapist. Also, the scale goes from -2 to $+2$, with 0 as the expected outcome. Goals can also be constructed for families as a unit objective, as opposed to goals for the individual family member. The ability to objectively assess outcomes of treatment by using this method is obvious. Another advantage is that the model requires specificity and clarification of the client's issues, which is advantageous to the client, the therapist, and the family.

The second study is somewhat similar in that problems are targeted during the intake process, and progress is determined at a later time on these specific areas. However, Bond, Bloch, and Yalom approached the problem somewhat differently. Rather than developing goals, these researchers constructed a simple list of specific problems for each client prior to therapy. To evaluate success in these areas, agreement from three sources (patients, therapists and independent judges) was examined relative to their appraisal of the effects of treatment after 8 and 12 months. This method was helpful because it provided a check or comparison on the different subjective perspectives of the effects of treatment. This is an uncomplicated way treatment personnel can obtain feedback on their counseling skills. The independent judges based their ratings on videotapes of the sessions. A team of three experienced clinicians viewed the pre-therapy tape and together constructed a list of the patient's main problems, prioritized on a 9-point scale of severity. They later viewed the patient again after eight months and rated each problem on a 9-point scale reflecting the degree of change, from 1 = "worst possible outcome" to 5 = "unchanged," to 9 = "best possible outcome." The procedure was then repeated with the 12-month tape. Patients and therapists completed the same procedure, but based their ratings on their experience in treatment, not on videotapes. All three groups also rated the sessions globally at eight and twelve months (i.e., "improved," "no change," "did not improve").

Table 12-1 Sample Goal Attainment Scaling

Outcome Value	Goals				
	Fear of Sex Involvement	Dependency on Mother	Decision-making	Social Functioning	MMPI—78
Goal Weights	20	30	20	30	10
Most unfavorable treatment outcome thought likely (−2)	Avoidant No dating No sex	Lives at home Does nothing without mother's approval	No new decisions made, still weighing same alternatives (job, vocation)	Institutionalized prison or hospital	Up at all over previous score
Less than expected success with treatment (−1)			Complains of being unable to make up mind	On probation Further arrests	Remains in double prime range
Expected level of treatment success (0)	Dating Petting	Chooses own friends, activities without checking with mother	Makes up mind on vocation, other major items	On probation No further arrests for peeping	Mid 60's T-score
More than expected success with treatment (1)	Some satisfactory intercourse	Returns to school		No contact with police, states peeping no longer a problem	
Best anticipated treatment success (2)	Regular dating Regular satisfactory intercourse Marriage	Establishes own way of life Chooses when to consult mother			40-60 T-score

THE RESULTS OF FAMILY THERAPY EVALUATIONS

Reviews of empirical research on family therapy outcomes have not been particularly encouraging (Sigal, Barrs, & Doubilet, 1976; Wells, Dilkes, & Trivelli, 1972). But as Lebow (1981) has argued persuasively, the global question "does family therapy work?" cannot possibly be answered in any one study, no matter how rigorous. Rather, he suggests, the knowledge base relating to the effects of family therapy must be constructed incrementally, using findings from more limited studies that address such areas as specific treatment techniques, counselor characteristics, treatment goals, or outcome criteria.

An even more basic question is the feasibility of applying rigorous research methodology to this area of the human services field, given the multitude of subject, counselor, and outcome variables that must be somehow controlled. Wells, Dilkes, and Trivelli contend that although clinical practitioners have only paid lip service to research endeavors in the past, all methods of therapeutic intervention can and must be submitted to experimental scrutiny. These authors do, however, concede that the clinical evaluations of professionals in the field do have a place. Lebow (1981) agrees:

Family therapy is also an art. Thus, research is only one tool that can help in the development of family therapy. Scientific findings will never take the place of clinical wisdom. The isolation of the effectiveness of techniques alone will not suffice. What can be hoped is that family therapy outcome research will aid in the continuing development of the art, as art and science become an intermingled process. (pp. 185-186)

Paul (1967) also concurs, believing that, as case studies accumulate, effective parameters for family therapy can be drawn even if not completely validated.

Indeed, the results of studies that rely on clinical evaluations to determine effectiveness indicate that family therapy does work. Wells, Dilkes, and Trivelli (1972) compared the results of family therapy studies (using clinical judgments) with similar global studies of individual psychotherapy. These results were tabulated along a four-point continuum, ranging from "improved," "some improvement," "no change," to "worse." The overall success rate (improved or some improvement) was 69%. The combined success rate for individual counseling was 66%.

What these two encouraging statistics indicate is that both individual and family therapy have been effective when evaluated subjectively. This is not hard and fast, valid data, but it may be as accurate (or more so) as studies using more stringent research methods due to the difficulty of applying methodological principles of evaluation to this treatment model at this time.

In summary, the growth and interest in family counseling as a new and effective model for therapy are in themselves exciting. This process is still evolving and its exact uses are in need of further refinement. However, the authors feel it is the model of choice for families with alcoholism or related problems, not only due to the traumatic effects problem drinking has on all family members, but also due to the authors' contention that the family, as a dynamic unit, should be perceived as the client.

Evaluation of Alcoholism Treatment

The idea of evaluating alcoholism treatment sounds at first to be a straightforward proposition. Does it work? However, at the present time, there is no clear-cut, comprehensive answer. As seen in the section on the evaluation of family counseling, both theoretical and methodological problems abound. First, definitions of program design are far from consistent. Residential or milieu therapy, for example, may constitute a variety of treatment models, lengths of stay, personnel qualifications, etc., making an across-the-board comparison of residential programs an "apples to oranges" situation. Also, population characteristics vary considerably; some programs primarily treat chronic, skid-row type clientele while others serve higher socioeconomic groups. Beyond this, consistent criteria for success have yet to be agreed upon. Some evaluation studies consider total abstinence the sole criterion for success while others take multiple factors (job stability, marital status, etc.) into account.

Nevertheless, many attempts have been made to evaluate alcoholism rehabilitation. The remainder of this chapter will cite a few examples of evaluation techniques that may be adopted by the reader. Results of existing evaluations will also be reported.

Godley (1982) has developed a straightforward procedure for evaluating treatment outcomes for residential alcoholism programs. Godley advocates the accumulation of concrete, quantifiable data that minimally includes: (1) reductions in drinking; (2) reductions in the use of institutional facilities; and (3) increases in productive life styling. He feels these are typical goals of alcoholism facilities that lend themselves to quantifiable measurement, but he also stresses that other criteria can be easily added.

The first variable, drinking behavior, can be determined by dividing the number of days in which drinking occurs by the total number of days in the pretest and/or followup interval. This will yield a percentage that can be compared before and after treatment and can show trends in drinking (versus simple abstinence or nonabstinence).

$$\frac{\text{No. of days drinking occurred}}{\text{Total no. of days in pretest or followup interval}} = \text{percent of days drinking}$$

The second variable, use of institutional facilities, can be determined in the same manner:

$$\frac{\text{No. of days in a hospital detox or other treatment facility}}{\text{Total no. of days in pretest or followup interval}} = \text{percent of days institutionalized}$$

The third variable, employment, is measured like the other two but must account for legitimate days off. The formula for determining time employed is:

$$\frac{\text{No. of days worked}}{\text{No. of days in pretest or followup period required for full-time employment}} = \text{percent of time employed}$$

Similarly, alcohol-related arrests are also a measure of alcoholism. In this particular case, however, it is recommended that a straightforward count of arrests be recorded rather than expressing it like the other variables. The rationale for this format change is that a client can be arrested and charged with an offense (e.g., D.W.I.) and not necessarily spend the night in jail.

Data Collection Procedures

Godley feels the best way to collect this data is by integrating it into the normal clinical routine. For example, pretest data can be collected on these measures at intake. This is not too awkward because at this point the counselor is interested in learning as much as possible about the new client. The pretest data is helpful as an extra assessment tool.

Similarly, followup data can be gathered as a routine function of the outpatient visit or the aftercare contact. Because of the possibility of relapse, it is always desirable to maintain contact with clients for a long period of time (i.e., 18 months). Contact points during this time frame afford the opportunity to collect data without creating a cumbersome new system. A sample format for data collection is shown in Exhibit 12-2.

Each client's data can be traced using this type of format. Also each client's data sheet can be transferred to a summary sheet, by converting ratios to a percent. An example of a summary sheet is shown in Exhibit 12-3.

Data can be summarized at pretreatment and subsequent three-month intervals by adding up each column for which data is available. This procedure also lends itself readily to computer systems.

A second evaluation technique is to examine objectives. This model helps program personnel define their mission in concrete terms and gives feedback on

Exhibit 12-2 Sample Data Sheet

Name or I.D. _____					

FROM	TO	Number of days drank	Number of days employed full-time	Number of days institutionalized	Number of arrests

the extent to which goals are being met. To be written properly, objectives should have three elements: (1) conditions stating how the objective is to be measured (a survey form, interviews, etc.); (2) a behavioral verb stating the nature of the objective (e.g., reduction of drinking, attendance at social activities, etc.); and (3) criteria, or levels of performance desired (reduction in relapse from six to zero times per year).

The following statement is an example of a behavioral objective for an alcoholic client. "Based on a monthly interview questionnaire, client x will reduce his or her relapse rate from two to zero times."

There are two additional elements that can make objectives even more meaningful. First, the objective should be time-limited, and second, objectives should be scaled so an approximation of the objective can be determined.

Evaluation Results

The results of evaluation studies of alcoholism programs are equivocal, unfortunately, owing to the many issues already presented.

First, Alcoholics Anonymous, the most pervasive of rehabilitation techniques, will be examined. Based solely on face validity, AA seems to be helpful to many alcoholics. The millions of recovering persons who attend regularly bear witness to this. However, more rigorous examination with this model is difficult.

What, for example, are the relapse rates for those who attend? Also, what happens to individuals who attend a few meetings and then drop out? Due to the anonymous nature of AA, detailed, controlled followup studies are next to impossible. Another contaminating issue is that AA is also incorporated into treatment programs that offer individual, group, and family counseling. Therefore, it is not possible to determine which variable is responsible for success (or lack of it). In short, definitive outcome studies of AA are not available.

Exhibit 12-3 Followup Data Summary Sheet

NAME OR I.D.	DRINKING MONTH						INSTITUTIONALIZATION MONTH						EMPLOYMENT MONTH						ARRESTS MONTH					
	PRE	3	6	9	12	18	PRE	3	6	9	12	18	PRE	3	6	9	12	18	PRE	3	6	9	12	18

On the other hand, aversive conditioning models, especially chemical aversion, have reported success rates of 60% abstinence after one year (Wiens, 1976). Even though this sounds impressive, many criticisms have been leveled at these claims. First, it is argued that those who choose or can afford this treatment are relatively intact, functioning members of society and would be successful in any program. Second, many of these models require six or seven "booster" treatments on an outpatient basis for one year following the initial treatment, which ensures the aversion to drinking for that first year. To be meaningful, drinking behavior must be studied with these clients *after* one year.

Other aversive models, particularly shock aversion, have unfortunately been shown by Nathan and Briddell (1977) to have short-lived and modest effects on clients.

An outpatient treatment model devised by Hunt and Azrin (1973) called the "community-based reinforcement approach" cited successes. According to the authors, patients (N = 8) who received standard hospital treatment plus community-based reinforcement drank less, remained employed longer, were hospitalized for a shorter period of time, and stayed longer with their families than standard treatment patients (N = 8).

The effect of many of the other approaches (i.e., transactional analysis, psychoanalysis, etc.) is still questionable. Isolating a "theory" of treatment to compare it with others offers major obstacles. A definitive answer to which model is the most effective cannot be provided.

REFERENCES

Bond, G.S., Bloch, S., & Yalom, I.D. The evaluation of a "target problem" approach to outcome measurement. *Psychotherapy: Theory, Research and Practice, 1979, 16*(1), 48-50.

Coleman, S.B., & Stanton, M.D. An index for measuring agency involvement in family therapy. *Family Process, 1978, 17,* 479-483.

DeWitt, K.N. The effectiveness of family therapy: A review of outcome research. *Archives of General Psychiatry, 1978, 35,* 549-561.

Glidewell, J.C., Domke, M.R. & Kantor, M.B. Screening in schools for behavior disorders: Use of mother's report of symptoms. *American Journal of Psychiatry, 1963, 56,* 508-515.

Godley, M. *Outcome measures for the evaluation of alcoholism treatment.* Unpublished manuscript, 1982. (Available from Alcoholism Counseling Services, Marion, IL).

Hunt, G.M., Azrin, N.H. The community reinforcement approach to alcoholism. *Behavior Research and Therapy, 1973, 11,* 91-104.

Kiresuk, T., Sherman, R. Goal attainment scaling. Community Mental Health Journal, 1968, *4,* 443-456.

Langsley, D.G., Flomenhaft, K., & Machotka, P. Follow-up evaluation of family crisis therapy. *American Journal of Orthopsychiatry, 1969, 39,* 753-760.

Lebow, J. Issues in the assessment of outcome in family therapy. *Family Process, 1981, 20,* 167-188.

Martin, B. Family interaction associated with child disturbance: Assessment and modification. *Psychotherapy: Theory, Research and Practice*, 1967, *4*, 30-35.

Mayer, J.E., & Timms, H. *The client speaks*. New York, NY: Atherton, 1970.

Minuchin, S., Montalvo, B., Gurney, B.G., Jr., Rosman, B.L., & Shermer, F. *Families of the slums*. New York: Basic Books, 1967.

Nathan, P.E., and Briddell, D.W. Behavioral treatment and assessment of alcoholism. In B. Kissin & H. Begleiter (Eds.) *The biology of alcoholism*. New York: Plenum Press, 1977.

Paul, G.L. Strategy of outcome research in psychotherapy. *Journal of Consulting Psychology*, 1967, *31*, 109-118.

Sigal, J.J., Barrs, C.B. & Doubilet, A.L. Problems in measuring the success of family therapy in a common clinical setting: Impasse and solutions. *Family Process*, 1976, 225-233.

Tittler, B., Friedman, S., & Klopper E. A system for tailoring change measures to the individual family. *Family Process*, 1977, *16*(1), 119-121.

Wells, R.A., Dilkes, & Trivelli, N. The results of family therapy: A critical review of the literature. *Family Process*, 1972, *1*, 189-207.

Wiens, A.N. Pharmacologic aversive counterconditioning to alcohol in a private hospital: One year follow-up. *Journal of Studies on Alcohol*, 1976, *37*, 1320-1324.

Woodward, C., Santa-Barbara, J., Levin, S., Epstein, N. Aspects of consumer satisfaction with brief family therapy. *Family Process*, 1978, *17*, 399-407.

Prevention

INTRODUCTION TO PREVENTION

Earlier in Chapter 5 the relevance of etiology in terms of diagnosis, treatment, and prevention was briefly discussed. A major point of the chapter was that the first step in prevention is understanding etiology. With etiology as it was discussed in Part I as a basis, it is now possible to discuss prevention from a family perspective.

This will be done in Part IV from two points of view. Chapter 13 will discuss prevention from the perspective of the public health model. Chapter 14 will examine the three levels of prevention—primary, secondary and tertiary. As is the intent of this book the family will be the focus of these chapters.

Chapter 13

Public Health Model and Implications for Family Therapy

VIEWING FAMILY TREATMENT AS PREVENTION

Family therapy can go beyond the remediation of current alcoholism and associated problems. The philosophy of viewing the family system as the client can stop the intergenerational cycle of alcoholism by also treating the alcoholics of the future—the children.

Similarly, because attitudes of self-worth and values surrounding alcohol use are formed at an early age, the involvement of young children in the overall treatment approach is essential. The development of positive self-worth and healthy values related to drinking and family relationships may indeed prevent children of alcoholics and their future families from experiencing the perils of alcoholism.

The goal is to free the offspring of alcoholics from the learned patterns that may lead them to abusive drinking in the future. This does not automatically occur for the child just because the parent enters treatment for alcoholism. The Booz-Allen and Hamilton (1974) report on needs and resources for children of alcoholic parents found that the treatment and recovery of the alcoholic parent did not appear to reduce the problems experienced by the children. In their study group, 22% of the alcoholic parents had received treatment. Most of these had recovered or had significantly reduced their drinking. However, the type and frequency of problems among those children whose parents had recovered were not significantly different from those children whose parents continued to drink heavily.

The children from alcoholic families involved in a study by Cork (1969) did not find that family life became significantly better when drinking stopped. For the majority of alcoholics, the recovery process only begins with treatment and abstinence from alcohol. For some it is many years before they can be a fully functioning effective parent. Without help, this may never happen.

Sometimes the alcoholism becomes an excuse for family problems. One client who recently brought her children in for therapy because they would not "behave" told her family therapist that "My children must learn to behave. I'm alcoholic, and my alcohol counselor told me I couldn't handle stress."

By the time many recovering alcoholics have developed the ability to model healthy behavior, their children have already established negative patterns. In other cases children have already left the home due to divorce or other reasons. Therefore, they may have only experienced the alcoholic parent's prerecovery behavior.

Many of these children will go on to become alcoholics themselves. It has been estimated that as many as 60% of alcoholics in treatment were raised in a home where there was at least one alcoholic parent. Many of those who do not become alcoholic themselves marry an alcoholic, and this pattern is known to repeat itself in second and even third generations. Even those children of alcoholics who do not become alcoholic or marry an alcoholic have been reported to continue into adulthood with problems relating to: (1) intimacy; (2) control; (3) responsibility; (4) identification and expression of feelings; and (5) trust (Black, 1979).

Why are these children of alcoholics not helped prior to the development of serious problems in adulthood? There are several reasons. Research has shown that alcoholism in a great majority of cases is not so much due to immediate stress as to earlier predisposition underlying some environmental stress (Moore & Ramseur, 1960). This environmental stress generally is identified as occurring within the family of origin. However, the major focus of treatment for the alcoholic has remained on the individual rather than the family (Cork, 1969). Because of the disturbed nature of family relationships, alcoholism therapists have found it easier to see the alcoholic without the family. The reasons for the lack of treatment of the children of alcoholics reported by Booz-Allen and Hamilton (1974) were: (1) alcoholism treatment programs do not present a substantial resource for children of alcoholics; (2) primary goals of these treatment programs do not include the family; (3) when family therapy is included it is done to help individual alcoholics reach their goals; (4) family therapy is usually adjunct to individual therapy for the alcoholic; and (5) the child is rarely seen in individual treatment.

There appears to be a host of potential sources of help—nuclear and extended families; friends; community contacts, such as school personnel, clergy, doctors, child and family agencies; alcoholism treatment programs; and specialized resources for the children of alcoholics, such as Alateen (although many are not used by children of alcoholics). Often the children are too young or too embarrassed to ask for help. In some cases, the alcoholic might stop the child from seeking help through these groups.

Al-Anon, Alateen, and Alatot are the principle resources available for the children and family of the alcoholic. Most children who have attended one of these groups feel they have been beneficial in helping them to adjust to living with an alcoholic. Unfortunately, only a small number of children ever attend.

Because these groups are associated with AA and alcoholism, many children feel stigmatized by attending them. They want to lose the stigma of parental alcoholism, not increase it. In addition, some children feel that these groups are juvenile, overly religious, and unsophisticated. Some children do not have confidence in the ability of their peers to help them solve problems, and still others are not ready to accept the independent, laissez-faire attitude toward the alcoholic parent (Booz-Allen & Hamilton, 1974). Also, these groups vary widely, depending on the individual makeup of the members. One lady who was in family therapy referred to her Al-Anon group as "Revenge Anonymous." This may have been a biased, subjective observation on her part. However, these groups, even though they all operate under basically the same guidelines, can be heavily influenced by their members. Just one member who has not worked through his or her anger toward an alcoholic can have a negative effect on the progress of the rest of the group.

Another problem with self-help groups is that they sometimes discourage members from seeking needed professional help, and sometimes they are seen as competition or as a substitute for family therapy. However, a family therapist with knowledge of the dynamics of alcoholism or an alcoholism counselor who does family therapy can use these self-help groups to augment and enhance family therapy. Family therapy should be regarded as complementary rather than a threat to patients' involvement in Alcoholics Anonymous, Al-Anon, Alateen, or Alatot. These groups, on the other hand, should not be thought of as a substitute for family therapy. The latter three groups are designed to help their members adjust to living with an alcoholic. They do this by helping the member to become independent of the alcoholic and by helping him or her to rely on the group rather than the alcoholic for support. One major difference between the two approaches is that the focus for change for the self-help group is on the group and the focus in family therapy is on the family.

Self-help groups and family therapy have several things in common. Both recognize that others in the family besides the alcoholic may suffer from the problems arising from alcoholism; and both make use of contact with significant others to facilitate change in drinking behavior. Furthermore, both operate on the assumption that family members can be a source of resistance to change by the alcoholic and can do things to trigger drinking by the alcoholic (NIAAA, 1978). The family therapist who uses both family therapy and self-help groups can have one reinforce gains made by the other.

There are two potential problems that the family therapist should be aware of when both approaches are used. First, as family members begin to work on different problems in either the therapy or the self-help group, there is a resulting rise in anxiety. This may cause family members to avoid facing problems by escaping to the other group. Almost all worthwhile movement in family therapy toward a fully functioning family system that meets the needs of all members will cause tension among family members. If family members are allowed to retreat to their own personal self-help group (e.g., Al-Anon, Alateen) and they do not work through the issue at hand, family therapy may suffer.

If the family therapist begins working with a family who is attending a self-help group and the therapist takes the focus off the alcoholic's drinking problems, the family may reject this approach and retreat to the self-help group, believing that the family therapist did not understand the problem. The family therapist should avoid shifting the focus and should assure the clients that alcoholism will remain the primary concern of treatment.

The family therapist who establishes a clear purpose for therapy, creates a nonthreatening atmosphere, and conveys a genuine concern for everyone in the family will not be in conflict with self-help groups. While interpreting, clarifying, and rephrasing family interactions, the family therapist can keep the focus on the family system (and the dynamics of that system) without understating concern for the problem drinking, as well as keep the focus on the family unit and not the individual member (State of Florida, 1977).

By helping the family system to function to meet the needs of the family members, the therapist can help establish patterns in children that can be carried into the future to their families, thus breaking the chain of alcoholism. Self-help groups, individual therapy, and other individual approaches to the treatment of alcoholism are justified in many cases because they are all that is available. However, they are not substitutes for the family and should not be thought of as appropriate substitutes. In the final analysis, a person can gain many positive things from sources other than the family (e.g., self-help groups, religion, etc.) but these cannot replace a fully functioning family system that meets the needs of its members. If treatment professionals are to be successful in the treatment and prevention of future alcoholism (and other problems) among the children of alcoholics, they must focus their major efforts on the family. Treatment approaches that focus on the individual are very likely to be less effective than family therapy, and they do not have a built-in prevention focus. The hope for the future lies in family therapy and family systems that work effectively since this is the best type of prevention.

Prevention involves many things. The family system is the major aspect of prevention, but it is not the only one. Perhaps the best way to examine all of the issues is through the public health model. The family should be integrated into this model with regard to each of the factors presented.

PUBLIC HEALTH MODEL

According to the public health model, alcoholism is seen as stemming from an interaction between three factors, the host, the agent and the environment (Nobel, 1981). The host in this context becomes the individual and his or her knowledge about alcohol, the attitudes that influence drinking patterns, and drinking behavior itself. All of these factors are influenced heavily by the family.

The agent is alcohol—its content, distribution, and availability. These areas are not directly influenced by the family but by cultural norms.

The environment includes the setting in which drinking occurs and the community mores that influence the drinker (Nobel, 1981). These are also factors influenced by the family.

Intervention at any or all of these points is considered appropriate for preventing alcoholism. Each of the three factors will be briefly examined, as well as traditional prevention efforts. Following this, the role of the family in each area will be discussed. It is important to note that any of the three factors may overlap or complement the others. However, the public health model is useful for understanding different prevention approaches.

The majority of formal prevention programs deal with the host. One approach involves providing the host with information about the dangers of alcohol. The original idea was to change peoples' attitudes by approaching the issue morally and referring to alcohol as "demon rum," etc. The moralistic approach has long been used by parents and others in positions of authority to control all types of behavior.

It is true that in families where there are extreme moral or religious sanctions against drinking, fewer children become drinkers. However, it is also true that such children who do choose to drink as adults have a disproportionately high rate of drinking problems, including alcoholism, when compared to children reared in families where moderate drinking is the model (Fillmore, 1972). It is probable that both guilt and the lack of an appropriate drinking model play a part in the higher rates of drinking problems for this group.

Another common approach to prevention with the host involves providing grim statistics about the consequences of alcohol abuse. The problem with this method is that many people simply cannot identify with statistics and believe "it won't happen to me." For example, it is widely known that there is a link between cigarette smoking and health problems, such as lung cancer and heart disease. But the smoker can easily rationalize that it only happens to others (a good thing for the tobacco companies). Perhaps one of the dynamics here directly involves the family. Children are warned so many times by parents about negative consequences that never happen, that as they grow older they become desensitized to such warnings. Any behavioral psychologist can confirm what writers of children's stories have known for years. A person can only hear "wolf" so many times without seeing a wolf before the warning becomes meaningless. An additional problem involved in providing factual information to the host has been lack of agreement among experts in the field. Many concepts of alcoholism have several sides and may become confusing to the public and professional alike.

A pertinent example is the "disease concept" of alcoholism. It is hard for the average citizen to accept all the information given him or her concerning alcoholism when much of it conflicts with his or her own experiences. People hear that alcoholism is an illness, alcohol is a drug. They may wonder, "Why don't we hear that heroin addiction is a disease? Isn't heroin a drug? Isn't nicotine a drug? Is smoking a disease? How about overeating? Doesn't that kill people as well?" A graphic example of this confusion was seen recently in an Ann Landers column. A lady wrote to Ann saying:

> Dear Ann Landers: We are hearing a great deal about the "disease" called alcoholism these days. Do you have the guts to print this? If alcoholism is a disease, it's the only disease that is bottled and sold. It is the only disease that requires a license to keep it going. It is the only disease contracted by the will of man. It is the only disease that produces revenue for the government. It is the only disease that provokes crime. It is the only disease that is habit forming. It is also the only disease spread by advertising. And the only disease not caused by a germ or virus. Can it be that it is not a disease at all? (Signed) I'm from the Show-Me State.

Ann Landers wrote back:

> Dear Missouri: The experts whose opinions I respect say that alcoholism is a disease. But you raise some interesting questions. (As seen in the *Lincoln Journal*. Reprinted with permission of Field Newspaper Syndicate.)

The experts that Ann Landers speaks of include no less than the American Medical Association (AMA), the American Psychiatric Association, the American Public Health Association, the American Hospital Association, the National Association of Social Workers, the World Health Organization and the American College of Physicians.

Although it may seem like a digression, it is important to make the points that the disease concept has not been backed up by research; it places the focus on the drinker not the family system; and the disease model leaves little prospect for prevention.

When the motto "alcoholism is a disease" was first adopted by the National Council on Alcoholism (NCA), some remarkably complex concepts were involved. The persons concerned knew that alcoholics were sick people who needed help and were worth helping. In a rather special context, the AMA defined the word *disease* in such a manner that the people at NCA felt they could conscientiously make the statement that alcoholism is a disease. Their motivation was clear and commendable. They wanted to take the stigma away from alcoholism so that alcoholics would come forward and be helped. If alcoholism is a disease, then it is not a manifestation of weak will or poor character (Cain, 1964).

Prior to this time, medical treatment of the alcoholic was less than adequate. Some physicians provided a dose of moralizing along with the medical treatment, but others ignored the condition and refused to treat the inebriated alcoholic at all. When there was treatment, it often constituted cruel and unusual punishment rather than sound medical principles (i.e., strapping the patient down during detoxification or withholding medication that would ease the process or both). In defense of the medical community, it only reflected the popular view of the time that alcoholism was a moral weakness that called for punishment.

Today many people in the medical community defend the "disease" concept and condemn those that would see alcoholism as "only a symptom." In regard to the disease concept Gitlow (1976) has written:

> But what of our reasons for retaining the title of "disease" for alcoholism. The ultimate reason for the designation of any individual as sick or diseased is for the singular purpose of separating him from the larger (normal) group in order to channel special resources to him. Whether the patient has a broken bone or is addicted, the "disease" label assists him in obtaining that special care which society reserves for its ill. (p. 6)

It seems Gitlow has disputed his own point by his example. We separate many people from the larger (normal) group without giving them the "disease" label and that includes those with broken bones. They are classified as injured not "diseased." If alcoholism can't be cured but only arrested, are recovering alcoholics who don't drink diseased?

The final reason Gitlow gives for acceptance of the disease concept is that it "establishes alcoholism as firmly within the province of the medical profession" (p. 6). Would he make such a point if he were a psychologist or social worker rather than a medical doctor? The bulk of alcoholism treatment is done by paraprofessional alcoholism counselors, not physicians, who are often not trained in the treatment of alcoholism. The authors agree with Gitlow that the alcoholic is sick and in need of treatment. However, other than the medical complications of withdrawal, the medical doctor is usually poorly trained in treating the condition of alcoholism. In a recent survey of medical schools, drug and alcohol abuse accounted for less than .6% of the average curriculum. This translated into 25.7 average hours over the entire four years of medical school (Porkorney, Putnam & Fryer, 1978). This is less than one day per year. Some medical schools offered no training at all in the areas of alcoholism or drug abuse.

Another major problem of the medical model or disease concept is that few strategies for prevention are suggested. Room (1978), a leading critic of the disease concept of alcoholism, points out:

> The logic of the disease concept requires that other preventive measures beyond casefinding be seen as utterly irrelevant to the behavior of the alcoholic, since the disease of alcoholism is defined by the individual's complete inability to control his drinking no matter what incentive or deterrents are brought to bear. (p. 48)

Given the medical model, the only logical prevention approach is to have everyone stop drinking. Few doctors would accept this approach to prevention either for themselves or their patients.

The disease concept also means the family approach is simply a matter of counseling the family members on how to adjust to living with the "disease" of the family member who is the identified patient. As was pointed out in the treatment chapters the authors do not see this as family therapy. It involves treating the patient and educating the family but it does not treat the family.

Although the disease model has done a great deal to provide respectable medical treatment for the alcoholic, the full ramifications of the acceptance of the disease concept are not yet understood.

Recently the disease concept has been questioned, and some possible negative results postulated. The limitations of the concept of alcoholism as a disease are summed up by Scott (1968) as reported by Cahalan (1970, p. 27).

> To assert that alcoholism itself is a disease runs the risk of obscuring the probable truth that it may be a symptom of a number of quite separate conditions; it also tends to direct the problem to medical practitioners who, with their tradition of requiring the patient to be the passive recipient of treatment, may perpetuate errors. Thus it is possible that some forms of alcoholism are not diseases of individuals but of society; some may drown themselves in alcohol as lemmings drown themselves in the sea, and both may be responding to social rather than personal cues. Epidemiological studies, for example, of the notable differences in hospital admissions for English and Scottish alcoholics, may be the appropriate corrective. Some forms of alcoholism should properly be grouped with other killing conditions such as obesity, smoking, posses- sion of a high-powered motor bicycle. Looked at in this way it may be bad psychology to call these persons "sick" and to be squeamish about such terms as "immaturity," "lack of wisdom," and "self- indulgence" where they are manifestly justified. Such terms as "self-

indulgent'' or ''unreliable'' may be objective descriptions, to be sharply distinguished from moral judgements such as "shameful," "wicked," etc. Addicts need someone who will call a spade a spade in a realistic fashion without adopting a punitive, moralistic, or superior attitude. They know their weaknesses only too well and do not regard them as an illness, though they may secondarily bring illness. Certainly excesses of every sort may lead to illness or even to death, but we should guard against labeling everything which may shorten life as a disease, and the person who deliberately incurs risk as necessarily sick. (p. 221)

Cahalan (1970) has concluded that the disease "alcoholism" has not been defined and there is no specific treatment for it. Physicians can hardly be expected to apply a nonexistent treatment to an undefined disease in a population that denies the disease and rejects the treatment. Similarly, people working in prevention are trying to prevent an undefined disease in an unwilling population.
Horman (1979) has written:

I submit that the disease model is invalid and that the problem of alcoholism can be defined only as a highly complex political and behavioral problem. I believe further that alcoholism is in and of itself symptomatic of deep and significant societal and psychological problems. Unfortunately we have come to label alcoholism as a disease when it is merely a symptom of underlying diseases. Because we have decided to classify alcoholism as a disease, we have decided the appropriate treatment objective for this disease is abstinence. It is unfortunate that we have given this complicated problem an easy label and an easy cure. (p. 263)

Perhaps the most poignant case for deliverance from the disease model was presented by Cain (1964) who stated:

The fact is, however, uncontrolled drinking is an enormously complicated human phenomenon: almost as difficult of comprehension as human psychology itself. In their desperation to understand, control and prevent it, professionals and laymen alike have fostered upon anything that seems to work . . . What we have in the final analysis is not one but two distinct concepts of "disease" when we say alcoholism is a "disease." These two concepts mingle most confusedly and slide back and forth most conveniently in our minds depending on what it is we want to believe at the moment.

Concept Number One: Alcoholism is a tangible physical entity-in-itself which the alcoholic "has" just as people have cancer, heart disease, and tuberculosis.

Concept Number Two: Alcoholism is a collective noun which states that a number of people in a given society indulge in uncontrolled drinking. This is just like saying crime is a disease, or illiteracy or anti-Americanism.

It is difficult to imagine how anyone could dispute Concept Number Two. Not even the most ardent devotee of Bacchus and John Barleycorn would seriously assert that he favors uncontrolled drinking.

On the other hand, after many years of scientific exploration of the hypothesis, there is not one iota of acceptable evidence to support Concept Number One. There is, to the contrary, an overwhelming mass of experimental data to support the contention that uncontrolled drinking is fundamentally psychological in nature and in etiology—with, of course, a concomitant constellation of physiological, sociological and spiritual factors. (p. 38)

Cain also points out as does our example from Ann Landers that those who are not alcoholic find it hard to believe that alcoholism is a disease. "If so, they opinion, secretly or publicly, alcoholics certainly seem to bring it on themselves" (Cain, 1964, p. 168).

From our perspective, one of the most disastrous effects of the disease concept is to take the focus off the family, both in terms of treatment and prevention. The disease concept of alcoholism provides a linear and singular cause approach that is contrary to the circular multicausal approach accepted by family therapists. In the disease model, treatment and prevention start and end with the alcoholism itself. While the family approach acknowledges that problems may begin with alcoholism, this is not a critical point because family therapists also believe that in many cases the alcoholism is the result of unresolved family problems. The point is, in most cases both family problems and alcoholism exist. In order to successfully treat the alcoholic, the focus must be on the family system and not just on alcoholism.

It would be less confusing and more to the point to call the distressing and disabling disturbance of alcoholism a condition rather than a disease. Alcoholism is not a condition of moral weakness but a condition with multiple causes that can best be treated and prevented with the focus on the family. The authors realize that our society is very susceptible to rigid black and white, either-or thinking, and that the primary resistance to rethinking the disease model comes from those who believe that the only alternative to this model is the moral weakness theory.

The authors believe that the majority of people in this country would gladly accept an alternative to both of these concepts. If we, as a country, would spend the time and effort we spend convincing ourselves that alcoholism is a "disease" on training parents and pre-parents to provide a positive nurturing family environment for their children while meeting their own needs through the family, we would be providing the best prevention effort to date for the host, as defined by the public health model.

There are three primary things that can be done with the host: (1) provide education; (2) change attitudes; or (3) change behaviors. The traditional methods mentioned, as well as many others, have proven to be largely unsuccessful at accomplishing any of the above. School systems traditionally teach about the problems of alcohol, yet the school is the breeding ground for adolescent alcoholism. Similarly, the attempt to change attitudes about alcohol use through mass media campaigns has been nullified by commercial advertisements sponsored by the alcohol industry. The picture is bleak but not hopeless.

The answer to successfully working with the host is found in the family, where most attitudes and values about alcohol are learned. Even more importantly, the attitudes people have about themselves, about their own worth, and their ability to deal with their environment come from their family. These are critical issues. They separate those who abuse alcohol from those who do not. They separate those who are mentally healthy from those who are not, and most importantly, they separate those who become successful parents from those who do not.

The prevention of alcoholism, or for that matter, the prevention of any of the situations in which human beings seek to destroy themselves, begins with the family. As early as the first six months of life, a baby is making decisions about his or her world. Is it a world that meets his or her needs or one that does not? Is it a world over which an infant has some control?

A baby reared in a home where its basic needs are met in a reasonable manner will have a very different view of the world than a child who has been neglected. The feelings of despair and hopelessness that are generated by a neglected child are the seeds of future alcoholism. Not every child who is neglected becomes an alcoholic, and not every alcoholic was neglected as a child. However, somewhere between childhood and alcoholism there were needs that went unmet, such as approval from others or learning to feel self-worth. A mentally healthy person is unlikely to drink alcohol when it becomes a physical threat and hurts those he or she cares about. Inappropriate drinking behavior fills some basic need for the individual, or it sends a message to others that there are needs that are not being met appropriately. Most of these unmet needs would not have become severe problems had they originally been met in the family.

There are many ways the family can prevent alcoholism in the host. The role of the family will be discussed in terms of individual prevention at the primary, secondary, and tertiary levels in the next chapter. Presently, it will suffice to say that prevention with the host is best begun in early childhood, through a family atmosphere that allows for the development of a positive self-concept, coping and social skills, and decision-making skills that will allow children to relate to the environment in a positive way. The family should provide an atmosphere where feelings of self-worth can develop while a healthy respect for others is maintained. Parenting skills are not the subject of this book, but they are crucial to the early prevention of alcoholism. For more information in this area consult works by Rudolph Dreikurs, A.S. Neil, William Glasser, Thomas Gordon, Haim Ginott and others who specialize in the area of raising children.

Outside the family, schools play the biggest role in the development of self-image. Schools have come a long way toward meeting the affective needs of students, but they still have room for improvement. For example, schools could spend more time helping students to learn conmunication skills rather than just teaching English. Students could be taught to deal with problems appropriately, rather than deny they exist. Most importantly, they could teach students (who are future parents) appropriate parenting skills. Many bad habits are passed on from generation to generation. Child abuse, incest, and alcoholism all run in families. Proper parenting skills can be learned, and the public schools would be an excellent place to begin. In addition, free daycare centers in high schools for children of working mothers would provide an excellent training site for students as well as a much needed service.

The prevention approaches that have been used in dealing with the host include: (1) teaching the problems of alcohol use and abuse; (2) providing information; (3) efforts to change behavior or attitudes; (4) the development of interpersonal skills among nonabusers; (5) providing alternatives to abuse; and (6) suggesting resources to help deal with related problems. All of these should be done quite naturally in the fully functioning family, and alcohol problems occur when they are not. Individuals are frequently motivated to engage in alcohol abuse by a perceived need to augment or to replace the constructive, pleasurable, and meaningful benefits that are naturally derived from healthy human development and an effective living environment, as these benefits relate to self-esteem, stress management, value integration, effective communication, recreation, decision making, and relating to other people.

Effective prevention efforts with the host or individual become attempts to promote healthy development around the areas just cited (McCord, 1981).

Many of those working in the field of alcoholism feel prevention efforts should be confined to the host. This idea comes from a narrow conceptualization of the problems in general and inadequate definitions of problems in particular. This singular focus on changing individual behavior leads to an almost total neglect of the larger environment (including the family). As was pointed out earlier, all of these issues are interrelated, and the relationship is not a simple linear one but one of mutual causality. One fuels and supports the other and in turn is affected in a similar fashion. The family supports the alcoholism, and the alcoholic behavior supports the dysfunctional family system. If this is not the case, the family will break up, as often happens when the wife is alcoholic. In this case, the behavior of the husband is strongly related to the environment, which makes alcoholism much less acceptable for women than for men.

The neglect of the role the environment plays in alcoholism has been summed up by Wallack (1981) who says:

The way we think about the nature of alcohol in society has not reflected a broad reaching effort to increase and enhance understanding but has indicated a need to reduce a complex problem to presumably manageable proportions. Disease concepts have been a convenient and popular way to organize thinking in this area. Such concepts have served to legitimate alcohol problems as a worthy recipient for treatment and minimize the moral onus associated with alcoholism. At the same time, however, the disease concept also serves to simplify the problem by locating the source as an individual deficiency seemingly independent of other influence. (p. 4)

Morgan (1981) has suggested that the disease model provides an out for society in dealing with serious social problems by creating a need to treat the individual and thereby legitimatizes the problem as based in the individual rather than based in the larger system of social relations (i.e., the family, the school system, the church, the community).

It is unfortunate that prevention efforts have focused on the individual (host). It is clear that prevention programs are more likely to be successful if they result from the combined efforts of families, schools, and communities. Very few programs that work exclusively with the host have demonstrated clear success or, for that matter, adequate evaluation designs. In addition, the relationship between alcohol information and its use is unclear. Let us next examine the problem of alcohol abuse from the perspective of the environment, both with regard to etiology and prevention. No group provides a better example for this than adolescents. They have problems with their environment that those 10 years ago did not have. Problems within the environment not only manifest themselves in alcohol and drug abuse, but in violent crimes, teenage pregnancy, etc., to the point that a significant number of the young people who have reached legal age are unable to function within reasonable limits.

Glenn (1981) has identified several reasons for the increase in these problems. First, it takes longer to achieve functional adulthood in the United States than it does in comparable nations, by about eight years according to some estimations. This is due in large part to assumptions we make about our children. These are reflected in child rearing practices as well as in how we educate our children and see their roles. As Glenn states:

> We do not need our kids. We definitely don't need them at 16. There are
> no jobs for them. There is nothing for them to do in this society. Those
> countries that need their young people have them solidly involved in
> important tasks by the time they are 16 years old. (p. 10)

Although contemporary teens mature physiologically faster and appear to be
developing higher I.Q.'s than adolescents 20 to 30 years ago, they have more
mental and physical problems. Unfortunately, today's society is equipped to
absorb them much later as functioning adults.

As an additional problem, Glenn cites poor moral and ethical decision making
due to a modern focus on situational ethics or feelings, rather than on true
moral-ethical values. He feels this puts adolescents in the position of being
expected to do things they do not perceive or understand. He claims this is due in
part to "adultism" that occurs when adults forget the childhood experience.

Slow development also appears to be related to a loss of role-taking opportunities. These involve carrying out tasks that are important to the welfare of the family
or some other group. This situation has resulted from many changes in our
environment, such as changes in the nuclear family (including a vast decrease in
the time the parents spend interacting with their children), reliance on television
rather than role-taking, and the lack of an extended family and close neighbors
(Glenn, 1981). Similarly, the peer group does not perform the task of role-taking
for the adolescent. A successful peer group operates at a high level of judgment,
but most adolescent peer groups operate on the level of situational ethics (which
hardly gives the adolescent a chance to learn and practice higher level judgments).
Peer groups operate on the assumption that "whatever we both want to do is
probably O.K." not on "is it fair for us to do this?"

The point is that when we (the family, society, etc.) make a child feel unappre-
ciated, unable to make a contribution, impotent, or unimportant, then problems
will exist. Prevention strategies that deal with the environment not only prevent
alcoholism, but rectify a vast array of other social problems.

Glenn has postulated four principles for parents, a basic set of tools that people
need to help children develop the ability to make decisions. First, he recommends
that parents think small and concentrate on routine things that accumulate over
time. For example, parents should let children make decisions that affect them
very early (e.g., Do you want milk or orange juice to drink?, How do you want your
eggs?). Besides giving children an opportunity to practice making decisions,
parents will find children respond much better when given a choice, even when
both alternatives are unattractive. Second, parents should become learners. In
times of change, learners do very well while the learned find themselves beautiful-
ly equipped to deal with a world that no longer exists. Many parents fit into the
learned category. Third, recognize common ground. There are commonalities for
all problems, and skills developed to deal with one situation will often apply to

another. It is helpful to generalize problem-solving techniques to new problems. (One of the authors learned a great deal about how to parent children from raising a St. Bernard). Fourth, it is important to learn to habilitate. Rehabilitation assumes the person was excellent before he or she developed the problem. If habilitation was used more generously, perhaps the problem would never develop.

More traditional prevention attempts with the environment include arranging settings where alcohol is consumed to minimize abuse (lighting, seating arrangements, music, food). Schoefer (1981), an anthropologist, has done research in this area and has found definite high/low risk factors related to drinking problems in the areas of:

- lighting
- space-design
- parking and lighting those areas
- male/female ratios
- music style via live/jukebox
- drinking styles
- age factors and social groups
- detox/emergency/taxi/referrals
- age regulations and ID checking systems
- hours
- crowd control
- beverage control
- art and decor
- bartender training/style
- food service
- alcohol breath devices
- serving regulations
- alcohol/driving education in place

These and other factors can and do affect the manner in which people drink in bars. There are vast differences between the atmosphere in drinking establishments in the United States and European countries. Take lighting for example. It would be difficult to find a pub in England that is as dark as most bars in the United States. Food is another area in which the two cultures are vastly different. There is a vast difference between a package of stale potato chips, served American style, and a portion of steak and kidney pie, or a sausage role served in most English pubs. In fact, in Madrid, Spain, each tasca or bar is known by the special hors d'oeuvre it serves. People go there more to eat than drink. The primary beverages served in most of Europe are beer and wine; a martini is vermouth on the rocks, no gin.

Perhaps most importantly, drunkenness and losing control of behavior when drinking are looked down upon in Europe.

Part of drinking behavior in this society stems from a Puritan background. Drinking is often seen as a clandestine experience—something someone should do only in the dark in order to keep from being discovered. The first drinking experiences of many adolescents occur before the legal age and involve an attempt to keep from being caught. Very few people teach their children how to drink, even when they become of age. Drinking is a behavior that is assumed children do not need to know about and adults should already know about. Here again, Europeans take a different approach. For example, in Germany, at high school functions, even those held at churches, beer is sold to teenagers. Drunkenness or inappropriate behavior is seldom a problem.

People should learn drinking values from their families. If these values are unrealistic or are not taught in the family, they will be learned elsewhere, such as in the adolescent peer group under illegal conditions. If this is the case, these values will probably lead to some type of problem drinking.

This approach to the environment has been called the sociocultural approach, and the major idea behind it is that eradication of drinking problems requires changes in the social norms around drinking. Certain patterns of drinking are associated with low levels of problem drinking. Approaches to drinking *not* associated with problems include:

1. reducing emotionalism about drinking and ambivalence about drinking norms
2. making a clear distinction between drinking per se and drunkenness
3. drinking in situations of restraint, that is, where drunkenness is out of the question
4. drinking when drinking itself was not the focus of the group's activities
5. drinking with food, both to integrate drinking with other activities and to reduce alcohol levels (Wilkinson, 1970)

Sociocultural approaches have led to the expectation that safe or responsible drinking should be the goal of alcohol policy. Although this cannot always be the case in this society because of religious beliefs, for those who choose this goal the five rules listed above are a good place to start to provide an appropriate model for children. Wilkinson (1970) also suggested the following regarding youthful drinking:

1. The minimum age for drinking should be 18 and not 21, and those under 18 should be allowed to buy drinks with their parents.
2. Drinking at home should be subject to no legal age limit.
3. Mild alcoholic beverages should be served at "teenage dances and parties" without being the prime means of entertainment.

4. There must be more alcohol education for responsible drinking.
5. Colleges must provide supervised drinking places for students.
6. Alcohol-related offenses for young people should be decriminalized.

Some readers may assume these changes suggested by Wilkinson would promote rather than prevent alcoholism. There are two sides to every issue, and perhaps many sides to this one. From this writer's perspective of having lived in countries where these ideas have been in practice for years, it is apparent that these approaches lead to a healthy integration of alcohol into society, resulting in fewer drinking problems among youths and adults.

Many of Wilkinson's suggestions are examples of prevention measures that deal with both the environment and the agent. The agent (alcohol) is most often controlled by laws. Historically, our biggest effort toward controlling the agent was prohibition. This approach not only proved to be unsuccessful as a means of controlling alcohol intake, but also deeply affected our society since criminal elements began to organize and prosper as a result of prohibition. When prohibition was repealed in 1933, this criminal element simply moved into illegal drugs, gambling, and prostitution. In retrospect, prohibition did a great deal more harm than good.

Other approaches to prevention via the agent include strict pricing policies (the more expensive alcohol the less people will drink), limiting on-premises drinking, lowering alcohol content of beverages (3.2 beer for those between 18 and 21), limiting the number of retail and wholesale outlets, and enacting and enforcing strict zoning regulations. There are also those who believe placing warning labels on alcoholic beverages would deter misuse. If cigarette warnings are any example, this process would seem to be a waste of money.

An effective prevention effort on the part of the family (concerning the agent) would be to encourage the use of beverages with a low alcohol content (beer or wine vs. straight drinks like martinis or Manhattans). It is also very important to provide alternatives for those who choose not to drink. People should be respected not for their choice to abstain from alcohol, but because each individual's opinions and values deserve respect. If children are taught to be suspicious of those who do not drink, it is unlikely that they will be abstinent as adults even if they feel abstinence is desirable.

Although prevention efforts most often involve only the host, these efforts are often not effective or have poorly identified outcome criteria. The role of the "disease model" in terms of prevention was examined in light of problems with this model, including distracting the focus from the family. Environmental factors and alcohol itself have been examined in terms of prevention. Finally, the high and low risk factors discussed in the etiology chapters will be examined in terms of primary, secondary, and tertiary prevention.

REFERENCES

Black, C. Children of alcoholics. *Alcohol and Research World,* Fall 1979, pp. 23-27.

Booz-Allen & Hamilton, Inc. *An assessment of the needs of and resources for children of alcoholics.* Prepared for the National Institute on Alcohol Abuse and Alcoholism. Springfield, Va.: National Technical Information Service, 1974.

Cahalan, D. *Problem drinkers: A national survey.* San Francisco: Jossey-Bass, Inc., Pubs., 1970.

Cain, A. *The Cured Alcoholic.* New York: John Day Co., 1964.

Cork, M. *The forgotten children.* Toronto: Addiction Research Foundation, 1969.

Fillmore, K.M. *Abstinence, drinking and problem drinking among adolescents as related to apparent parenting drinking practices.* Unpublished manuscript, University of Massachusetts, 1972.

Gitlow, S.E. Alcoholism: A disease. In Bourne & Fox (Eds.), *Alcoholism Progress in Research and Treatment.* New York: Academic Press, 1976.

Glenn, S. *On prevention.* Presentation to seminar sponsored by the Nebraska Prevention Center, Omaha, Nebraska, February, 1981.

Horman, R.E. The impact of sociopolitical systems on teenage alcohol abuse. In H. Blane & M.E. Chafetz (Eds.), *Youth, Alcohol and Social Policy.* New York: Plenum Press, 1979.

McCord, W.J. *Developing prevention opportunities: A single state agency perspective.* Paper presented to Conference on Developing Prevention Programs, Lincoln, Neb., April 27, 1981.

Moore, R.A., & Ramseur, F. A study of the background of 100 hospitalized veterans with alcoholism. *Quarterly Journal of Studies on Alcohol.* 1960, *21,* 51-67.

Morgan, P. *Alcohol, disinhibition, and domination: A conceptual analysis.* Paper presented to Conference on Alcohol and Disinhibition, Berkeley, California, February, 1981.

NIAAA Information and Feature Service. *Family therapy seen complementary to Alcoholics Anonymous, Al-Anon.* National Clearinghouse for Alcohol Information, IFS No. 49, July 11, 1978.

Nobel, E.P. Action on prevention of alcoholism at the national level. *Preventing Alcoholism,* Smithers Foundation, 1981.

Porkorney, A., Putnam, P., & Fryer, J. Drug abuse and alcoholism teaching in U.S. medical and osteopathic schools. *Journal of Medical Education,* Vol. 53, October, 1978, pp. 816-824.

Room, Robin. *Governing images of alcohol and drug problems: The structure sources and sequels of conceptualizations of intractable problems.* Doctoral dissertation, Dept. of Sociology, University of California, Berkeley, 1978.

State of Florida. *The family secret: Tips on counseling.* Public document, 1977.

Schoefer, J. Presentation on Prevention of Alcoholism, University of Nebraska, 1981.

Scott, P. in Cahalan, D. Problem drinkers: A national survey. San Francisco: Jossey-Bass, Inc. Publishers, 1970.

Wallack, L.M. *The problems of preventing problems.* Paper presented to Conference on Developing Prevention Programs, Lincoln, Nebraska, April, 1981.

Wilkinson, R. *The prevention of drinking problems: Alcohol control and cultural influences.* New York: Oxford University Press, 1970.

Chapter 14

Primary, Secondary, and Tertiary Prevention and Implications for the Family

Caplan (1974) first conceptualized the model of primary, secondary, and tertiary prevention. Caplan's definition of primary prevention included early diagnosis, but secondary prevention in alcoholism calls for early diagnosis. Primary prevention for alcoholism is identification of those who are "high risk." Perhaps this accounts for the confusion in the field that exists about the difference between treatment, intervention, and prevention. The greatest confusion seems to center on the distinction between primary and secondary prevention (Swisher, 1980). This chapter will indicate how tertiary or secondary prevention for a parent may or may not be primary prevention for the children of that parent. This chapter will also demonstrate how very important the family role is in the primary, secondary, and tertiary prevention of alcoholism.

Primary prevention, as it is used in the field of alcoholism, applies to new cases. Ideally, it occurs before abuse and involves such factors as government alcohol policy, public education and changes in customs, and values or mores that promote more satisfactory drinking. It also involves offering alternatives to drinking as well as opportunities for personal and social growth. The focus is often on those identified as high risk (e.g., children of alcoholics). Secondary prevention is the early identification of prodromal drinking as described by Jellinek (1960), or the provision of treatment or rehabilitation for these individuals so that they do not develop more serious, long-term problems. Tertiary prevention involves the treatment of serious cases (leading to recovery) so they will not contaminate others by social influence, modeling, or setting bad examples (Smart, 1978). As mentioned earlier, some confusion exists about primary and secondary prevention. However, the definition of tertiary prevention is clear-cut. Alcoholics or alcohol abusers seek treatment and hence become "cases" or patients. They are self-defined. In some instances, tertiary prevention also includes institutionalization and/or detoxification. In any case, it is clear when tertiary prevention is taking place.

This is not true, however, with primary and secondary prevention. In fact, there seems to be little agreement even about the goals of primary prevention. Personal opinions, values, and judgments all help make up an individual's idea of the goals of primary prevention. Most people will agree a proper goal might be to reduce alcohol abuse. But what is alcohol abuse? A medical doctor may define it as using alcohol to the extent that it causes physical problems. The law enforcement officer may define alcohol abuse as drinking and driving or drinking under age. The social scientist might define alcohol abuse as that which is harmful to the individual or to society.

The latter of these definitions has been chosen here. Primary prevention should prevent alcohol use that is harmful to the individual and/or society. To be more specific, primary and secondary prevention should prevent adverse consequences like those proposed in Rockefeller's *White Paper on Drug Abuse* (Rockefeller, 1975). These include: (1) illness and death; (2) acute behavioral effects (e.g., paranoia); (3) chronic behavioral impairment (e.g., apathy); (4) intellectual impairment; (5) injury or death associated with conditions of use (e.g., nutrition); developmental difficulties (e.g., adolescent crises); (6) barriers to social acceptance; and (7) adverse consequences to society. This type of prevention effort is best done with the complete cooperation between the family and all of the community resources, incuding schools, churches, and local and national governments. Such an effort may seem all but impossible. However, the family plays a more important role than all of these other resources put together. Furthermore, the family is a social system that can be controlled and changed as necessary by its members. The school system, the community, or the church may not be as flexible or as responsive to individual needs. The best place to begin primary prevention is in the family. Starting with the assumption that alcoholism is a complex condition, what is the role of the family in primary prevention?

As seen earlier in the etiology section, the family plays an important role in the development of risk factors for alcoholism in each of the three areas of risk, physiological, sociological, and psychological. The child of an alcoholic parent may have a risk profile that is high in all areas. See Figure 14-1.

Primary prevention involves early identification of high risk individuals and attempts to move the high risk factors to low risk.

In the physiological area of risk, it is almost impossible to make a change in level without providing the child with a new genetic background. However, the physiological area is very useful in the identification of individuals at risk. Once high-risk children are identified, prevention efforts can focus on the two areas that can be changed—the sociological and psychological areas. The goal becomes to make these two risk areas as low as possible. The individual in Figure 14-1 would look like Figure 14-2 after a successful prevention effort.

Before we discuss how to lower risk factors in the sociological area via the family, let us mention one possible area of primary prevention in the physiological

Figure 14-1 Alcoholism Risk Figures

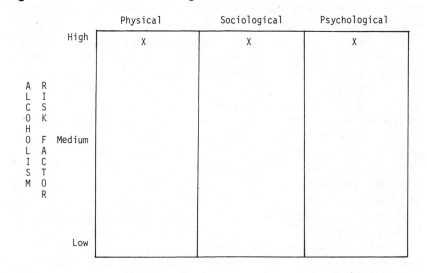

Figure 14-2 Alcoholism Risk Factors

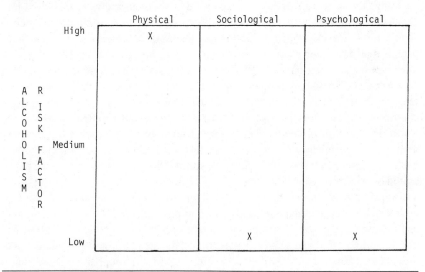

risk area. Several of our clients have given histories of drinking problems that occur only on specific and identifiable occasions. Something about these situations triggered abusive drinking in these clients. For one college student, it was finals week. For one woman, it was the Christmas holidays. For another man, it involved visiting his family of origin. These clients were all successfully placed on Antabuse several weeks before the precipitating event and were then taken off the drug shortly thereafter. Antabuse is a drug that makes any use of alcohol impossible without many adverse physical symptoms (i.e., vomiting, cramps). It temporarily makes a person at very low risk physically for alcohol use or abuse and can be used as a preventive method quite effectively under the right circumstances. Best results occur when the individual wants to take the drug and assumes responsibility for self-administration. It is not implied here that it is not worth looking into the reasons these people drink to excess on these occasions or that therapy would not be worthwhile. However, if Antabuse works to keep them from having alcohol-related problems, why not use it on these occasions?

Primary prevention in the sociological area means dropping a person's risk level in that area from high risk to low risk. As stated in Chapter 4, there are a number of reasons a person would be at high risk in this area. Among those are: (1) having parents who have strong moral or religious views against drinking; (2) having a parent or parents who are alcoholic; (3) coming from an ethnic background that is at high risk for alcohol abuse; (4) belonging to a social group or having social values that allow for alcohol abuse; and (5) being in a position in society that is inconsistent with the individual's self-image.

If any or all of these conditions exist, the family is the place to begin to neutralize them. If parents have strong moral or religious views against drinking alcohol, it is important that they discuss these views with their children. Parents should provide them with their rationales for making the choice. One of their parents may have been alcoholic, or the choice may be based on a religious belief. They could also point out that it is a personal choice each individual must make. Parents must discuss the pros and cons as they see them and should listen to what their children think without disparaging their opinions. They could provide their children with rules for appropriate drinking and point out people as role models who drink without problems. They could discuss possible problems associated with choosing to drink. However, they must try to keep an open mind and not make their children feel wicked, guilty, or sinful if they choose to drink since those attitudes lead to problems.

If a parent is alcoholic, he or she should get treatment, preferably in a family-oriented program. Parents should discuss their problem openly with their children and inform them of the risks they might incur as a result of parental alcoholism. They should try to make sure their parenting skills are the best they could be, and they are well advised to take a course in parenting. In addition, parents should look for high-risk factors in their children and take corrective action. For example, if they feel their children might be suffering from low self-esteem, activities could be provided to help reverse this problem. Children should be given many opportunities to experience success. Above all, parents should communicate with their children.

If parents are themselves children of alcoholics, they should try not to accept responsibility for their parents' problems but instead help as much as they feel they need to. If these parents are still drinking it is important to confront the parents with their feelings. Condemnation or punishment is not advised. Personal feelings should be presented in this form, "When you drink, I feel . . ." or "Your behavior when you drink makes me feel . . ." They should *not* say, "You're an SOB when you drink" (even if it's true). It is also helpful to provide alcoholic parents with some alternatives. For example, they may be asked if they would prefer inpatient or outpatient treatment. A person can be 70 years old but may still be affected by an alcoholic parent. However, even if the parents are dead, rehabilitation can include reconstructive therapy to deal with past issues. Parents leave their mark, which can be positive, negative, or both. It is difficult for individuals to develop to their full potential if there are unsolved problems with alcoholic parents.

With regard to high-risk ethnic backgrounds, primary prevention also begins in the family. The first problem becomes recognizing the high-risk group and then examining some of the reasons the risk factors are high. Irish Catholics are an example. Survey data ranks Catholics nationally and locally the highest among religious groups for prevalence of alcohol-related problems. As Father Martin puts it in his film, "Chalk Talk," "any time you find four Catholics you'll find a fifth." Among American ethnic groups, the Irish rank the highest or near the highest in terms of heavy intake and loss of control (Cahalan, 1970; Cahalan & Room, 1974).

Although there has been much speculation as to why Irish Catholics have such high rates of drinking problems, some of the most often repeated reasons include studies that portray marriage among the Irish as an uneasy practical alliance providing little affection or intimacy. Sex and procreation were reported as duties rather than joys or expressive activities. Irish women, in their roles as mothers and wives, have traditionally been controlling matriarchs on whom sons and husbands were dependent (Messenger, 1969). Stivers (1978) has postulated that heavy drinking became a significant characteristic of the cultural as well as masculine identity of the Irish male. Greeley (1972) has presented a discussion of sexual relations and affective characteristics of Irish-Americans. He says that "the Irish are generally not very good at demonstrating tenderness or affection for those whom they love" (p. 114). He also describes the domination of the Irish-American mother who rules her family by her strong will or by subtly manipulating the sympathies and guilts of her husband and children. Ablon and Cunningham (1981) have presented case studies that substantiate these claims and provide an even clearer picture of the special problems related to problem drinking in this population.

After the identification of problems, primary prevention focuses on corrective measures in these areas. For example, Irish males might be taught how to express affection or how to communicate with their spouses. Each problem would be addressed with family involvement where appropriate, and by doing this, the cycle would soon be broken. Alcoholism would stop passing from family to family through the generations. The key here is to identify specific problems and address them. For example, if Native Americans drink heavily because they do not identify with the primary culture, they could be helped to relate or to have an acceptable culture of their own. If adolescents abuse alcohol because they feel alienated and powerless, they must be provided with something to do. Perhaps, a year or two of public service for all 18-year-olds might not be a bad idea.

Sociological high-risk question number four is "Do you consider your friends to be heavy drinkers?" This indicates a logical prevention approach. Change friends. If a person's friends drink to excess, chances are he or she will also. Parents should provide their children with good role models. Very few heavy drinkers are good role models when it comes to modeling drinking. A single person who wants to cut down on drinking should find some new friends who drink less or do not drink, or they could go to places where heavy drinking is not acceptable. As pointed out earlier, one of the reasons AA works is that it changes the social group of the individual. There are over 50 million people in the U.S. who do not drink. If people think they or members of their families have drinking problems because of their associates, they could find new friends who drink less.

Risk question number five is a psychological problem. In terms of primary prevention, it is a matter of matching up what people think they are with what they think they should be. For families this means not placing personal expectations on children. Parents should be satisfied if the children are happy with what they are doing. Also, parents should see that children get adequate vocational guidance and should provide children with many chances to try different things while they are growing up. These approaches can help children make difficult career choices later in life. If parents or other members of the family are unhappy with the way things are going, they should make plans to change things and work on their plans. If nothing seems to help, they should see a therapist or someone else who can help. Parents should take responsibility for their lives and teach their children to do the same.

In terms of the sociological primary prevention and the family, in Chapter 4, the reader should reexamine the fourteen variables that impact on an individual's decision to drink, the six social psychological variables that determine the level of drinking maintained, and the eight characteristics of drinking groups that have low incidences of alcoholism.

Perhaps the risk area that is the most amenable to primary prevention is the psychological area. Primary prevention in this area can be done with those identified as high risk, such as children of alcoholics, or it may be done with children prior to the development of a risk factor. This includes working with a child from early development to produce an adult that is low risk. Either way, the family is the key to this type of prevention. Although there are many sociological variables involved in prevention, there are only a few in the psychological area. In their most basic form, these factors involve producing a person who feels good about himself or herself and others and who can function positively in the environment. In other words, he or she begins and continues to have successful life experiences.

Alcoholics are often characterized as having low self-esteem, an inability to cope, an inability to relate to others, poor decision-making abilities, unhealthy dependencies, and a low tolerance for tension. All of these somehow relate to the statements above. Primary prevention should involve providing a person with a positive self-image and skills to maintain successful life experiences. More specifically, children that were raised to have high self-esteem, good coping skills, good ability to relate to others, good decision-making abilities, independence, and a high tolerance for tension would not become alcoholics.

In Chapter 4, seven inadequacies of psychologically high-risk people were listed as follows: (1) low identification with viable role models; (2) low identification with and responsibility for family processes; (3) high faith in miracle solutions to problems; (4) poor intrapersonal skills; (5) poor interpersonal skills; (6) poor systemic skills; and (7) poor judgmental skills. The key to prevention here is to strengthen or develop intrapersonal and interpersonal skills; develop systemic skills (function in a system) and problem-solving abilities; and strengthen identification with the family and viable role models.

These approaches to primary prevention seem straightforward enough. However, the problem arises in their implementation.

The family is the logical place to teach such skills, and the parents are the ones to do the job. However, many parents are poorly prepared to raise their children in this manner, particularly if they have not developed these skills themselves. This is generally the case if their own parents never developed these skills. In multigenerational alcoholism, poor parenting skills are passed along from generation to generation. There is no room for blame here. Often the parents who are causing the most harm are the ones who are making the most sincere effort to be good parents.

The problem with the implementation of programs to prevent parents from poor parenting is that they are most often voluntary. The parents who need the training the most are the ones least likely to attend this training. Parents who are often doing the best parenting job are the ones who go to parent training programs.

The research concerning the effectiveness of parent training programs as prevention is very limited because too many problems with definitions and design have rendered the results of most research unusable. However, this approach can be accepted at face value, and research can be done later to substantiate productivity. For example, the acceptance of AA as the primary model for treatment programs is based almost entirely on face validity. If it is accepted that the family is the most effective agent in primary prevention, what can be done about parents who reject the training?

There are two places to begin alcoholism prevention via parent training. Alcoholism treatment programs must be solidly based in a family therapy model that has as its primary goal the development of a family system in which each member meets his or her needs. The parents learn to parent, and the children in turn learn how to lead meaningful, successful lives. They feel good about themselves and others, and they learn to find something to do in their lives that they feel is worthwhile. However, this will only prevent children of parents who are in family treatment from becoming alcoholic.

The other area in which this country can begin a prevention effort that will not only prevent alcoholism and drug abuse, but many of society's ills, is in the public schools. The schools should teach parenting skills, but the hard part here is designing and implementing a program to teach effective parenting to students. However, someone figured out how to teach English, math, and history in public schools, and it is very likely someone could figure out how to teach parenting. Many good programs have already been developed to teach adults how to parent, and with some minor adaptation, these could be used in the school system. A good school program would take into consideration the different values among students and would also recognize that adolescents, even juniors and seniors in high school, would find it hard to imagine themselves as parents. Even if they are able to do this, often their preconceived ideas about how life will be when they are parents are overly optimistic, imagining only the "fun" aspects of parenting. The dirty diapers and 3:00 a.m. feedings are often forgotten until reality overtakes imagination.

It would not be too much to ask to have students spend one hour per day for their final three years of school to learn a skill that would make not only their lives but the lives of their children more meaningful and more satisfying with fewer major problems (including alcoholism).

The first year of the program could be spent teaching communication skills (not English). The students could learn to identify and express their feelings. They could learn listening and reflecting skills and learn how to express both negative and positive emotions in an appropriate manner. In the second year, they could learn developmental psychology in a meaningful context. They could begin to learn parenting skills like setting limits, how to handle misbehavior, discipline, building a child's self-esteem, answering difficult questions (e.g., Why is the sky blue? What is it like to be dead? Is God married? Why does Grandpa drink so much?) and many more. They could also learn to meet the psychological needs of a child. This would be like receiving an owner's manual with a child, something many parents have wished for at one time or another. The final year of the program would be a handson placement experience. The public schools could offer daycare free of cost or at a reasonable rate for single parents, working mothers, or anyone who needs it. High school students would be responsible for taking care of the children who are in daycare and that would include changing diapers, etc. Such a program might also have a pleasant side effect of reducing teenage pregnancy. The program would be required for both males and females.

The end result of a program like this would be to give future parents the skills to develop families that function as families should, meeting the needs of each member and helping each other to develop and grow both physically, emotionally, and intellectually.

Blum (1972) and his associates have done an indepth study on the role of the family in the origin and prevention of drug use. The findings are equally applicable to alcoholism. They found that no excellent family (as rated by clinicians as superior or good) was in the high-risk category. However all troubled and pathological families were in the high-risk classification. Children from the excellent families stated that they derived self-confidence from their feelings of worth. In summary, Blum states:

> In excellent families, the inner joy and strength is visibly expressed in harmony and in happy adjustment. In the troubled or pathological families, pain and chaos may take a variety of forms, all of which visibly reflect disharmony, disconnect and a search for elusive meanings and gratifications. Risk taking drug use by youngsters is to be seen in this light. (p. 21)

According to Silberman (1971), author of *Crisis in the Classroom*, the proper kind of education helps students to, "develop the knowledge and skills they need to make sense out of their experience—their experiences with themselves, with others, with the world—not just during adolescence, but for the rest of their lives" (p. 74).

The type of parenting classes mentioned above would provide just this type of education. It seems ironic that the most sensible and productive form of alcoholism prevention need not mention the word alcohol. But that appears to be the case. The most outstanding factor is that it would cost little more than is spent on education at the present time. With some small shifts in priorities, the program could be underway. It is time for such a program for the sake of the future of the family and for the primary prevention of alcoholism.

Another reason to provide individuals with parenting skills is that functional families can be productive in the secondary and tertiary prevention of alcoholism. As stated earlier, secondary prevention involves the early diagnosis of the alcoholic or problem drinker and treatment and rehabilitation. Tertiary prevention is treatment of serious cases. A functional family, by definition, would be one that can identify problem areas and seek assistance for those problems. A nonfunctional family would ignore or hide the problem. As pointed out in Chapter 4, treatment for the alcoholic does not always imply primary prevention for his or her children. However, treatment for the alcoholic can be viewed as secondary prevention for that alcoholic, just as treatment for the chronic alcoholic can be seen as tertiary prevention. In both cases, a strong family system can be helpful. One of the reasons for the low success rate among chronic alcoholic treatment programs is that often all family ties with the alcoholic have been broken.

In many cases, reestablishment of ties with either the family of origin or the nuclear family will aid in the treatment of the chronic alcoholic. If this is not possible, reconstructive family therapy using surrogate family members can enhance treatment. Unresolved issues of the past with parents, even if the parents are no longer alive, can be addressed. Past hurts, frustrations, and feelings of guilt can be discussed. If these feelings are not resolved, there is very little likelihood of a successful treatment. The individual is tied to the family just as human beings are tied to their environment. The 55-year old chronic alcoholic may still carry perceptions of his or her family of origin that developed at the age of 5, and 5-year-olds do not always have accurate perceptions. A small child may hear his parents fighting and may think it is his fault. If the parents later divorce, the child may feel responsible for the divorce, a heavy burden for someone to carry for life.

Just as a strong family system will carry on after the loss of a member, it will similarly continue to function and support its members during the loss of one member to alcoholism. When that individual reaches treatment, this family can be a great support and make the likelihood of successful treatment more realistic.

In summary, when the family is involved at all levels, prevention is more likely to be successful. The goal of primary prevention is to lower risks in the sociological and psychological areas and/or to raise children who are not high risks to begin with. The family plays a major role in such prevention, and the family is also important in secondary and tertiary prevention. In fact, it may be said that the family is the key to the prevention of alcoholism.

SUMMARY

Alcoholism is a widespread problem that has been frustratingly resistive to treatment efforts. In many respects, the development and maintenance of alcoholism are still a mystery, and effective treatment and prevention are yet to be discovered. However, this is not meant to disparage the gains that have been made by dedicated practitioners and researchers in the field. This book should add to the knowledge base and act as a helpful guide for the reader.

This book has attempted to place alcoholism and its treatment into a family perspective. It is the strong belief of the authors that this conceptualization is critical to an effective understanding of the problem. In addition, prevention of alcoholism was also shown from a family perspective.

It was the authors' goal to provide, first of all, an overview of current thinking on the causes or nature of alcoholism, coupled with treatment approaches based on these theories. Although this information may be familiar to some readers, it was necessary to set the stage with background information on which the major themes of the book could be built.

Following this, alcoholism etiology was described in terms of the family of origin and the nuclear family. Many reasons for the generation-to-generation transmission of alcoholism were explored. Much space was also given to treatment strategies for alcoholic families. Both the theory behind these techniques and specific applications were examined.

Finally, prevention efforts within a family perspective were delineated. The authors' goal was to provide an informative and useful document to the field of alcoholism treatment.

REFERENCES

Ablon, J., & Cunningham, W. Implications of cultural patterning for the delivery of alcoholism services. *Journal of Studies on Alcohol,* 1981, *9,* pp. 185-205.

Blum, R., & Associates. *Horatio Alger's children: The role of the family in the origin and prevention of drug risk.* San Francisco: Jossey-Bass, Inc., Pubs., 1972.

Cahalan, D. *Problem drinkers: A national survey.* San Francisco: Jossey-Bass, Inc., Pubs., 1970.

Cahalan, D., & Room, R. *Problem drinking among American men.* New Brunswick, N.J.: Rutgers Center of Alcohol Studies, Monograph No. 7, 1974.

Caplan, G. *Support systems and community mental health.* New York: Behavioral Publications, 1974.

Greeley, A. *That most distressful nation: The taming of the American Irish.* Chicago: Quadrangle Books, 1972.

Jellinek, E.M. *The disease concept of alcoholism,* New Brunswick, N.J.: College and University Press, 1960.

Messenger, J.C. *Inis beog: Isle of island.* New York: Holt, Rinehart & Winston, Inc., 1969.

Rockefeller, N. *White paper on drug abuse.* Washington, D.C.: Government Printing Office, 1975.

Silberman, C. *Crisis in the classroom.* New York: Vintage Books, 1971.

Smart, R.G. Priorities in minimizing alcohol problems among young people. In H. Blane, & M. Chafetz (Eds.), *Youth alcohol and social policy.* New York: Plenum Press, 1978.

Stivers, R. Irish ethnicity and alcohol use. *Medical Anthropology,* 1978, *2,* 121-135.

Swisher, J.D. Background paper for Conference on *Developing Prevention Programs in Treatment Agencies and Settings.* Prevention Issues, April, 1980, Lincoln, Nebraska.

Index

About the Authors

GARY LAWSON is a professor of Counseling Psychology at the University of Nebraska. His specialty area is alcoholism counselor training. He has 12 years of experience in the field of alcoholism, including directing an inpatient alcoholism treatment center. Dr. Lawson has published articles on alcoholism and presented related materials both regionally and nationally. He also has a private practice in psychology and does family therapy.

JAMES PETERSON is a professor of Counselor Education at the Rehabilitation Institute at Southern Illinois University and has developed a specialty area on alcoholism as part of a graduate program in rehabilitation counseling. Dr. Peterson has been an alcoholism counselor and has directed an alcoholism facility. He has also published several articles on alcoholism and presented related materials at national professional conventions.

ANN LAWSON, MA, MFA, is the Director of the Lincoln and Lancaster County Child Guidance Center, Children From Alcoholic Families Program (Lincoln, Nebraska). This is an innovative family-based prevention and treatment program for children who have alcoholic parents. Ms. Lawson is a child and family therapist. Her work is based in a family systems approach with emphasis on prevention. She has blended her dual backgrounds of art and counseling psychology to create a unique approach to treatment of the alcoholic family and has presented this treatment method at national conventions and regional workshops.